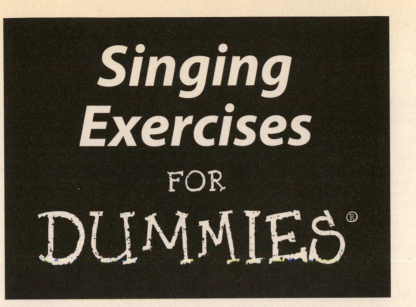

Singing Exercises

FOR DUMMIES®

by Pamelia S. Phillips, DMA

WILEY

John Wiley & Sons, Inc.

Singing Exercises For Dummies®

Published by

John Wiley & Sons, Inc.
111 River St.
Hoboken, NJ 07030-5774
www.wiley.com

For general information on our other products and services, please contact our Customer Care Department within the U.S. at 877-762-2974, outside the U.S. at 317-572-3993, or fax 317-572-4002.

For technical support, please visit www.wiley.com/techsupport.

Wiley publishes in a variety of print and electronic formats and by print-on-demand. Some material included with standard print versions of this book may not be included in e-books or in print-on-demand. If this book refers to media such as a CD or DVD that is not included in the version you purchased, you may download this material at http://booksupport.wiley.com. For more information about Wiley products, visit www.wiley.com.

Library of Congress Control Number: 2012940019

ISBN 978-1-118-28108-6 (pbk); ISBN 978-1-118-32822-4 (ebk); ISBN 978-1-118-32823-1 (ebk); ISBN 978-1-118-32824-8 (ebk)

Manufactured in the United States of America

10 9 8 7 6 5 4 3 2 1

WILEY

About the Author

Dr. Pamelia S. Phillips is the Conservatory Director and Chair of Voice and Music at CAP21 (Collaborative Arts Project 21). Dr. Phillips earned her Doctorate of Musical Arts and Master of Music in Vocal Performance from Arizona State University and her Bachelor of Music Education from Arkansas State University. Her performances range from contemporary American Opera premieres to guest performances with major symphonies.

Performances include title roles in *Carmen, Tragedy of Carmen, Dido and Aeneas,* and *Lizzie Borden,* the Witch in *Hansel and Gretel,* Giulietta in *The Tales of Hoffmann,* Dorabella in *Cosi fan tutte,* Mum in *Albert Herring,* Constance in the world premiere of *She Stoops to Conquer,* Lady with a Hat Box in *Postcard from Morocco,* Frau Bauer in *Dora,* Beatrice in the stage premiere of *Garden of Mystery,* Mrs. Cornett in *Tobermory,* staged performance of *From The Diary of Virginia Woolf,* Gloria Thorpe in *Damn Yankees,* Gymnasia in *A Funny Thing Happened on the Way to the Forum,* Liebeslieder singer in *A Little Night Music,* and Lady Thiang in *The King and I.* Symphonic performances include Berlioz's *Le mort de Cléopâtre* with the Bronx Symphony, Mahler's *Fourth Symphony* with the Centre Symphony, *Das Lied von der Erde* and Mahler's *Third Symphony* with the New York Symphonic Arts Ensemble, and guest artist with the Phoenix Chamber Symphony, Scottsdale Fine Arts Orchestra, Putnam County Chorale, and the National Chorale.

Dr. Phillips has taught at CAP21, Wagner College, Arizona State University, Scottsdale Community College, and South Mountain Community College. She is also the author of *Singing For Dummies,* 2nd Edition (Wiley).

Dedication

To my husband, George.

Author's Acknowledgments

I would like to gratefully acknowledge Project Editor Jen Tebbe for her vision and sense of adventure with this new series, Copy Editor Amanda Langferman for patiently editing until it was exactly right, Acquisitions Editor Michael Lewis for allowing me to continue writing for this audience that I just adore, and Technical Editors Mary Anne Scott and David Kelso for checking my accuracy.

Thank you to my husband, George, for tolerating all the nights and weekends that I spent writing and for singing the figures so I could test the recording equipment.

Thank you to my parents for attending numerous concerts over the years and embracing my passion for singing.

Thank you to my students and colleagues who sang so beautifully on the CD and for all your encouragement.

Thank you to my voice teachers: Julia Lansford, Jerry Doan, Norma Newton, and Judith Natalucci.

Publisher's Acknowledgments

We're proud of this book; please send us your comments at http://dummies.custhelp.com. For other comments, please contact our Customer Care Department within the U.S. at 877-762-2974, outside the U.S. at 317-572-3993, or fax 317-572-4002.

Some of the people who helped bring this book to market include the following:

Acquisitions, Editorial, and Vertical Websites

Project Editor: Jennifer Tebbe

Acquisitions Editor: Michael Lewis

Copy Editor: Amanda M. Langferman

Assistant Editor: David Lutton

Editorial Program Coordinator: Joe Niesen

Technical Editors: Mary Anne Spangler Scott, David Kelso

Vertical Websites: Jenny Swisher, Josh Frank, Melanie Orr

Singers: Todd Alsup, Rachael Ferrera, Bailey Frankenberg, James LaRosa, Heather Petruzelli, Dr. Christopher Roselli, Jacob Samuels, Bailey Seeker, Erik Sparks, Dr. Pam Phillips

Piano Arrangements: Joel Waggoner

Pianists: Joel Waggoner, Dr. Pam Phillips

Sound Design: Matthias Winter

Editorial Manager: Christine Meloy Beck

Editorial Assistants: Rachelle S. Amick, Alexa Koschier

Cover Photo: © iStockphoto.com/Monika Olszewska

Cartoons: Rich Tennant (www.the5thwave.com)

Composition Services

Project Coordinator: Patrick Redmond

Layout and Graphics: Carrie A. Cesavice, Joyce Haughey

Proofreader: Betty Kish

Special Help
Danielle Voirol

Publishing and Editorial for Consumer Dummies

    Kathleen Nebenhaus, Vice President and Executive Publisher

    Kristin Ferguson-Wagstaffe, Product Development Director

    Ensley Eikenburg, Associate Publisher, Travel

    Kelly Regan, Editorial Director, Travel

Publishing for Technology Dummies

    Andy Cummings, Vice President and Publisher

Composition Services

    Debbie Stailey, Director of Composition Services

Contents at a Glance

Table of Contents

Introduction

Singing is an amazing sport that can provide you with hours of entertainment. But developing your singing skills takes time and practice. This book is here to help you expand your singing technique with exercises specifically designed to address the most common aspects of singing. These exercises provide a great practice routine for you to use every day or when you need to brush up on a skill. Whether you want to sing just for fun or you have dreams of breaking out as a singing sensation, *Singing Exercises For Dummies* is for you.

About This Book

Whether you sing pop music or you're auditioning for the local chorus, *Singing Exercises For Dummies* has what you need to refine your singing technique. The exercises in these pages, which range from easy to pretty hard, cover the most common topics in singing and are designed for any type of singer singing any style of music. They're also the same type of exercises that you may expect to sing during a voice lesson or in a singing class. If you can't afford to pay for lessons on a regular basis, this book can help you continue to refine your technique on your own at home.

In addition to exercises, Chapters 5 through 14 also feature practice pieces — short songs I've written to help you practice applying a specific singing technique. They all have accompanying audio tracks and a singer who demonstrates the correct sounds for you so you know the sound that goes with the text that you read in the chapter. The combination of exercises and practice pieces provides a variety of ways to practice your technique.

The audio tracks are demonstrations of the music figures you see in the chapters. Some of the tracks have only the piano playing the figure for you so that you can make the sounds on your own; the text in the chapter lets you know which tracks you won't hear a singer on.

I've organized the material so that you don't have to read the book from cover to cover. Instead, you can review the table of contents to find the technique you want or need to work on most and head straight to that section. For example, if you have trouble transitioning between different vocal registers, you can proceed directly to Chapter 11 for help. Or you can work through all the practice exercises for a complete vocal workout that builds on itself.

Conventions Used in This Book

I use common singing terms throughout this book, but I define them for you in case you haven't seen them before. You can also expect to see the following conventions:

- ✔ **Key signatures:** Each figure includes a key signature so you know exactly where to sing that particular pattern. Don't worry if you don't know key signatures; for those patterns with audio tracks, you can still follow along with the piano and/or singer.

- ✔ **Pattern repetitions:** Most figures in the book show all the repetitions of the patterns, but some larger figures show only the ascending or descending versions of the patterns. Rest assured that you can hear all the repetitions on the audio tracks.

- ✔ **Phonetic spellings for vowels:** The English alphabet has five vowels — *A, E, I, O,* and *U* — but each of those vowels may make more than one sound based on how they're combined with other vowels or consonants in a word. I use the phonetic spellings of the various vowel sounds to help you understand exactly which vowel sound you're supposed to make. (***Note:*** The sound the letter *a* makes in the word *cat* is different from the *a* in the word *father*. When you see this a, know that the vowel sound you're going for is like the *a* in *cat*.)

✔ **Practice exercises and other figures:** Some of the figures in this book help you practice a particular exercise, and some of them provide basic singing information or practice for you. A black box with a track number tells you which exercises have an accompanying audio track. If you don't see a black track box, you know that example is a figure that's explained in the chapter but doesn't have audio. ***Note:*** A lot of the time, music is written in treble clef for guys even though they sing the notes an octave lower. Guys, when you see the music written in treble clef, just know that you sing it down an octave unless instructed otherwise. In some exercises in the book, I ask you to sing the music as written — not down an octave.

✔ **Singers on the tracks:** Many of the exercises have accompanying audio tracks where a singer demonstrates the sounds of the patterns for you. I include both male and female singers, as well as different voice types. The text accompanying each exercise tells you whether you hear a singer or you get to practice the figure on your own.

✔ **Song lists:** At the end of most of the chapters in this book, I include a list of songs that you can use to help you practice the different techniques covered in the rest of the chapter. If a song's text is gender specific or if it's for a role that's gender specific, I mention that gender. Otherwise, I list *either*. You can work on any song you like, but you may want to note the gender-specific information if you want to perform the song. To help you learn a song, I recommend you get the sheet music first so you can practice singing along with the notation without hearing a recording. You can find sheet music at your local music store or online.

What You're Not to Read

Throughout the text, I include helpful tips for performing each exercise, but if you're in a hurry and you just want to get to singing, feel free to perform the exercises along with the audio tracks. You can always go back to the tips later.

Foolish Assumptions

I made the following assumptions about you when writing this book:

✔ You really like singing and want some help with developing your technique.

✔ You have some prior knowledge about singing — whether from singing in a choir, taking lessons, or reading my book *Singing For Dummies* (Wiley) — and you want to take your skills to the next level.

✔ You sing all kinds of music and don't limit yourself to just one style (such as classical, country, pop, or gospel).

✔ You'll use the audio tracks for a long time, which is why the exercises range from really easy to pretty hard. That way, they can keep you challenged now and later.

How This Book Is Organized

This book is organized into five parts, each of which contains specific topics about singing. Each chapter in the part contains details about how to develop that part of your singing technique with exercises that correspond to the explanation.

Part 1: Preparing Your Body for Practicing

Practicing singing is like practicing any other sport because you need to warm up your body and voice. After all, your singing voice will last longer during your practice session and won't tire out as easily if you take the time to warm up beforehand. Chapter 1 is all about knowing what to do when you warm up.

Chapter 2 helps you explore breathing so you can develop the physical coordination you need to manage any phrase in your song. It lists all the places that move when you breathe and explains how to control all those shifting muscles. The rest of the part is about vowels and consonants. Chapter 3 guides you on shaping vowels, and Chapter 4 helps you practice the proper articulation for consonants.

Part 11: Making Your Music Magical with Variety

Musical variety is what makes a song memorable. This part helps you discover several musical elements that can make your song sound great every time you sing it. Chapter 5 tells you all about the most common intervals you find in songs. Knowing how to recognize intervals and sing them allows you to get your new song ready fast.

Chapter 6 helps you explore the most common rhythms seen in songs. The notation on the pages of classical music is exactly what you're supposed to sing. The rhythms in contemporary radio songs are often just suggestions because contemporary singers don't always sing what's on the page. However, if you don't know what's written on the page, you won't know how to change the rhythm to make it sound the way you want it to sound.

Chapter 7 describes the elements you can use to make your songs unique. In it, you explore dynamics and discover what you need to do physically to sing softly or loudly. You also find out about the symbols that you see above the notes that tell you how to sing the notes — short or long, detached or connected — or even when to stop singing. This chapter also helps you work on improvisational techniques.

Part 111: Working Out Your Range

The chapters in this part work out the various areas of your singing voice from top to bottom. Chapter 8 explores your chest voice — the lowest part of your singing voice. Chapter 9 moves way up the scale and explores your head voice — the high part of your singing voice. Chapter 10 moves to the middle area of your voice to help you work on your mix. (*Mix* is a word that you hear a lot in singing, and it can be used in a lot of different ways; Chapter 10 tells you what it means to mix and how to do it.)

Last but not least, Chapter 11 helps you figure out how to move between registers. When singers say they cracked when they tried to sing the high note, they're really saying they didn't know how to handle the register transition. This chapter helps you practice moving between registers so you can smooth out the transitions.

Part 1V: Advancing Your Singing Technique

Advancing your singing technique requires that you know not only the basics of singing but also how to finesse your tone. You make a unique sound when you sing, but you can always decide to change your tone, and Chapter 12 tells you how. Chapter 13 gets you moving fast with patterns for agility. *Agility* in singing is the ability to sing a phrase that has a lot of notes that move quickly. You need a combination of skill and courage to sing the notes quickly, and this chapter is full of exercises that get you on your way. Chapter 14 is all about *belting* — singing with really forward resonance and a mixture of some head voice and chest voice. You want to know how to belt well so your voice stays healthy.

Part V: The Part of Tens

One of the hallmarks of a *For Dummies* book is the Part of Tens, and this book is no exception. Chapter 15 has you covered if you want to develop your practice routine from the first session when you try out the song to the performance. Chapter 16 is full of answers to those questions you just don't know whom to ask (like "What shouldn't I eat before a performance?").

This part also houses a helpful appendix that tells you all about the various audio tracks found on this book's CD. If you can't remember which track had the exercise for making a smooth crescendo, for example, turn to the appendix to find out quickly. When you flip to the chapter you need (in this case, Chapter 7), just look for the black box that tells you which track goes with which exercise.

Icons Used in This Book

The three icons you see in the left-hand margin throughout the book are as follows:

This icon is to remind you of the fundamental concepts of singing.

This icon highlights particularly helpful advice about singing the exercises.

This icon reminds you about what not to do and warns you about potential problems.

Where to Go from Here

If you're wondering where to head first, you can always start with Chapter 1 and explore the chapters in order. Or you can move around and explore sections that interest you now. If you go that route, feel free to group exercises together to create your own practice routine to suit your interests.

The exercises on the audio tracks are played at the tempo that's best for practicing. After you know the exercise, you can sing it without the audio tracks at any tempo that you find interesting or challenging. Save any exercises that you find too challenging for later, or break them into parts and work on only the easiest parts now. You can always sing along with the first portion of the track and then rewind and start over. As your skill develops, you may find that those harder exercises get more comfortable. If an exercise isn't in the right key for you, feel free to explore the exercise to get all the notes and then sing in the key that suits you best.

This book contains a lot of information and a lot of options for structuring your practice sessions. Don't be afraid to dive right in, and enjoy exploring your technique!

Part I

Preparing Your Body for Practicing

The 5th Wave   By Rich Tennant

"Okay—you're relaxing your neck _too_ much."

In this part . . .

This part has information to help you develop your warm-up and get your body ready for practicing. You may be tempted to just rush through your warm-up, but I'm telling you now, "Don't!" After all, the warm-up can make a big difference in your practice session when you know how to use it. Start by physically preparing your body with stretching and positioning. Then focus on mastering the physical coordination necessary for proper breathing while singing. Take your time working through the chapter on breathing to make sure you know exactly what to do for any phrase.

Shaping your tongue and lips for vowels and consonants is something you do every day whether you're singing or not. However, you have to be more precise with your lip and tongue movements in singing if you want your audience to understand you. So be sure to review the chapters on vowels and consonants because they contain lots of exercises to help you practice making just the right shapes and sounds.

Chapter 1

Warming Up for Singing

The sequence of every practice session you do as a singer includes a warm-up (both physical and vocal), your vocal exercises, and then the application of the skills you work on during your vocal exercises to your songs. Warming up the body before you warm up the voice helps get the muscles flexible so your warm-up takes less time. If you warm up your body first, that early morning practice session becomes much more productive because you can get to your vocal exercises more quickly.

In this chapter, you explore the steps of a warm-up for singers. You find out how to warm up your body, stretch your muscles, and maintain good balance by releasing tension. Each section has you warm up a different part of the body with one or more stretches and balance exercises. Then at the end of the chapter, I give you a vocal warm-up that both prepares your voice and lets you take stock of your body.

After your vocal warm-up, you're ready to start working on the practice exercises in this book that help you develop technique. You can look through the table of contents to find a topic that interests you and dive right in, or you can move on to Chapter 2 to work on breath control and then explore the rest of the chapters in order. You may want to take a quick look at Chapter 15, which can help you set up productive practices, before you start exploring other chapters.

Preparing Your Instrument: Stretching Out from Head to Toe

Warming up and stretching your body before a vocal warm-up helps you feel like your body is flexible and open from head to toe. Feeling *open* means that you feel as if you have a lot of space inside your body that you can open for sound to resonate. Although your body is full of muscles, organs, and tissues, the stretching and releasing of tension that you do during your physical warm-up can make you feel like you're creating an open area between the organs.

Remember whatever physical sensation you feel after you stretch so that you can create that same opening every time you start your warm-up. After you get your body warm, you want to maintain the feeling of flexible movement throughout your practice session.

Don't feel like you have to follow every part of this chapter word for word during your warm-up. You know your body better than anyone, so use the information I present here as a guide for structuring the warm-up that best suits you. For example, you can use your yoga routine or your cardio workout at the gym to get your body warm and your blood pumping. Even your power walk around the neighborhood can get your body quickly warmed up and ready to stretch. Then you can use the stretching sequence in this chapter to help you stretch just the right muscles to get flexible for singing.

Make notes of any stretches in the chapter that may be more than your body can handle. Here are some ways to modify the stretches to work for your body:

- ✔ If standing for long periods of time isn't comfortable for you, feel free to modify the stretches and do them seated in a chair. Practicing your singing in a chair can help you really focus on the movement and not worry about holding up your whole body.

- ✔ Lower-back problems or balance problems may prevent you from comfortably leaning over or stretching. When an exercise calls for stretching, feel free to alter the movement to get the stretch that feels good for your body. Start with a limited amount of movement and gradually add more as you explore what's comfortable and safe for your body.

Opening and Positioning the Lower Body

To create the most efficient movement in your body for singing, you need to line up all the parts of your body and evenly distribute your weight, starting at your feet and moving all the way up to your head. When you do so, no one muscle has to work harder than necessary for singing. As you work through the lower-body stretches and balance exercises in the following sections, notice how the stretch affects the weight distribution throughout your body. It's easy to forget all about your legs and feet when you sing since they're so far away from your mouth. However, taking the time to balance your weight on your legs and feet gets you better prepared for singing by increasing flexibility in your torso.

If you're getting ready to sing in a performance, do your practice sessions in the shoes you plan to wear at the performance. Guys, even the slight heel on your dress shoes may change your alignment. Ladies, wearing high heels changes your balance quite a bit. Hence, I don't recommend wearing stilettos for any performance because they offer such little support on the tiny heels. Choose heels that are more solid for better support and remember that you need to keep your feet flexible inside your shoes. If your feet lock, you may lock muscles all the way up your back.

Connecting your feet to the floor

Three points on the bottom of each foot help you balance your weight to keep the muscles throughout your body flexible. You need to know where these three points are so you can balance when you practice singing and stay balanced when you perform on the stage.

Stretch

While standing or sitting, lift your toes up and then curl your toes down to stretch the muscles in your feet and toes.

Balance

To balance the right way on your feet, you need to distribute your weight evenly on three points of the feet: the heel, the point under the little toe, and the point under the big toe. To help you find the right points, take a few minutes to work through the following steps, which can help you identify the right (and wrong) sensations to feel when balancing on your feet for singing. I recommend that you do this sequence without shoes so you can really feel the connection between your feet and the floor.

1. **Rock slightly forward so that you're balancing your weight on the balls of your feet.**

   As you lean forward, you should feel a tightening sensation along the back of your body. You don't want to feel this sensation when singing.

2. **Lean back so that you're balancing more on the heels of your feet.**

   Leaning back creates tension in the front of the body. You don't want to feel this tension when singing.

3. **Lean on the outsides of your feet (from the heels to the little toes).**

   As you lean on the outside of each foot, notice that you feel most of the weight in your heel at the back of the foot and at a point underneath your little toe. Leaning on the outsides of your feet tightens the muscles along the outsides of your legs.

4. **Lean on the insides of your feet (from the heels to the big toes).**

   As you lean on the inside of each foot, you should feel most of the weight in your heel at the back of the foot and at a large point under your big toe. Leaning on the insides of your feet tightens the muscles on the insides of your legs.

The points you identified in Steps 3 and 4 (the heel and the points under the big and little toes) are the points you want to balance on when singing. You can roll your feet around on the floor to feel these three points even more distinctly. Just follow these steps:

1. **With both feet flat on the floor, gently press each heel to the floor.**

2. **Roll to the point under your little toe and press that point to the floor.**

3. **Roll to the point under your big toe and press that point to the floor.**

Rolling through these three points helps you figure out where the middle of your foot is and how you need to situate your feet to make sure you're spreading out the balance equally. Work through these three steps several times until you can feel the sense of balance. After you know what that balance feels like, you can roll through the three points at the beginning of each warm-up just to remind yourself to balance on the three points.

 Balancing equally on the three points of the foot is a lot like using a tripod for a camera. Forming a tripod helps you feel grounded or connected to the floor. To make sure you're making a solid tripod, lift your toes while you're standing with the rest of your feet flat on the floor. You're more aware of the three points of your feet when your toes are lifted. Keep in mind that the toes are there to help you balance, but they shouldn't be tight. After you feel the points, find the same sensation of balance with your toes released.

To release any tension in the feet and reconnect with the floor, take a breath and release into your feet. Imagine that you have a mouth on the bottom of each foot that opens when you inhale; that's what the release into your feet should feel like. It also feels as if the feet were spreading out and then reconnecting with the floor.

Balancing on the ankles and knees

The ankles and knees are pretty far away from the mouth, but how you balance at both of these places helps you keep muscles flexible in your torso. Use the visuals I mention in the following sections to help you explore and remember the sensations you should feel when positioning your ankles and knees.

Stretch

To stretch the ankles, sit in a chair with one foot lifted off the floor. Draw an imaginary circle with your toes and gradually allow the circle to grow larger and then smaller. Reverse the direction of the circle. Repeat with the other foot.

To stretch the knees, bend your knees to warm up the joints. Bend them in a way that's comfortable for you. Don't worry if you can bend your knees only slightly. As long as you bend **or** move them enough to warm up the joints, you're good to go. Another way to warm up your knees is to sit in a chair and move your feet to touch underneath the chair and stretch the muscles around the knees.

Balance

To position your ankles for maximum balance, stand or sit in a chair with your feet well balanced on the floor. Your heels are behind your ankles, and each ankle should feel like a camera on a tripod, the tripod being the three points on the bottom of the foot (the heel, the point under the big toe, and the point under the little toe).

Balancing the knees requires that you keep your knees straight but not locked. Bending your knees makes you shorter, and locking your knees tenses up the muscles around the knees. To feel the locking sensation, push your knees back. Now release the muscles in your thighs and feel your knees move forward just enough to release but not bend. That's where you want to be when singing.

To make sure you're getting the right balance of weight in your knees, imagine that your knees are lengthening or opening. This lengthening sensation is the opposite of what it feels like to sink into the knees or feel heavy in the knees.

Distributing weight in the legs and hips

Singers often forget about their legs when they sing. But you need to focus on both your legs and your hips during your stretching and warm-up to remind yourself to keep your hips balanced and your legs flexible. *Note:* Women often sink into their hips because their hips are wider than their shoulders. But when they sink into their hips, they end up slouching and allowing the chest to fall and the hips to push forward. If you have this problem, pay close attention to the following sections, which help you lift up out of your hips so that you can evenly balance weight throughout your torso.

Stretch

To stretch out your legs, lean on your left leg and stretch the right leg out to the side to stretch the inside of the leg. Do the same thing with the other leg. For a slightly different stretch, squat on one leg while keeping the other leg out to the side. The leg that's out to your side can be balancing on either the heel or the inside of the foot. You can try one stretch and then the other to feel which one helps you stretch the most.

While standing, make small circles with your hips. Pretend to hula hoop very slowly. As you continue the circles, allow the circles to grow larger. Reverse the direction of the circles and repeat. Then sit in a chair and rock your pelvis forward and backward several times. Finally, lift your left hip while keeping your right hip on the chair; then do the same thing with your right hip.

Balance

You need to distribute your weight evenly on both legs. You don't want to lean on just one leg because the opposite side of the body will tense from the unequal distribution, and that tension will affect your singing. Also, if you don't balance your hips and instead move your buttocks forward, you'll feel the muscles along your sides tighten. Tightening along your sides tightens your ribs and affects your breathing.

To help you achieve the right balance in your legs and hips, inhale and visualize your legs opening from the hips all the way down into your feet. If that visual doesn't work for you, imagine that your legs and hips are a shock absorber or bed spring that lengthens on the inhalation. The lengthening helps you evenly distribute the weight in your legs and hips instead of pressing down through the legs and sinking into the hips. Just placing your awareness on your legs helps you release tension and lengthen.

How you position your feet affects the amount of balance you achieve in your legs. So be sure to stand with your feet parallel and about hip-width apart; doing so allows you to feel the muscles in your legs engaged but not tense. If you stand with your toes pointed out, you tense muscles on the outsides of your legs. Likewise, if you stand with your toes pointed in, you tense muscles on the insides of your legs.

If you know one of your legs is longer than the other, try standing with the longer leg slightly in front of the shorter leg. You may find that this position helps you balance your weight more evenly because the legs feel like they're the same length.

Positioning the Upper Body for Easy Movement

How you position the parts of your upper body matters a lot when you're singing. Holding your arms tightly at your sides directly affects your back alignment and your ability to breathe successfully during your song. How you balance your head affects the muscles in your neck that you use for singing. This section helps you stretch and position the torso and upper limbs. As you work on balancing your upper body, make sure you stay connected to your legs and feet to achieve better alignment throughout your entire body.

Lengthening your spine

The spine is made up of 33 vertebrae, which divide up into sections of the spine: 7 vertebrae in the cervical spine (neck), 12 in the thoracic area (the chest), 5 in the lumbar area (lower back), 5 that are fused together in the sacrum (pelvis), and 4 in the tailbone. The discs between the vertebrae are like cushions that keep the vertebrae from rubbing against each other. With this many vertebrae, several muscle groups function together to move the spine. You need to stretch all the muscles that move the spine before you sing because the ribs are attached to the spine and you want the ribs and the spine to be flexible so you can develop good breath coordination for singing.

Stretch

Stand upright or sit upright in a chair. Raise your arms over your head and reach high to the sky with your right hand; then reach high with your left hand. On each side, feel the stretch all through your back and ribs and down into your hips.

Now lean to the right and lift the left arm over your head. Stretch as far as you comfortably can to the right to stretch the ribs on your left side. Inhale and then stretch a little bit farther as you exhale. Repeat the same leaning stretch on the left side.

While standing or sitting, lean back enough to feel a stretch in your abdomen. *Note:* If you have back problems, you may be more comfortable rocking your pelvis forward to stretch the abs.

Balance

Your spine curves naturally at your lower back and in your neck. You want to maintain this natural curve as you sing because it helps you stay balanced. On the inhalation, visualize your spine lengthening and the discs between the vertebrae expanding. Feel your head move toward the ceiling and your tailbone move toward the floor on the inhalation. You should experience a feeling of buoyancy, not pressing down.

Releasing the shoulders

Stretching the muscles around the shoulders helps you feel the right position of the shoulders, as well as the relationship between the shoulders and the arms. Your shoulders sit on top of your rib cage with the collarbone, or _clavicle,_ connecting the shoulders to the arms. Feel along the collarbone from your neck out to your shoulder. At the end of the collarbone, you can feel the top portion of the shoulder blade as well as the edge of the bone of the arm. Knowing how to position your shoulders and arms helps you keep all the muscles that you need for singing flexible and ready to move.

Stretch

While standing, raise your right arm over your head so that your fingers point toward the ceiling. Then make forward circles to the side of your body; your arm points to the ceiling, then in front of you, then down to the floor, then straight behind you, and finally, back to the ceiling. Then reverse the direction of the circles. When you get the hang of making the circles with one arm, try making the same circles with your other arm at the same time, only make the circles in the opposite direction. Twist your torso to correspond with the movement of both arms circling at the same time in opposite directions. If swinging the arms in opposite directions is too complicated, start by moving one arm at a time and then try moving both arms in the same direction and then in opposite directions.

Lift your right arm and place it across your chest with your left hand at your right elbow. Use your left hand to gently grasp your right elbow and bring it closer to your body. Take a breath; as you exhale, bring your right arm closer to your body to stretch the right shoulder. Repeat this stretch with your left arm across your chest.

Place both arms behind you and grasp your hands. After connecting your hands, lift your hands higher to stretch your shoulders. Reach only as far as you can comfortably go. If you can't comfortably stretch both arms behind you, stand in a doorway with both arms out to your sides. Allow your arms to touch the walls on the side of the doorway as your body moves a little farther through the doorway. Take one step forward to see what stretching your shoulders feels like. If you can take one step comfortably, take one more step for a little more stretch of the muscles. Just be mindful of what your body can handle; you don't want to force the muscles to stretch too far.

Balance

To find just the right position of balance for the shoulders, move your shoulders up and then drop them down. Press them down and then release them. Doing so can help you figure out how far up or down your resting position needs to be (it should be in the middle). Move your shoulders forward and then release them. Then move your shoulders back and release them. Doing so can help you determine how far forward or back your resting position needs to be. Note that it shouldn't be fully forward or back; it should be in between.

Why is finding a balanced resting position for your shoulders so important when singing? It's all about the breath. With each inhalation, the shoulder blades release down and out. If your shoulders hunch or round forward, your chest is partly collapsed, making the release and opening of the torso for the breath more difficult. If your shoulders thrust back too far, you can feel the muscles around the shoulder blades tighten. Roll your shoulders forward and then back to find the center; that's where you want to be when you sing.

Balancing the head and neck

The balancing of your head directly affects the muscles in your neck, and because the main vocal muscles you use when singing are in your neck, you need to take some time in every warm-up to stretch and balance your head. Your head is designed to balance on the end of your spine. The specific shape at the end of the spine allows the head to balance perfectly so that it can move in any direction. Stretch your neck muscles to release them and then explore what balancing the head feels like. Also, take some time to stretch the tongue and jaw so that they're ready to sing when you are.

Stretch

While standing or sitting, drop your head toward your chest. Take a breath; as you exhale, drop your head a little farther toward your chest. Move your head slightly to the left to stretch the muscles in your neck at an angle. Take another breath; as you exhale, drop your head a little more to the left. Move your head slightly to the right of center. Take a breath; as you exhale, drop your head a little farther to the right.

Lift your head and look left as if you were looking over your left shoulder. Turn your head slowly so that you don't stretch the muscles too quickly. Take a breath; as you exhale, turn your head to look over your right shoulder. These stretches are great because they increase the flexibility of your neck muscles and warm them up so they're ready to help balance your head, which weighs about the same as a bowling ball. No wonder you need your neck muscles to be strong and flexible!

To stretch your tongue, stick your tongue forward and out of your mouth. Feel the stretch from the tip of the tongue all the way to the back of the tongue, which curves down your throat. If your tongue won't stick out of your mouth, then place the tip of your tongue against your bottom front teeth and roll the tongue forward. To stretch the jaw, close your mouth and open your jaw by opening your back teeth. You want your jaw to drop by opening the space by your ear, not by pushing down your chin. Opening the space by the ear helps keep the space in the back of the mouth and throat open. Find out more about dropping the jaw in Chapter 12.

Balance

Move your head forward in front of your body and then back behind your body. Where you want to balance your head is right in between too far forward and too far back. After you get your head in the right forward/back position, focus on balancing it on the curve of your cervical spine without letting it press down into your neck. Your head should feel buoyant as if it were made of helium; it shouldn't feel like it's pressing down into your neck and shoulders.

Managing the arms and hands

When you sing, your arms probably hang down at your sides most of the time and then gesture when you want to emphasize something important. As you warm up, you want to eliminate any tension you feel in your arms and hands so the tension can't spread to your back or any other area in your body.

Stretch

Stretch your right arm out to your side and point your fingers to your right. Draw circles in the air as if you were drawing circles on the wall on your right side. Switch to the other hand and repeat the stretch. When you're comfortable making circles, try drawing figure eights in the air with your right hand. Allow the whole hand to move to make large figure eights in the air instead of just drawing small figure eights by pointing your fingers. Draw the figure eights with the opposite hand.

Balance

While standing or sitting, allow your arms to hang at your sides. Notice the effect this position has on the muscles in your arms and hands. You should feel a sensation of suspension, not one of pressing down or feeling heavy.

Because you may want to gesture during your songs, you need to be aware of how you move your arms and hands as you sing. If you move your arms out to your sides, you have to engage the muscles in your back, which is okay as long as you don't tighten or grip the back muscles in the process.

At no point when you're singing should you tighten the muscles in your back or anywhere else in your torso; if you do, you'll impair your ability to breathe smoothly and deeply.

Intentionally tighten the muscles at your elbows. As you tighten these muscles, notice that you also tighten the muscles across your back. As you release the elbow muscles, you release the tension in your back. Although you may not think the elbows are connected to the back, any tension in your elbows affects your ability to release the back and ribs for breathing.

Intentionally tighten the muscles in your hands. As you tighten these muscles, notice that you tighten all the way up your arms and into your lower back. Release this tension and notice the open sensation you feel in your torso. That's the open feeling you want when singing.

When you gesture during a song, be sure to notice how you shape your hand during the gesture. Tightening the muscles in the hands as you sustain a gesture can cause you to tighten across your back. Feel free to move your hands as you sing, but focus on keeping the muscles flexible rather than squeezing or locking them.

Putting It All Together with a Vocal Warm-Up

After your body is warm, you're ready to warm up your voice. The exercise in this section, featured on Track 1, allows you the chance to sing a short phrase that gradually moves up the scale. It doesn't go very high, but it goes high enough to get the voice going before you go back down the scale. I use this sequence every time I warm up.

Notice that the pattern in this exercise includes the word *hum;* this word indicates that you should hum the pattern rather than sing it. Humming sounds like you're sustaining the sound of an *M* consonant. Humming is a great way to gently warm up the voice.

As you sing through this exercise, use the following steps to help coordinate your awareness of how you're using your body. In the beginning, you may need several tries to get each step just right. Play the track as many times as you need to and take your time getting through each step.

1. **As you take a breath before the first measure, open all the way down into your feet.**

   As you inhale, check in with your feet to make sure you feel a balanced connection between them and the floor. Visualize a mouth on the bottom of your foot and pretend that you need to open your feet to take in air. This visual helps you remember to maintain flexibility and movement in your feet as you sing. **What not to do:** Don't grip your feet on the floor or tighten your toes. Tightening your toes tightens the muscles along the back of your body.

2. **Open the space around your ankles.**

   Pretend each ankle contains a shock absorber that springs up and opens as you inhale. **What not to do:** Don't sink into your ankles, or you'll feel like your body is really heavy.

3. **Open the space around your knees.**

   On the next inhale, breathe into your knees. Feel an opening around the knees and balance the weight evenly throughout the body. The bones in your knees should feel oily and glide easily. **What not to do:** Don't sink into your knees. If you sink into your knees, the weight of your body will be supported only by your legs and knees, and you'll feel much heavier.

4. **Open the space around your hips.**

   Feel the muscles around your hips expand and open with the inhale. If the muscles in your pelvis are tight, you'll most likely feel tension up your back and through your legs; you can do a few pretend hula hoops or sit in a chair and lean forward to stretch the muscles in your hips. **What not to do:** Don't sink into your hips. If you sink into your hips, you'll feel more pressure and tension in your hips; plus, you'll look like you're slumping.

5. **Open your spine.**

   Feel the sensation of lengthening the spine on the inhale. You want the discs in between the vertebrae to expand and open, not press down. **What not to do:** Don't push up to force the spine to stretch, but don't allow your posture to slump either. Both positions cause your muscles to tighten to hold you up.

6. **Open your neck and head.**

   On the next inhale, pretend that your throat is expanding in all directions to open. This expansion feels as though your neck is lifting and opening on the inhale. As your neck opens, you should feel a release of the muscles in your head. **What not to do:** Don't let your head be heavy. Notice any pressure you feel in your neck and eliminate it by opening the neck more. Also don't let the muscles in your head tighten; if they do, the inside of your throat will also tighten.

7. **Open your eyes.**

   You want the eyes and all the muscles around the eyes to release and open as you inhale. On the next inhale, open your eyes as if your eyes were mouths and you had to take in air through your eyes. When the space around the eyes releases and opens, you should also feel a releasing sensation in your throat because all those muscles are connected. **What not to do:** Don't squint. Squinting tightens the muscles throughout the head.

8. **Open your jaw.**

   On the inhale, allow your jaw to drop and release. You want your jaw to be very flexible so that it can move freely when you sing. **What not to do:** Don't press the jaw tightly. This tight sensation creates a very tight tone.

9. **Release your elbows.**

   On the inhale, allow your elbows to release and notice that the muscles around the torso move more freely when you eliminate any tension in your elbows. **What not to do:** Don't tighten your elbows as you inhale or at any time when you sing. Tension in the elbows causes tension throughout the torso, which affects your breathing.

10. **Release your hands.**

    On the inhale, allow your hands to release and notice that your tension-free hands help you maintain tension-free arms. If you want to gesture or point for emphasis as you sing, feel free to do so. Just don't tighten your hands in the process. **What not to do:** Don't tighten your hands at any time as you sing.

11. **On the inhale, release from the toes all the way up to the skull.**

    Notice that you can open the body and keep it free from tension by keeping it in motion (which you do simply by breathing in and out while singing) so that no muscle group has a chance to tighten or hold.

Chapter 2

Practicing Breathing Exercises

In this chapter, I introduce you to the muscles that need to move as you breathe while singing. You need to develop the coordination of these muscles to sing long phrases in your songs. After all, you don't want to run out of breath in the middle of a phrase, and breathing between the syllables of a word doesn't sound very smooth. You also need to be able to control the muscles in your body so you can control the amount of air you release when you sing. When you have good breath coordination, you can work on any style of music and sing with confidence — especially if you need to sing and dance.

I divide the exercises in this chapter into two categories: inhalation and exhalation. When you're confident that you can successfully manage your inhalation, move on to the exhalation exercises to refine your coordination.

Note: If you haven't read Chapter 1 yet, you may want to check it out before you dive into this chapter. In it, you find lots of information about your body alignment, which directly affects how your body moves for breathing.

Moving the Breathing Muscles for Singing

You may think that all you have to do to sing a phrase is fill your lungs with air, but you can't just fill your lungs any way you want. You have to be able to inhale quick breaths without letting your audience hear you as you open your whole body, including your lungs.

In the following sections, you explore opening and moving four areas — the ribs, the abs, the sides, and your hips and pelvis — one at a time. Knowing how to move the muscles in these areas allows you to control your inhalation. Later in this chapter, you practice opening all these areas at once. Focusing on inhalation first allows you to develop the coordination you need to get that quick breath between phrases. When you get the coordination down, you can move on to working on exhalation (see the later section for details).

Physically working out can help your singing. For example, cardiovascular workouts strengthen the lungs. When the muscles around your lungs get stronger, your singing benefits.

Opening the ribs

The rib cage is designed to protect the lungs. When you move the ribs, you move the lungs, so you need to be able to flex open the muscles between your ribs to open your lungs for singing. Work through the following sequence to develop coordination for moving your ribs:

1. **Place your hands on your ribs.**

   You can either place your palms against your ribs with your fingers pointing to the front of your body or with your fingers pointing behind you and your thumbs pointing forward. Use whichever position is more comfortable for you.

2. **Try to open the ribs so that your ribs move laterally out to the sides of your body.**

   You can either open your ribs with an inhalation of air or just try to move the ribs. Just by flexing open the rib cage (specifically, the external intercostal muscles in between the ribs), you draw air into your lungs. You may need to try this step a few times to figure out how to stretch out the muscles between the ribs.

3. **Continue to practice opening the rib cage to see whether you can expand the ribs a little farther each time.**

   Your muscles may feel tight if you haven't stretched open your ribs before. Be patient and work slowly to get the muscles to open a little more each time.

If you can't feel your ribs moving, try the following tips:

- ✔ **Some people say their ribs open when they yawn, so try placing your hands on your ribs and yawn to notice if the ribs open.** Then see if you can find that same motion without the yawn.

- ✔ **Lie on your side with your elbow bent and your wrist under your head and place your other hand on your ribs.** As you lie on your side, breathe and notice the motion of your ribs. You should feel them expand out away from your body.

- ✔ **Visualize your ribs opening from the inside out.** Take a breath and send the breath into your ribs. Pretend that the breath fills and opens the ribs rather than the lungs. The more you move the ribs while visualizing them opening, the more you can open them later without having to use an image.

- ✔ **Lie down and take a long, slow breath.** Lie on the floor on your back with your knees bent and your feet flat on the floor. As you take the air in slowly, notice the sensations you feel along your upper back. You may feel only a slight movement at first. Continue to explore the sensations in your back as you inhale while lying on your back, and you'll gradually feel more motion along your upper back or ribs.

- ✔ **Sit in a chair and lean your elbows on your knees.** Take long, slow breaths and notice which muscles move as the air enters your body. You should feel an opening in your sides and back as your ribs open. If you feel your chest rising, allow your ribs to open to the side or across your back to expand for the inhalation instead of lifting your chest. Watch in a mirror to make sure your ribs are opening to the side. You want the chest or sternum to be up rather than collapsed (but not thrusting up) so that the ribs can flex and open.

After you discover the movement of opening your ribs, explore getting even more expansion of the rib cage as you inhale. You may need several weeks to explore the expansion of the ribs before you can successfully move your ribs for singing. Remember that each time you work on the movement, you're gaining more control over your muscles.

Releasing the abs

In addition to opening the ribs, you need to be able to release your abdominal muscles, or *abs,* when you inhale. The abdominal muscles are the muscles above and below your belly button. When you inhale, the abs release out and down. You can see the abs moving during the inhalation, and they feel like they're dropping open to make room for the air to fill your lungs. However, you don't want to rely only on your abs to control your inhalation, especially if you need to move around while singing because you need the abs to help you dance.

Here are some ways to help you feel the release of the abs:

✔ **Take a breath and imagine that you're sending the air all the way down to your belly button.** This visual helps you feel the release that happens throughout your torso on the inhale. The release should feel like a dropping sensation, as if the abs were dropping along with everything else inside your torso.

✔ **Place your hands on your abs to feel the release that happens at and below your belly button.** As your lungs fill with air on the inhale, the organs inside your torso drop down to give your lungs room to expand. As your abs release and drop, you may also feel a release in your sides.

✔ **Wait a few moments before you take the next breath.** After you exhale, count to ten before you inhale again. When you don't take your breath until you really need it, you feel your abs drop down fast to allow air into your body as quickly as possible.

Practice allowing the abs to release on the inhalation. Although the release may be slow in the beginning, you can use the exercises later in this chapter to help you speed up the inhalation so you can get the breath you need throughout your song.

Many singers are nervous about releasing their abs because they don't want to look fat. If you share this concern, practice releasing your abs for breathing when you're alone at home and no one else can see. The more you explore the movement of the abs, the more you realize that it's about releasing the abs smoothly, not flopping them down and creating a big belly.

Moving the sides

As the ribs open and the abs release, you also want to open the area just below the rib cage on the sides. The muscles along the sides of the body just below the ribs are called the *internal* and *external oblique muscles*. The obliques are primarily responsible for controlling the exhalation, but you need to open or expand them during the inhalation to get them ready to control the exhalation.

To feel the opening in the obliques, try moving into different positions the next time you practice singing. For example, follow these steps to try out a squat position:

1. **Squat down and either keep your heels on the floor or balance on the balls of your feet.**

   If the squat isn't comfortable for you to maintain, sit in a chair and lean forward to put your elbows on your knees.

2. **Practice opening your ribs.**

   You may feel more movement in the ribs from the squat position than you do from a standard standing or sitting position because you don't have to worry about holding up your body.

3. **Continue to open all the way down your sides.**

    When the sides open, you may also feel an opening sensation low in your back. Continue to explore this opening sensation until you can feel an opening all the way from the top of your rib cage down your sides to your hip bone.

In the beginning, you may feel only a slight opening in your sides. Don't worry; just continue to explore the expansion of the muscles in your sides until you can not only feel but also see the movement of the muscles. You want to be comfortable with stretching out your side muscles so that in the middle of a song you can deliberately create a slight opening for short phrases and a larger opening for long phrases.

Releasing into the hips

You may not think the hips have anything to do with breathing, but in actuality, the release of the muscles in the hips allows you to release everything else in your torso. To practice releasing into the hips, try out these two techniques:

✔ **Sit in a chair with your knees apart and lean forward to rest your elbows on your knees.** While in this position, take a breath and allow the muscles along your back to release all the way down into your hips. This release should feel like a dropping and opening sensation happening inside your body.

✔ **Pretend that you have on a really tight shirt and open your back enough that you can either rip open the back of the shirt or really stretch out the back of the shirt all the way down to your hips.** The stretching sensation you feel is a combination of the opening of the ribs, the stretching of the sides, and the releasing into the hips.

If you're not sure whether you're opening or stretching the right muscles in and around the hips, give the following two tips a try:

✔ **Tighten all the muscles in your hips and pelvis, including the pelvic floor muscles.** As you tighten these muscles, notice that you feel tight all the way up the back and along your sides. After you figure out what tight hips feel like, you can use that feeling to make sure your hips are released (and not tight) when you breathe during singing. That way, the rest of your torso can also be ready for expansion (rather than tension).

✔ **Sit in a chair and rock your pelvis on the seat.** In other words, allow the bones that you're sitting on to tilt backward and then forward. As you rock your pelvis, notice what happens to your breath. Most singers feel that their breath flows into the body when the pelvis rocks backward and that they automatically exhale as the pelvis rocks forward. After rocking your pelvis, the muscles around your hips may feel more flexible and you may be more aware of how they move when you inhale.

Take It In: Shaping Inhalation

Inhalation is the process of opening the body so that air can fall in. When singing, you don't want to try to pull in air as you inhale. Instead, just open the muscles in the ribs, abs, sides, and hips, and the air will fall in naturally.

In this section, I help you develop control over the muscles of inhalation. After you work through the exercises I present here, put the muscle coordination you develop to the test as you sing through the rest of the practice exercises in this book as well as your own songs.

Controlling the movement of your ribs

The tips I describe in the earlier section "Opening the ribs" help you practice opening the ribs in general. In this section, I help you develop control over the movement of the ribs so that you control how much air you take into your body. If you only open slightly, you take in a small amount of air. Opening more brings in the air you need for longer phrases. Follow these steps to develop control over your rib movement:

1. **Open your ribs slowly as you inhale for four counts and then exhale for two counts.**

   As you inhale, notice how much your ribs move. Allow the ribs to open or expand more each time you slowly inhale. Continue to work on this step until you can see and feel the movement of the ribs. Then move on to Step 2.

2. **Increase your inhalation to six counts and then exhale for two counts.**

   As you inhale for six counts, your ribs should move out farther than they did in four counts. Your goal here is to slowly develop control over the opening of the ribs and to gradually stretch the muscles so they can open more.

3. **Increase your inhalation to eight counts and then exhale for two counts.**

   As you inhale for eight counts, your ribs should move out even farther than they did for six counts. However, you don't want to inhale so much that your ribs and lungs feel like they may explode. Opening the muscles around the ribs farther isn't the same as trying to fill up the lungs with a huge amount of air.

You may need to work on these steps for a few weeks before you develop the coordination you need to fully open the muscles in your ribs.

Adding suspension to develop coordination

The normal movement of the body when breathing is a quick inhalation with very little movement in the torso, a short exhalation, and then a pause before it all begins again. This process is the opposite of what you want for singing. In its place, you want a quick but broad expansion of the body for the inhalation and a very slow exhalation during the phrases you sing. Because the body is used to making a quick exhalation right after you inhale, you have to resist this natural movement of the body when you sing and instead practice a *suspension,* or resistance to the quick collapse of the body, in between the inhale and exhale. This suspension is especially necessary when you want to sing long phrases.

Here's how to explore suspension:

1. **Open your ribs slowly as you inhale for four counts and then pause for four counts.**

   When you get to the pause, don't inhale or exhale — just wait. This pause helps you discover the sensation of suspension. The muscles feel like they're ready to collapse at any moment, but you don't let them.

2. **Exhale and notice how quickly the rib muscles collapse to their resting position.**

3. **Open your ribs as you inhale for four counts, suspend for four counts, and then exhale.**

   Remember that the suspension is a sensation of moving at any moment, not holding your breath. Holding your breath feels tight and causes your throat to close.

4. **Inhale for four counts, suspend for six counts, and then exhale.**

5. **Repeat Steps 3 and 4 and continue to extend the suspension for up to ten counts as long as your body doesn't tighten.**

   If you feel your body tighten as you move past six counts, release the air and know that six counts is your limit for now.

When you're comfortable with the sensation of suspension in your ribs, try this exercise by opening the other areas of your torso (the sides, abs, back, and hips).

Opening the torso for quick inhalation

Sometimes in a song, you have to take a quick breath to stay on track. In this section, you develop the physical coordination to inhale quickly (in one count) while finding the same opening of muscles that you find in the preceding section when you inhale for four counts. Follow these steps to help you discover how to open the torso for quick inhalation. If you find that you can't open your muscles efficiently, take a look at the previous sections on moving the breathing muscles.

1. **Sit in a chair and lean forward with your elbows on your knees.**

2. **Open your body for inhalation by opening your ribs, sides, back, and abs.**

   Take your time and practice opening all four areas separately. You may need to exhale and then inhale to feel the movement of the muscles. When you're confident that you can open each area separately, try opening two of the areas at one time. For example, practice taking a breath by opening your ribs and releasing your abs at the same time. Continue to explore opening two areas at the same time until you've opened your ribs, sides, back, or abs together with another area. Then practice taking a breath and opening three of the four areas. Try simultaneously opening your ribs, abs, and sides or any other combination.

3. **Practice inhaling again by opening the entire torso down through your hips.**

   Notice the coordination you need to move all your torso muscles at the same time. You may need to practice this step for several days before you can move on to Step 4 and open your entire torso within a limited amount of time (six counts). Don't get too frustrated; it's better to work slowly and develop the coordination instead of rushing through and trying to force the muscles to move.

4. **Practice opening the muscles throughout the torso (ribs, sides, back, and abs) in six counts and then exhale.**

   As you count to six, you should feel all the muscles in the torso slowly opening for the inhalation.

5. **Practice opening the muscles throughout the torso in four counts and then exhale.**

   Practice this step several times to make sure you can create the same kind of opening and movement of the muscles that you made in six counts in Step 4.

6. **Practice opening the muscles throughout the torso in three counts and then exhale.**

   Your goal is to achieve the same opening in three counts that you achieved in six counts, so you may need to spend several days practicing this step before you move on to Steps 7 and 8.

7. **Practice opening the muscles in the torso for two counts and exhale.**

   To open the muscles in two counts, you really have to develop control over each of the muscles by themselves before trying to open them all at once. If you have this control, you shouldn't be tempted to try to pull in air. Opening the muscles the right way naturally brings air into the body so that you don't have to stress about the inhalation itself.

   When you're confident that you can open all the muscles in just two counts, move on to Step 8.

8. **Practice opening the muscles to their full expansion in one count.**

   Remember that the goal isn't to open the body to make it huge but to open it sufficiently so that air flows easily into the lungs. You may need to count one, two, and then open the spaces on the third count. If you just try opening in one count, you may open too fast and end up gasping. If you get the speed of the counts down first, opening in one count will make more sense.

Be sure to spend plenty of time developing your muscle coordination for your inhalation before you start working on your exhalation in the next section. Check out Chapter 13 if you want some practice inhaling and opening your torso in one count while singing a pattern.

Let It Out: Controlling Exhalation

Exhalation is the process of moving the air out of the body. When you sing, you exhale and the breath passing through your throat helps you make sound. Hence, singing a phrase requires a consistent flow of air. The way to control the air is to control the movement of the muscles. Specifically, every exhalation in singing involves controlling the muscles that you open during inhalation. During the inhalation, you open the ribs, abs, sides, lower back, and hips. You use the same muscles during the exhalation, but you can move them in one of two ways:

   ✔ You gradually move the muscles during the exhalation back to their normal resting position.

   ✔ You suspend the muscles or keep them open for a short period of time before gradually moving them back in.

If controlling exhalation is new to you, I suggest that you start with the first section on developing muscle coordination. When you're confident that you can feel the gradual movement of the muscles during the exhalation, you can explore using muscle isolation in the second section to help you with really long, challenging phrases.

How successful your exhalation is determines how clear your tone is. If you have a breathy tone, too much air is escaping while you're singing. It's natural for breath to move out of your body as you sing, but you're letting too much air move out if you have a breathy tone. Turn to Chapter 12 for exercises that get you working on tone.

Developing muscle coordination

Developing muscle coordination is the most important step for managing exhalation for singing. This section helps you develop that muscle coordination, but it assumes that you can open the body for the inhalation quickly. If you can't open the body quickly, see the earlier section "Opening the torso for quick inhalation" for help.

Trying to control your entire torso is difficult, so the following steps have you work on controlling the movement of only one area at a time. After you've explored the individual areas, you can coordinate two and then three areas and then the entire torso.

1. **Open the ribs as you inhale for three counts.**

2. **Exhale by making the *SH* sound for three counts, allowing only the ribs to move during the exhalation.**

   Your *SH* sound should be a steady sound, not a wobbly one. A steady *SH* means that your breath is moving steadily; a wobbly sound means that the muscles aren't moving smoothly and the breath is moving out in spurts.

3. **Inhale for three counts and then repeat Step 2, this time exhaling for four counts.**

4. **Inhale for three counts and then repeat Step 2 for six, eight, ten, and then twelve counts.**

   Move to a higher number of counts only when you can successfully manage the previous number three times in a row. Watch the second hand on a clock to make sure you're counting at a consistent speed. The goal isn't to exhale for tons of counts but to mimic the kind of control over exhalation that you need for singing your song. Working up to an exhalation of ten to twelve counts simulates the length of an average phrase in a song.

When you can control the movement of the ribs for at least six counts, repeat the previous steps by opening the abs, then the sides, then the back. If for any reason you can't really feel the movement of the sides or the back, combine the movement of the ribs with the area that you're struggling to feel. Remember that this coordination takes time to develop and these steps alone may take you several weeks of practicing.

After you've worked on each area of the torso separately, explore opening them all at the same time. Open the torso with an inhalation on three counts and exhale by gradually moving the muscles back in for the designated number of counts. Start with an exhalation on *SH* for four counts and then move on to six, eight, and ten counts. That pattern looks like this:

✔ Inhale for three counts; exhale on *SH* for four counts.

✔ Inhale for three counts; exhale on *SH* for six counts.

✔ Inhale for three counts; exhale on *SH* for eight counts.

✔ Inhale for three counts; exhale on *SH* for ten counts.

After you're confident that you have control over the muscles you use during the exhalation, you can explore adding some basic suspension. Using suspension with the exhalation means you delay the movement of the muscles. You stay open as if the breath could move without your having to push the muscles in. Follow this pattern to practice adding suspension to your inhales and exhales:

✔ Inhale for two counts, suspend for four counts, exhale on *SH* for four counts, and suspend for four counts.

✔ Inhale for two counts, suspend for six counts, exhale on *SH* for six counts, and suspend for six counts.

> ✔ Inhale for two counts, suspend for eight counts, exhale on *SH* for eight counts, and suspend for eight counts.
>
> ✔ Continue exploring the number of counts that your body is comfortable making. The goal isn't to get to a hundred but to gain enough control that you can handle just about any phrase length in your song.

Singers often say that they feel like they need to exhale before they can inhale again. This feeling is very typical because your body wants to exhale in a shorter amount of time than the long period of time required in the preceding list. When singing, you don't move all the air out of your lungs on the exhalation; you move just enough to sing the phrase. To prevent feeling like you're holding on to air or overfilling the tank, release the muscles in your torso instead of trying to suck in air for the inhalation.

Isolating muscles for extra-long phrases

Gradually moving the body in as you exhale works very well for most phrases, but you may need some extra help with those really long phrases. Using muscle isolation during exhalation helps you feel as though you have several tanks of air that empty one at a time. In this section, you explore keeping the ribs out while the abs and sides move in. After the abs are finished moving, you move the ribs. Try out the following steps to start developing control for those really long phrases:

1. **Take a breath and allow your torso to expand as you open your ribs, sides, abs, back, and hips.**

2. **As you start the exhalation, let your abs move first.**

   You can practice the exhalation on the *SH* as you do in the preceding section so that you can hear and feel the steady flow of air. Allow the abs to gradually move in, but leave the ribs open. You may need to practice this step a few times before you're able to isolate the movement of the abs and ribs.

   If you have a hard time isolating the movement on a slow exhalation, practice opening for the inhalation and then quickly exhale, focusing on moving your abs and leaving your ribs open. Inhale again and then quickly exhale by moving only the abs while keeping the ribs open. After you explore this quick movement several times, you should start to feel the isolation of the muscle groups. Specifically, the ribs should feel like they're suspended in motion while the abs are moving.

   When you're confident that you can exhale on the *SH* and leave the ribs open while the abs move, move on to Step 3.

3. **Inhale again and exhale slowly on the *SH*, first allowing the abs to move in while the ribs stay open and then allowing the ribs to slowly move in after the abs have moved as much as they can.**

   Your abs can move only so much, and you should feel when they just don't have any more movement left. That's when you want to start allowing the ribs to move in.

This kind of muscle isolation takes some practice, but when you get the hang of it, you'll be glad you did! For me, discovering this movement in my body has changed my breath control completely. Those longer phrases are now a whole lot easier because I feel like I have two tanks of air to draw from. You may not need this length of breath control for every style of music you sing, but you never know when you may want to try something new.

If you're struggling with a particularly long phrase in your song and just can't quite make it all the way through, then work backward to figure out the problem. Instead of starting at the beginning of the phrase, start closer to the end. If the phrase is eight measures, then practice your breath control on the last two measures. When you're confident on how you use the breath on the last two measures, then work the last four measures. You notice that the last four measures seem easy because you start them at the beginning of the breath cycle instead of when you're almost out of air. When the four measures feel solid, then sing the last six measures until you can manage the breath. Then try out the full eight measures. You now realize how long the phrase is and how steady the flow of air should be.

Singing Practice Exercises with Long and Short Phrases

The exercises in this section help you develop the physical coordination you need for controlling your breath in a song. In these exercises, you get to apply your breath coordination as you sing short phrases and then long phrases. You need to practice both so you're ready to handle any phrase in your song.

Practicing short phrases

This exercise, featured on Track 2, helps you practice using your muscle coordination to sing short phrases. In this exercise, notice that you have the option of practicing the pattern on a lip trill or a tongue trill or practicing it using a vowel and a consonant *(mee):*

✔ **Lip trill:** If working on breath coordination is new for you, I suggest you start this exercise by using a lip trill because the lip trill gives you some resistance so that the breath doesn't just blow out. The *lip trill* sounds like a buzzing of your lips combined with sound from your voice. Listen to the singer on Track 2 demonstrate the sound. When you use the lip trill, you want the lips to vibrate as the air flows out, but you don't want the lips to flop around.

To get the lip trill just right, place your fingers at the corners of your mouth and gently pull the corners out a little bit. This slight rounding movement of the lips helps you release just the right amount of air during the lip trill. Sometimes when the entire lip is involved in the lip trill, you blow out too much air.

✔ **Tongue trill:** The *tongue trill* is when you move air over the roof of your mouth and allow your tongue to vibrate as the air moves out of your mouth. If you can roll your *R,* then you can make a tongue trill.

✔ *Mee:* As you sing *mee,* you want the same steady flow of air you use for the lip and tongue trills. The voiced consonant *M* helps you get the tone started, and a steady flow of air helps keep the tone clear. You hear the singer demonstrate *mee* for you in the third measure.

Listen to the singer demonstrate the lip trill, tongue trill, and *mee* for you on Track 2. After you hear the pattern all the way through and are confident that you know the length of the phrases, then play the track again and sing along, using the lip trill or tongue trill. Then after two or three practice sessions, try singing *mee.* As you sing through the exercise, keep your hands on your sides to check the movement of your ribs, sides, back, and abs. You want to feel the body open for the inhalation and then gradually move in during the exhalation as you're singing.

Practicing longer phrases

Before you jump into this exercise, which is featured on Track 3, make sure that you've developed pretty good breath control (see the rest of this chapter for details). This exercise contains only a few notes, but you really have to practice your breath control to sing it slowly the way it's written. Don't be tricked by how easy the exercise looks; at such a slow tempo, it provides a great challenge for you.

Before you sing the first note in this exercise, make sure you really open your body for the inhalation. As you sing through the pattern, keep your hands on your sides to make sure the air flows consistently as your muscles slowly move back in as you exhale. You may want to start by singing only a few repetitions of the pattern and then stopping for a moment. After all, repeating the long phrases for a while is challenging.

You can use a lip trill for this exercise, or you can sing *mee* or *nooh*. I recommend that you try the lip trill (or tongue trill if the lip trill is difficult for you) first and then sing the *mee* or *nooh* so you can compare the flow of air on the trill versus on a consonant and vowel.

The singer demonstrates the sounds of this exercise for you on Track 3. Listen as the singer demonstrates the lip trill first and then *mee* and *nooh*. After you know the speed of the pattern, play the track again and sing along, using the lip trill. When you're confident you have a consistent flow of air on the lip trill, switch and sing either *mee* or *nooh*.

Testing your breath control

This exercise, which you can hear on Track 4, challenges you by changing the length of the pattern. The exercise contains a short pattern that repeats a different number of times on each line. The original pattern appears on the first line. Then on the second line, you see the pattern repeating two times, and on the third line, you see the pattern repeating three times.

After you're familiar with the exercise as a whole, you can decide how many times you want to practice it in a row. Keep in mind that you want to challenge yourself just beyond your comfort zone. If you can successfully make it through three repetitions, then practice singing through three repetitions for a few days before moving on to singing four repetitions. When you're comfortable singing four, move on to singing five.

Notice that the music for this exercise says *lip trill, tongue trill,* or *mee*. The lip trill and tongue trill can both help you discover how to move the breath and recognize the resistance from the lips or tongue, so I suggest you start there. For both of these options, the breath should move steadily instead of just blowing out at the beginning of the phrase. When you're comfortable controlling the air, you can switch and sing *mee*. Remember that you want the muscles to be in motion and not locked or held. If you find that you're holding your breath or holding the muscles in your torso, go back to a shorter exercise to practice the fluid motion and then return to the longer one.

As you sing the longer repetitions, think about where you're going in the phrase rather than where you've been. Thinking too much about the note you're singing now makes each note feel vertical, but thinking about what's ahead makes the phrase seem like it flows easily and isn't so long.

Singing along with the track helps you work your way up to singing longer phrases as well as alternating between long and short patterns. Listen to the singer demonstrate the first three lines of the pattern for you on Track 4. The pattern plays one time, then twice, then three times, and then the numbers start to alternate. Here is the full listing of the number of times the pattern repeats: 1, 2, 3, 1, 3, 2, 4, 3, 5, 2, 6, 3, 5, 2, 4, 1, 4, 2, 6, 1. When you're confident you know how many times to repeat the notes, play the track again and join in.

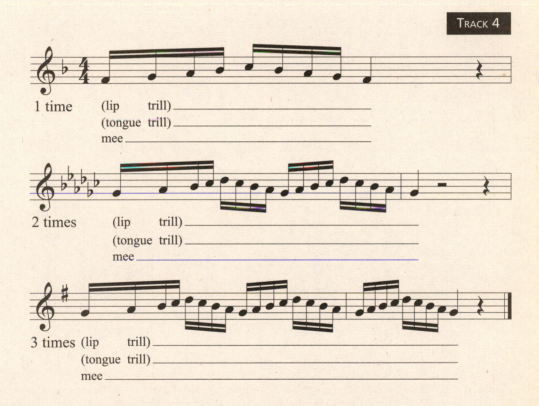

Songs for Extending Breath Control

The songs in this list have long phrases to help you practice your breath control. You may need to practice these songs for several weeks to be able to sing the long phrases. You can use the exercises from the sections "Practicing longer phrases" and "Testing your breath control" to help you develop the physical coordination you need for the more challenging phrases.

- ✔ "Sure on This Shining Night" by Samuel Barber (either)
- ✔ "A Dream Is a Wish Your Heart Makes" from *Cinderella* by Mack David, Al Hoffman, and Jerry Livingston (either)

- "I Never Has Seen Snow" from *House of Flowers* by Harold Arlen (female)
- "Silent Noon" by R. Vaughan Williams (either)
- "Chanson indoue" ("Song of India") from *Sadko* by N. Rimsky-Korsakov (either)
- "Morgen!" ("Tomorrow!") by Richard Strauss (either)
- "I Have a Love" from *West Side Story* by Leonard Bernstein (female)
- "Come to Me, Bend to Me" from *Brigadoon* by Frederick Loewe and Alan Jay Lerner (male)
- "Ribbons down My Back" from *Hello, Dolly!* by Jerry Herman (female)
- "Calm as the Night" ("Still wie die Nacht") by Carl Bohm (either)

Chapter 3

Shaping the Tongue and Lips for Vowels

- -

In This Chapter

▶ Shaping the mouth for the main types of vowels

▶ Getting some practice with front, back, middle, and combination vowels

- -

No matter what style of music you sing, you need to sing your vowels precisely so that your audience can understand you. Although the exact articulation needed for classical singing is quite different from what's needed for pop singing — the classical singer needs the best and most precise articulation possible at all times, while the popular singer can do without that same overemphasis of words — articulation is still critical to both styles. After all, your listeners will tune you out if they can't understand you.

In this chapter, you explore the various vowel sounds based on how you shape the mouth to create them. I explain how to position your tongue and how to shape your lips so you can apply this knowledge in the chapter's exercises.

I recommend that you speak the words in each exercise before you sing them. Speaking through the text gives you a chance to practice making the exact shapes before you try singing and shaping. You want your audience to understand your words, so take some time to practice making the shapes and then sing through the text in the exercises.

Coordinating the Tongue and Lips for Back Vowels

You form the *back vowels* — *ooh, OOh, oh, aw,* and *ah* — by arching the back of your tongue and creating very specific lip shapes. The tongue arches to its highest point on the *ooh* vowel and then gradually lowers for *OOh, oh, aw,* and *ah*. The lips create a specific shape for the back vowels, but the shape is more open when you sing the higher notes. Because you need to open the space in the back of the throat and mouth for the higher notes, the lips have to lengthen as the jaw drops. The following list provides examples of words that contain back vowels and walks you through how to shape your lips for each back vowel:

- ✔ To sing the *ooh* vowel (as in *shoe* and *new*), allow your lips to pucker forward (that is, to move forward away from your front teeth) and to round to a small opening.

- ✔ The *OOh* vowel (as in *took, shook,* and *crook*) requires that your lips pucker and open just slightly farther than they do for the *ooh* vowel.

- ✔ For the *oh* vowel (as in *go* and *no*), your lips round into a circle.

- ✔ For the *aw* vowel (as in *awful* and *slaw*), your lips are slightly rounded and open into a wider circle than the circle they make for the *oh* vowel.

- ✔ For the *ah* vowel (as in *father* and *gaga*), your lips are slightly rounded but without the protrusion that they made for the *oh* or *aw*.

REMEMBER

For all the back vowels, the tip of the tongue continues to touch the bottom front teeth. If the back of your tongue feels tight when you make the back vowels, you're pushing up the tongue rather than raising it. To fix this problem, allow the space in the back of your mouth and throat to release; then you can raise the back of your tongue without having to tighten the muscles. You'll feel some movement in the muscles as you arch your tongue, but that basic movement is different from tension.

The following sections explain how to make the five back vowel sounds and offer some exercises to help you practice them. I've paired the vowels together to help you make just the right shapes and sounds.

Shifting the arch around for ooh and ah

This section focuses on the back vowel with the highest arch, *ooh,* and compares it to the back vowel with the lowest arch, *ah.* It's easier to feel the vibrations of resonance on the *ooh* than on the *ah.* But if you know what the strong sensations on the *ooh* vowel feel like, you can keep those strong vibrations going when you sing *ah.*

These two vowels differ in both tongue arch and lip shape. The *ooh* vowel has a high arch in the back of the tongue, while the *ah* vowel has just a slight arch. When making the arch in the back of your tongue for the *ooh* vowel, your tongue should feel higher in the back than it is for the *ah* vowel but not tighter.

When you move from the *ooh* to the *ah,* your lips round for the *ooh* and release to an open and only slightly rounded position for the *ah.* But the corners don't pull to change the shape into an *ah* vowel. Instead, the corners of the lips should remain free and relaxed for the *ah* vowel.

TIP

Speak through the following pairs of words to feel the changes between the *ooh* and the *ah: to father, blue drama, new armada,* and *two Mazdas.*

Use the sequence of vowels in the following exercise to practice making the shape change from *ooh* to *ah.* Listen to the piano on Track 5 and sing along first with just the vowels and then with the full phrases in the second line.

TRACK 5

Altering your lip shape for oh and ah

This exercise pairs *oh* and *ah* so you can practice making specific shapes with your lips and tongue. The *oh* and *ah* are similar in lip shape, and if you aren't precise with that shape, your *oh* will end up sounding like an *ah*. Get out your hand mirror or stand in front of a stationary mirror to check the shape change of your lips for the vowels *oh* and *ah*. Remember that the lips open more for the *ah* vowel than they do for the *oh* vowel. Be very aware of maintaining the shape of the lips when singing the *oh* vowel and how much opening there is in the lips compared with the *ah*.

Note: In speaking, you may not notice that the lips change shape and form a *diphthong* (combination of two vowels in one syllable) for the *oh* vowel. You want only a shadow of the second vowel *(oh-ooh)*. If you change the shape of the lips too quickly in a song when you're sustaining a note, you hear a distinct second vowel *(ooh)*. See the later section "Singing Combination Vowels" for details on diphthongs.

When you change from the *oh* vowel to the *ah* vowel, notice how the arch at the back of your tongue drops slightly from the *oh* down to the *ah*. You can't see this arch change in a mirror because your lips are rounded for the vowel, so you have to trust that you can feel the right shape and hear the right sound.

You can feel the change in the arch and observe the movement of your lips by speaking through the following word pairs: *go father, those llamas, no drama, slow Brahms,* and *old tacos.*

Use the following exercise to practice shaping the *oh* and *ah* vowels. As you sing the vowel sounds in the first line and the full phrases in the second line, watch the shape of your lips in a mirror to make sure you're changing from a rounded puckered circle for the *oh* to a more open rounded shape for the *ah*. The piano plays this exercise on Track 5.

Tackling the tricky vowels aw and OOh

The vowels *aw* and *OOh* are very tricky because, first of all, the lip and tongue shapes aren't familiar for most singers and, second of all, these two vowels tend to blur with other vowels. The shape of the *OOh* vowel is in between the shapes for the *ooh* and *oh* vowels. The highest arch you make for the *ooh* drops slightly to make the sound of *OOh* (as in *took*), and the lips open slightly but not as much as they do for the *oh*. The shape for the *aw* vowel is a little more open (as in the word *thaw*) than the shape for the *oh*. Specifically, the arch for *aw* is slightly lower, and the lips are slightly more open and rounded.

The following word pairings, which move from *OOh* to *aw* in the first seven pairs and from *aw* to *OOh* in the last seven pairs, help you practice making the right shape and sound for these two vowels: *would thaw, cook slaw, good law, wool shawl, could claw, foot fraud, good awning, Paula should, raw sugar, thaw cookies, pawn books, saw wood, small soot,* and *wall hook*.

When you feel comfortable making the shapes and sounds of both the *OOh* and the *aw*, sing the following pattern along with the piano on Track 5. Start by singing just the vowel sounds in the first line and then move into singing the full phrases in the second line.

TRACK 5

Singing through the five back vowels

The following exercise, which you can hear performed on Track 6, allows you to practice making all the back vowels. Practice speaking through the text before you sing along with the singer on Track 6 to check the position of your tongue and lips. Then sing the exercise several times each time you practice, focusing on the shapes of the vowels so that each practice session brings you closer to absolute clarity of vowel sounds and shapes. If you aren't sure how to shape any of the consonants, turn to Chapter 4.

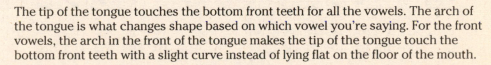

Positioning the Tongue for Front Vowels

The *front vowels* — *ee, ih, ay, eh,* and *a* — get their name from the fact that you have to arch the front of your tongue to create the appropriate sounds. The following list explains how to properly arch your tongue to sing each of the front vowels and notes a couple of words that contain each of the various vowel sounds:

✔ The *ee* vowel (as in the words *see* and *we*) requires the highest arch in the front of the tongue. To create this vowel sound, rest the tip of the tongue at the bottom front teeth, and raise the sides of the tongue in an arch to touch the inside of the upper teeth while the back of the tongue stays released. Say the word *me*. Do you feel your tongue make this shape?

The tip of the tongue touches the bottom front teeth for all the vowels. The arch of the tongue is what changes shape based on which vowel you're saying. For the front vowels, the arch in the front of the tongue makes the tip of the tongue touch the bottom front teeth with a slight curve instead of lying flat on the floor of the mouth.

✔ The *ih* vowel (as in the words *miss* and *mitt*) has the next highest arch. For this sound, the sides of the tongue continue to touch the upper side teeth, but the arch in the front of the tongue drops down a bit.

✔ The *ay* vowel (as in the words *day* and *they*) still has an arch in the tongue, but it drops slightly from its position for the *ih* vowel. The *ay* is a diphthong (two vowels sounded one after another in one syllable) and moves from this shape back to the higher arch for the *ih*. You can find more information about diphthongs in the later section "Singing Combination Vowels."

✔ The *eh* vowel (as in the words *met* and *bet*) still has an arch in the front of the tongue, but the sides of the tongue no longer touch the upper side teeth.

✔ The final vowel *a* (as in the words *ask* and *bath*) has a slight arch in the front of the tongue. Because the arch for the *a* vowel is lower than it is for the other front vowels, it may not feel much like an arch, but it shouldn't feel like tension either.

REMEMBER

When shaping any of the front vowels, be sure to keep your lips released; don't pucker them or else your front vowels will sound like different vowels.

Speak through the following list of words to feel the high arch for the *ee* vowel and the gradual lowering for each subsequent front vowel: *me, miss, may, met,* and *mask*. When you're confident that your tongue can move into the right positions, check out the following sections, which feature exercises that get you singing each of the front vowels in turn.

Dropping the arch between ee and ih

Some singers can find great clarity of tone when singing an *ee* vowel but have difficulty finding the same clarity when they move to the *ih* vowel. The problem is usually that they drop the arch of the tongue too far for the *ih*. Although the arch is slightly different for the *ee* and *ih*, it doesn't drop that much. To see what I mean, practice alternating between these two vowels in the phrases *he missed, she wished, free dish,* and *clean fish*. The arch of the tongue should rise for the *ee* vowel and lower slightly for the *ih* vowel, but the sides of the tongue should still touch the top teeth for the *ih* vowel.

In the following exercise, you alternate between singing *ee* and singing *ih*. Start by reading through the vowel sounds in the first line and the words in the second line. Then play Track 7 and sing the two lines along with the piano.

TRACK 7

Moving between ee and ay

Technically, the *ay* vowel is a diphthong, meaning it's a combination of two vowel sounds that happen in one syllable — *ay* and *ih*. When you move from the *ay* sound to the second vowel, your tongue moves back up to the shape for the *ih* vowel.

When singing *ay,* you don't want to linger too long or accent the second vowel too much. Lingering on the second vowel would sound like *dayeeee* instead of just *day*. As you speak or sing the word *day,* the second vowel happens at the last moment and it's very short. Practice saying these phrases to move smoothly from *ee* to *ay: we pay, she may, free day, read late,* and *three ways*. As you speak through the word with the *ay* vowel, you hear and feel that your tongue moves back to the shape and sound of the *ih* on the end of the *ay* vowel.

Use the following exercise to practice moving between the vowels *ee* and *ay*. First, read through the vowel sounds in the first line; then read through the full words in the second line. When you feel comfortable moving from one vowel to another, sing the sequence of vowels along with the piano on Track 7.

TRACK 7

1. ee ay ee ay ee   ee ay ee ay ee
2. She pays. She pays me.   He gave. He gave three.

ee ay ee ay ee   ee ay ee ay ee
We stay. We stay free.   She pays. She pays me.

ee ay ee ay ee   ee ay ee ay ee
He gave. He gave three.   We stay. We stay free.

Distinguishing between ee and eh

To make a clear sound when singing the *eh* vowel, you need to make a very specific shape with your tongue. Otherwise, you sound as though you're trying to sing the *ee* vowel and doing a very bad job. For the *eh* vowel, the tip of the tongue stays against the bottom front teeth, but the sides of the tongue no longer touch the upper side teeth as they do for the *ee, ih,* and *ay* vowels. When you move between *ee* and *eh,* the sides of your tongue may feel like little wings as they move up for the *ee* vowel to touch the inside of the side teeth and then move down for the *eh* vowel to rest level with the space between the teeth. If you feel the sides of your tongue moving all the way down to the floor of your mouth and touching the side gums, your arch is falling too far. To feel what the change in the arch should feel like from *ee* to *eh*, practice saying the following phrases: *he fed, free eggs, three hens,* and *she left.*

The *eh* vowel isn't a diphthong, so don't add another vowel to words like *met* and *bet.* Some regional accents add a second vowel into the mixture and say *meh-uht.* But the right sound is *meht* without the additional second vowel.

Practice shaping for the *ee* and *eh* vowels by reading through the first and second lines of the following exercise. Then play Track 7 and sing along with the piano.

TRACK 7

1. ee eh ee eh ee   ee eh ee eh ee
2. We met. We met Lee.   She bets. She bets three.

ee eh ee eh ee   ee eh ee eh ee
See vet. See vet please.   We met. We met Lee.

ee eh ee eh ee   ee eh ee eh ee
She bets. She bets three.   See vet. See vet please.

Comparing eh and a

The *a* vowel can be a tricky one to shape just right without creating tension in the tongue. Comparing *eh* and *a* can help you feel the right shape for both vowels and keep them tension-free. The *eh* has a slightly higher arch than the *a* vowel. If you say the phrases *bed bath, men chant, red plant,* and *pet calf,* you can feel that the shape of the two vowels is similar and that the *a* vowel has a slightly lower arch than the *eh.* What you shouldn't feel is an arch for the *eh* vowel and then tension in the *a* vowel. To help you find just the right shape for the *a* vowel, say the two words again but pretend that they're the exact same shape. Pretending they're the same shape helps you realize that the two vowel shapes are very similar and that there's only a slight difference in the arch of the tongue. Sometimes singers have difficulty singing the *a* vowel because the shape spreads or gets too wide. The corners of the lips shouldn't spread or tighten; instead, they should be released when you make the sound of *a.*

Try speaking through the text of the following exercise to feel the difference in shape between the two vowels. After you speak the text, listen to the piano play the exercise for you on Track 7. When you're confident that you know the pattern, play the track again and sing along.

TRACK 7

1. eh a eh___ a
2. Beth, ask ten___ staff.

Wet half said___ Lance.

eh a eh___ a
Let last ten___ pass.

eh a eh___ a
Beth, ask ten___ staff.

eh a eh___ a
Wet half said___ Lance.

eh a eh___ a
Let last ten___ pass.

Singing through the five front vowels

This exercise, which you can hear a singer demonstrate for you on Track 8, helps you practice singing all five front vowels. Be sure to apply proper breath coordination (I cover this in Chapter 2), open the space in the back of your mouth and throat (see Chapter 12 on tone for help with opening this space), and let the tongue articulate the consonants while the space in the back of your mouth stays open (see Chapter 4 for guidance on articulating consonants). You can watch yourself in the mirror to make sure all these things are happening at once. If they're not, you may need to focus on getting the vowel sounds correct first and then try adding the other technical skills to the accurate vowel sounds.

TRACK 8

We   did   pay   bets   last.

Gee   this   way   gets   vast.

She   missed   Jay's   friend   Lance.

Me   miss   may   met   mask.

Alternating between Front and Back Vowels

In songs, you sing a variety of vowels that may bounce back and forth between front vowels and back vowels. Knowing the correct shape for every vowel allows you to accurately sing all the vowels in a song at a fast pace. Therefore, you need to be familiar with all the vowel shapes and practice how to make them so you know exactly what to do when you see different sequences of vowels in the songs you sing. To get some practice with alternating between front and back vowels, speak the following word pairs a few times in a row: *we do, do we?, she took, should we?, hit Paul, call in, Playdoh, go away, his casa,* and *calm him.*

The following exercise really mixes up the vowels so you can practice moving between front and back vowels. Before you start singing along with the piano on Track 9, I recommend speaking slowly through the text to feel the change in the arch of your tongue. The arch in the front of your tongue should rise for a front vowel and then drop as the arch in the back of your tongue rises for a back vowel. Take your time to make sure you drop the arch in your tongue just the right amount for each vowel. Your lips also move from a neutral position for front vowels to a rounded position for back vowels. To help you make sure your lips are changing shapes the way they should, watch them in a mirror as you work through this exercise.

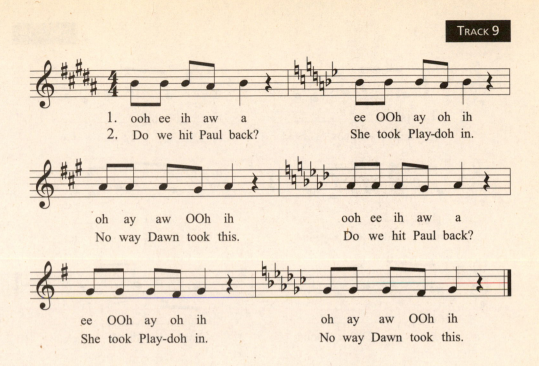

Presenting the Middle Vowel, Uh

The *uh* vowel is the only one that requires a slight arch in the middle of the tongue. This vowel comes in long and short versions. One *uh* sound is longer and is usually sustained (think of the words *cup, other, ugly,* and *trouble*); the shorter *uh* sound is often found in pre-fixes or suffixes and is called a *schwa* (think of the words *about, around, attempted, sofa, pizza,* and *tonight*).

Both the long and short versions of the *uh* vowel require a slight arch in the middle of the tongue, but they don't require shaping the lips. You should feel as if the middle of the tongue were arching toward the front of the mouth rather than straight up. What you don't want to do is allow your tone to fall backward and down your throat when you sing an *uh* sound. To help you figure out the right sound for the *uh* vowel, sing the word *father* and sustain the first syllable — *fah*. The height in the resonance on this *ah* vowel is similar to the height you want for the *uh*.

Sing along with the piano on Track 10 to practice making the *uh* sound. The first line shows the words *short* and *long* to tell you whether the sounds in the words in the second line are short or long. The curved line connecting the third and fourth notes in some measures tells you to sing legato or to smoothly connect between notes. As you sing, focus on moving the tone forward rather than backward.

TRACK 10

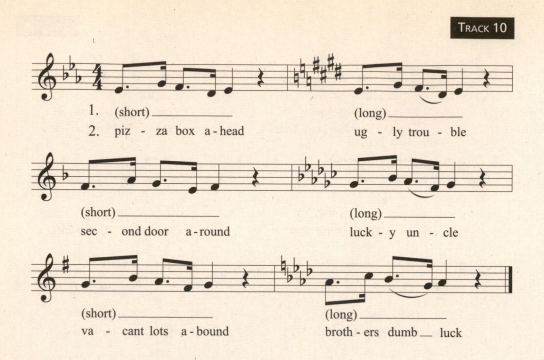

1. (short) _____   (long) _____
2. piz - za box a - head   ug - ly trou - ble

(short) _____   (long) _____
sec - ond door a - round   luck - y un - cle

(short) _____   (long) _____
va - cant lots a - bound   broth - ers dumb __ luck

Singing Combination Vowels

Diphthongs are groups of two vowels that combine together to make one sound, such as in the words *boy, pie,* and *cow.* Most of the time, the first vowel is the one you sustain as you sing. The exception is in words, such as *you* and *hue,* in which you sustain the second vowel. You need to practice speaking and singing both types of diphthongs so you can clearly make the sound of each vowel at just the right time. (**Note:** Southerners tend to drop the second vowel of diphthongs when they speak. If you're from the South, you need to realize that you drop that vowel in conversation and then make a conscious choice to put it back in when you sing a song that requires a neutral accent, such as a classical song.)

English has five diphthongs. Two of them — *ay* and *oh* — are vowels that I cover earlier in this chapter with the front and back vowels. The other three diphthongs are *awih* (as in *boy, toy,* and *joy*), *ahOOh* (as in *now, cow,* and *wow*), and *aih* (as in *my, tie,* and *dye*), and here's how you make them:

✔ For the *awih* diphthong, you move through the vowel *aw* (as in *all*) to *ih* (as in *him*). Notice that *aw* is a back vowel with an arch in the back of the tongue and *ih* is a front vowel with an arch in the front of the tongue. To practice this diphthong, arch the back of your tongue for *aw* and then release the back of your tongue and arch the front of your tongue for *ih.* The lips change from the rounded shape for *aw* to the neutral shape for *ih.* The following words contain examples of this diphthong: *boy, toy, joy, royal, noise, spoil, hoist, oil, enjoy, Joyce,* and *voice.*

✔ The diphthong *ahOOh* combines the vowels *ah* and *OOh,* although linguists disagree slightly on the first vowel sound for this diphthong. For the purpose of singing, move through a vowel that's brighter than the *ah* in *father* but not as bright as the *a* in *cat* and then progress to the second vowel of the diphthong (*OOh* as in *would*). For this diphthong, you need to create a slight arch in the back of your tongue for both vowels. The arch is lower for the first vowel and higher for the second vowel. The following words contain examples of this diphthong: *now, cow, how, wow, brown, owl, prowl, ground, loud, arouse, allow, gown, lounge, sound,* and *around*. **Tip:** Watch your lips in the mirror as you move through the two vowels in this diphthong. You want neutral lips for the first vowel and closely rounded lips for the second vowel.

✔ For the *aih* diphthong, you move through the vowel *a* (as in *ask*) to the vowel *ih* (as in *chin*). The lips are neutral throughout the whole diphthong because both vowels are front vowels. The arch in your tongue is very slight for the first vowel and then arches a bit higher for the *ih* vowel. The following words contain this diphthong: *buy, nine, pies, light, tiny, pine, sublime, chimes, decried, time, Friday, ice, nice,* and *tripe*.

Related to the diphthong is the *triphthong,* a group of three vowels in a row linked together to make one sound. The third "vowel" in the triphthong is actually the consonant *R*, which is sometimes considered to be a vowel because it can make a vowel sound. The two triphthongs you may encounter are *ahee-r* (as in *retire, sire, hire, liar, conspire,* and *fire*) and *ahOOh-r* (as in *shower, hour, devour, power,* and *flour*).

Here's your chance to work on singing diphthongs. Speak through the text to practice making the shapes of each diphthong and then sing along with the piano as it plays the following exercise for you on Track 11.

Songs for Singing Vowels Precisely

If you're interested in checking out real-world examples of singing precise vowels, check out the songs in the following list. The classical songs have long, sustained vowels, and the other songs have sustained vowels for that style of music. **Note:** Long, held-out notes aren't very common in popular music, but the songs in this list have longer phrases that allow you to practice creating precise vowels.

- ✔ "The Impossible Dream" from *Man of La Mancha* by Mitch Leigh and Joe Darion (male)
- ✔ "The First Time Ever I Saw Your Face" by Ewan MacColl (either)
- ✔ "I'll Know" from *Guys and Dolls* by Frank Loesser (either)
- ✔ "I Swear" by Gary Baker and Frank J. Myers (either)
- ✔ "Autumn Evening" by Roger Quilter (either)
- ✔ "I Will Always Love You" by Dolly Parton as sung by Whitney Houston (either)
- ✔ "You Don't Have to Say You Love Me" by Pino Donaggio, Vito Pallavicini, Vicki Wickham, and Simon Napier-Bell as sung by Dusty Springfield (either)
- ✔ "Bridge Over Troubled Water" by Paul Simon as recorded by Simon and Garfunkel or Linda Eder (either)
- ✔ "I Know That My Redeemer Liveth" from *The Messiah* by G.F. Handel (female)
- ✔ "Hero" by Mariah Carey and Walter Afanasieff (female)

Chapter 4

Articulating Consonants Accurately

• •

In This Chapter

▶ Identifying the four types of consonants and shaping the lips and tongue to sing through them

▶ Putting your consonant skills to the test with a few practice exercises

• •

It's a singer's nightmare: You're singing your heart out on stage, and the audience members are turning to each other wondering what in the world you're trying to say because all they're hearing is a bunch of gobbledy-gook. You may think you're being perfectly clear with each and every word, but unless you're creating the right shapes with your tongue and lips to form your consonants, audiences will have a difficult time understanding you.

This chapter is here to help you avoid ever finding yourself in this situation. In it, you meet groups of consonants that have similar shapes and discover exactly how to move your tongue and lips to be understood. Most of the consonant pairs in this chapter are *cognates,* meaning the two consonants have the same shape but one is voiced and the other is unvoiced. The other consonants that I pair together help you distinguish between similar consonants so you can practice being very precise in your songs.

As you work through this chapter, notice the shape you make to create the sound of each consonant as well as the shape you make to say the name of that consonant. In many cases, the way you say the name of a consonant isn't the same way you say its sound in words. For example, the name of the letter *C* sounds out like the word *see,* but the actual sound of the consonant in words sounds like *S* or *K.*

I recommend that you speak the words in each exercise before you sing them. Speaking through the text helps you practice making just the right shapes, and you want just the right shapes when you sing so your audience understands you. Take your time speaking through the text to feel the shapes and movement of your lips and tongue and then use those precise shapes when you sing through the figures.

Note: I don't group the consonant *H* with the other consonants in this chapter because you make the *H* sound simply by moving air (not by moving the tongue or lips). But if you're wondering how to sound this consonant, think about consciously moving air over the roof of your mouth. Don't just blow out the air; if you do, you'll end up blowing out too much air. Instead, pay attention to exactly how much air you move so that you can create just the right sound for the *H.*

Touching on the Tip Consonants

Tip consonants (sometimes called *alveolar consonants*) — *D, L, N, R, S, T,* and *Z* — get their name because you form them when the tip (or end) of your tongue meets your *alveolar ridge,* the hard ridge at the front of the mouth. Locate your alveolar ridge by moving the tip of your tongue to touch behind your upper front teeth and then running it along the curve of the gums behind the teeth. A little farther back, just beyond the curve of the gums, you should feel a ridge where the gums make a seam. That's the alveolar ridge — where your tongue connects to make the sounds of the tip consonants. If you're having trouble finding your alveolar ridge, feel where the roof of your mouth is still curving up; that's it.

Practicing touching the tip of your tongue to your alveolar ridge can help you develop the coordination necessary for singing tip consonants. Grab a hand mirror or position yourself in front of a mirror so you can see exactly what's happening with your tongue as you follow these steps:

1. **Open the teeth slightly and let the tongue rest on the bottom of the mouth with the tip touching the bottom front teeth.**

2. **Lift the tip of the tongue to touch the alveolar ridge and let it drop back down to the bottom of the mouth with the tip touching the bottom front teeth.**

   When you lift the tongue, the tip should touch the alveolar ridge but not the upper teeth. When you accurately land on the ridge, your tongue curves slightly to touch the tip (not the *blade,* or the part just behind the tip) to the ridge while the back of the tongue stays released — not pushing up or tense. You don't want to push up the tongue so you feel a tightening sensation when you lift the tongue.

3. **Lift the tip of your tongue to touch the alveolar ridge and let it drop back down five times.**

   The tip of your tongue should be resting against the bottom front teeth when you start and end the lift.

The following sections contain exercises that allow you to focus on moving the tip of your tongue precisely to sing through the various tip consonants. Look for directions under each heading to know which track to use for singing the musical figure. Also, note that the first line in each exercise shows the consonant followed by a vowel sound, and the second line shows a list of words that use the featured consonants so you can practice singing them.

Exploring the voiced consonants L, N, and D

The *voiced* tip consonants — *L, N,* and *D* — are produced by adding vocal sound at the same time the tip of your tongue touches the ridge on the roof of your mouth. For example, when you say *dad,* you have to add sound to the letter *D* before you get to the vowel. Singing voiced tip consonants requires you to shape the tip of your tongue precisely, touching the alveolar ridge at the same time you make the sound with your voice — all in time with the music. You want to say *dad,* not *uhdad.*

The lips are not involved in making the *L, N,* and *D* consonant sounds. As you make these sounds, the space inside your throat and mouth stays open as the tip of the tongue moves to touch the alveolar ridge. After you pronounce the consonant, the tip returns to rest against your bottom front teeth.

If you just touch your alveolar ridge with the tip of your tongue without adding the sound of your voice, the sound won't carry to your listeners and they'll have a hard time telling the consonants apart.

Play Track 12 and sing along with the following exercise. Practice the consonant sounds first; then practice the actual words.

TRACK 12

1. loh noh doh noh loh   loh noh doh noh loh
2. Live ___ near ___ dawn.   Laugh ___ now ___ Dan.

loh noh doh noh loh   loh noh doh noh loh
Lose no days on land.   Lease nine dain-ty lines.

Distinguishing between voiced D and unvoiced T

If you're not careful with your articulation, your *D*s may be mistaken for *T*s. As you discover in the preceding section, *D* is a voiced consonant, but young singers often mistake it for an unvoiced consonant. (You produce an *unvoiced* consonant by momentarily stopping the flow of air and making no voiced sound. The sound of an unvoiced consonant, such as *T*, comes from the flow of air as opposed to your voice.) Even if other people your age are changing the sound of consonants, you need to be able to switch gears and make your consonants precise when you're singing. After all, singing "that tute is hot" doesn't deliver the same kind of punch as "that dude is hot."

To shape the *D* and the *T*, you have to create a seal by lifting your tongue and touching the edges of it to the roof of your mouth. The sides of your tongue touch the inside of the upper teeth, and the tip of your tongue touches the alveolar ridge but not the front teeth. The tip of your tongue moves slightly to open the seal.

To sing through the *D*, you have to combine the sound of your voice with the opening of the seal. The *T*, on the other hand, requires that you release air to make the sound. While the sides of the tongue continue to touch the teeth, the tip moves to open the seal and a small amount of air passes over the tip of the tongue. If you blow out too much air and release the sides of the tongue, you create what's called a *wet T* or a *T* that splatters. But if you create the seal and then allow a very small release of air, you create the perfect sound for the *T*.

To help you distinguish between the *D* and *T*, play Track 12 and practice singing through the consonants listed in the first line of the following exercise. Then try singing the words in the second line. You may want to record yourself to make sure you're clearly distinguishing between the voiced *D* and the unvoiced *T*.

1. dooh tooh dooh tooh dooh   dooh tooh dooh tooh dooh
2. Do   to. Do____ to.   To   do. To____ do.

dooh   tooh dooh tooh dooh   dooh tooh dooh tooh dooh
Dream____ trip._____   Try____ draw - ing.

Sounding out the voiced R

R is a voiced consonant, but it's a tricky one because sometimes it stands alone and other times it's paired closely with a vowel. (You may actually find *R* listed as a vowel sometimes because you can sustain the sound just as you do with vowels; see Chapter 3 for more on vowels.) How you sing an *R* depends on its placement in the word:

✔ **When the *R* appears at the beginning of a word (called an *initial R*), you lift and curl the tip of your tongue toward the alveolar ridge as you make the sound with your voice.** You shape the tongue for the *R* at the same time that you make the sound, and then you move to the shape and sound of the first vowel. The sound of the consonant *R* is like *uhr* before the first vowel in the word. Words that have an initial *R* include *rose, rabbit, rainbow, round, reach, ricochet,* and *run.*

✔ **When the *R* appears in the middle of a word (called a *medial R*), you place the tip of your tongue against the bottom front teeth and arch the middle of your tongue toward the alveolar ridge as you make the sound with your voice.** Words that have a medial *R* include *snare, bird, corner, burn, are,* and *sure.*

As you sing the voiced *R*, notice what the rest of your tongue is doing as you arch it for the medial *R*. Singers often tighten their tongues to create the medial *R* sound, which is why choir directors sometimes tell their students to take out the *R* in the word and just sing the vowel. However, if you take out the *R*, you leave out one of the sounds in the word. So the better solution is to figure out how to sing the *R* without tightening the tongue, which you can do by working through the following exercise.

The first measure in this exercise contains words that start with *R,* the second measure features words that have an *R* in the middle, and the third and fourth measures mix the two. The piano plays this pattern for you on Track 12 so you can sing along.

When *R* follows a vowel (as it does in the words *here, their, poor,* and *sports*), you can hear two vowels that sound like a *diphthong,* or two adjacent vowel sounds in the same syllable. (I cover diphthongs in Chapter 3.) The problem is that singing a vowel and then arching the tongue for a medial *R* may cause you to retract the tongue or pull the tongue down the throat. Because you want the tongue to curl toward the alveolar ridge while the back stays steady, some linguists recommend using the tip of the tongue for both initial and medial *R*s. Experiment with both while recording yourself and looking in the mirror to see which technique works best for you. Try the experiment with a high note and a low note.

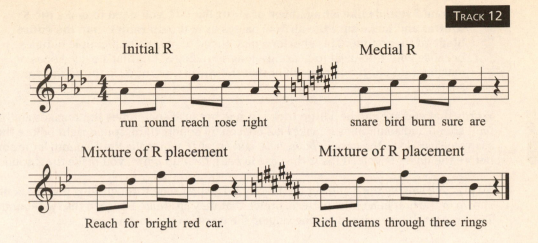

Singing unvoiced S and voiced Z

Two consonants that require really specific shaping of the tongue are *S* and *Z*. Practicing them together helps you distinguish between the two sounds so you can make really specific sounds in your song. You articulate both consonants by placing the tip of your tongue near your alveolar ridge, but the *S* is unvoiced and the *Z* is voiced.

To successfully make the voiced sound of the *Z*, you need to hold the tip of the tongue close to (but not touching) the alveolar ridge. Holding the tip of your tongue close to the alveolar ridge long enough to get the voiced sound of the *Z* to come out takes some strength and coordination. Don't worry if your tongue wiggles a little bit; that just means it isn't used to holding that shape and needs some practice. (The exercise later in this section can give you just the practice you need.)

To shape the unvoiced *S* properly, like in the word *its,* lift your tongue to the roof of your mouth and allow the edges of the tongue to create a seal on the roof of your mouth. As you make the seal, the sides of the tongue should touch the upper teeth and the tip of the tongue should be close to, but not touching, the upper teeth. To give the *S* just the right sound, let a very small stream of air pass over the tip of the tongue.

Make sure that you don't let too much air pass over the blade of your tongue when you're singing through your *S*. If you do, your *S* may sound more like *SH* or the soft sound in the German word *ich.*

If you hear a lisp or a whistle in your *S,* try the following tips to get the hang of shaping the *S* properly:

- **If your *S* whistles, the tip of your tongue is too close to your teeth.** Create the seal between your tongue and the roof of your mouth by placing the tip of your tongue on the alveolar ridge and then bringing the tip a tiny bit forward to allow the air to pass right over it.

- **If your *S* sounds too much like *TH,* the tip of your tongue is in front of your teeth or touching the back of your teeth.** Make sure you create the seal between your tongue and the roof of your mouth by touching the alveolar ridge and not your teeth. For the *S* to sound right, the air needs to pass over the tip just a tiny bit forward of the alveolar ridge.

✔ **If your *S* sounds like a huge blast of air or like *SH*, you need to make the *S* shorter and make sure the airflow passes over the tip rather than the entire blade of the tongue.** This shorter *S* may sound funny the first couple of times because you're so used to hearing a long-sounding *S*, but that's okay. Focus on making the *S* short and remember that the vowel (not the *S*) is the sound you sustain.

Words that end in *s* can be a little tricky to sing because sometimes the *s* makes an *S* consonant sound and sometimes it makes a *Z* consonant sound. If the sound right before the final *s* is voiceless (as is the case in *bites, bets,* and *snacks*), you make the *S* sound. If the sound before the final *s* is voiced (as is the case in *bees, his,* and *pays*), you make the *Z* sound.

To practice singing the *S* and *Z*, play Track 12. The first time through, sing just the sounds shown in the first line of the pattern; notice that they alternate between the two sounds. Then repeat the exercise, this time singing the words in the second line.

TRACK 12

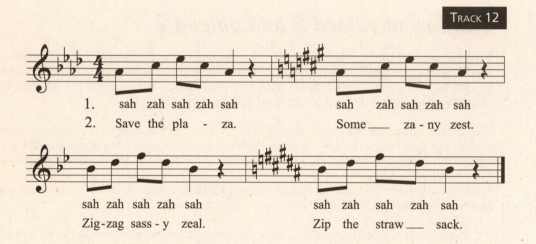

Moving the tip of the tongue to the teeth for TH

As I explain in the earlier section "Distinguishing between voiced *D* and unvoiced *T*," you make the *T* consonant by touching the tip of your tongue to the alveolar ridge, but the *TH* sound is entirely different. In fact, *TH* is the only consonant combination that requires the tongue to articulate on the teeth, and it can be either voiced or unvoiced.

✔ To create the unvoiced *TH*, place the tip of your tongue on the bottom edge of the upper front teeth and move air between the tip of the tongue and the teeth.

✔ To create the voiced *TH*, use the same movements you use for the unvoiced *TH*, except add the sound of your voice when the tip of your tongue touches the upper front teeth and you move the air. Adding your voice creates a vibrating sensation at the tip of the tongue.

To know when to sing through the voiced *TH* and when to sing through the unvoiced *TH*, you have to memorize which words use which *TH* sounds. Use the following exercise to help you practice singing through the unvoiced and voiced *TH*. Practice speaking through the text in the pattern to make sure you're making the right *TH* sounds. Then play Track 12 and sing along with the piano as you work through the first and second lines.

TRACK 12

1. this   thief   this___   thief   this   thief   this___   thief
2. These___   thir - ty   thieves.   Thirst - y   broth - er.

this   thief   this_____   thief   this   thief   this___   thief
This thief thinks they're thin.   Faith - ful   moth - er.

Singing through the consonants *L, N, D, T, S, Z,* and *TH*

The following exercise, which you can hear performed on Track 13, combines all the consonants covered in the previous five sections. Look closely at the words and practice speaking through the combination of consonants and vowels to make sure you hit the right spot for each consonant.

Touching your tongue to your teeth for the wrong consonants creates a thick sound that slows down your tone. When you sing *L, N, D,* and *T*, be sure to place the tip of your tongue on the alveolar ridge, not your teeth. For the *S* and *Z*, place the tip of your tongue near the alveolar ridge, but don't let your tongue touch it. For the *TH*, allow the tip of your tongue to touch the upper front teeth. Another thing that can mess up your tone is letting the back of your tongue tighten when it should be relaxed. So make sure you move the tip of your tongue to touch the alveolar ridge without tightening the back of the tongue at the same time. See the earlier sections for more details.

TRACK 13

Daf - fy   ze - bras   no   lon - ger   think   straight.

Then   the   zig - zag   stays   down   near   the   line.

Daf - fy   ze - bras   no   long - er   think   straight.

Then   the   zig - zag   stays   down   near   the   line.

Arching Back for Soft Palate Consonants

You create the *soft palate consonants* — *K, G,* and *NG* — by raising the back of your tongue to meet your *soft palate,* the soft tissue at the back of the roof of your mouth that rises when you yawn. The *hard palate* is the hard part of the roof of your mouth that goes from the upper teeth to the soft palate. Articulating these consonants where the hard palate ends and the soft palate begins allows you to leave the space in the back of your mouth open. This is important because keeping the space open gives the tone enough space to resonate.

Articulating *K, G,* and *NG* at the very back of the soft palate encourages you to close down the space in the back of the throat, which is a big no-no. Closing down the space causes a tighter, more constricted sound.

Keeping the space in the back of the mouth (behind the tongue) open is especially important when you sing soft palate consonants on high notes. To get an idea of what keeping this space open feels like for any consonant, try adding a vowel in front of the consonant to feel the openness of the vowel. Then focus on maintaining that open space as you sing through the consonant.

Practicing voiced G, unvoiced K, and voiced NG

G is a voiced consonant and *K* is unvoiced. Practicing the *G* and *K* together helps you make just the right sound when you sing your song. Adding the *NG* to your practice session helps you get familiar with the similarities between the *G* and the *NG.* To compare the sounds of these consonants, speak them several times. Do you feel the vibrations of sounds you make when you articulate the *G* and the *NG?* What about the movement of the air flowing over the roof of your mouth when you say the *K?*

To create the right sound for the *G* consonant, you need to use just the right amount of pressure. In other words, you need to move the tongue enough that the back of it touches the roof of the mouth right where the hard and soft palates meet to make the *G* sound, but you don't want to press so hard with the tongue that the *G* sounds like a grunt. So when creating the *G,* focus on touching the roof of the mouth with the tongue rather than pressing the tongue up.

For the *K,* you need to be aware of how much air escapes when you make the sound. The goal is to move enough air through your mouth that the consonant can be heard. To do so, let the back of the tongue touch the roof of the mouth where the soft and hard palates meet and move just enough air to make the sound of the consonant *K.* If you stop the airflow for too long in the process or if you have to push with your body to make the sound, you'll cause pressure that makes it feel like the *K* explodes or pushes out.

Like with the *G,* you make the *NG* by touching the tongue to the roof of the mouth where the hard and soft palates meet, but the sound you create for the *NG* is a little different from that of its voiced *G* counterpart. *NG* is a sound you could sustain by keeping the tongue touching the roof of the mouth. In contrast, you don't sustain the *G.* Even though the back of the tongue lifts to create the *NG,* you don't want to add pressure or tension to the tongue, and you want to keep the space open in the back of your mouth behind the tongue.

Play Track 14 and practice singing the consonants *G* and *K.* Note that *G* sounds like itself in the words *go* and *give,* but in the word *George,* it sounds like a *J.* (I explain how to sing the consonant *J* in the later section "Puckering for voiced *J* and unvoiced *CH.*")

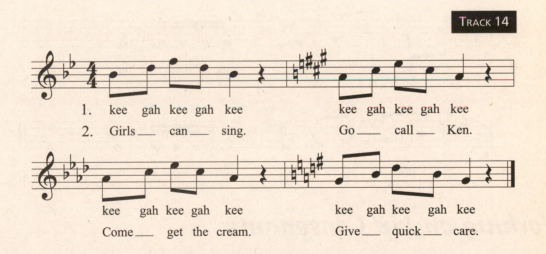

The consonants *X* and *Q* are related to the consonant *K.* When you say the name of the consonant *X,* you say the *eh* vowel and then make a *K* sound followed by an *S* sound. The *X* itself has several sounds, depending on the word. For example, *tax, except,* and *exercise* all use a *K* sound. But *X* also makes the sound of *GZ* in *exert* and *Z* in *xylophone.* The name of the *Q* consonant sounds like a *K* followed by two vowels *ee* and then *ooh.* The *Q* itself sounds like a *K,* as in *quick, queen,* and *plaque.*

Singing through the consonants K, G, and NG

The following exercise, which you can hear on Track 15, gives you a chance to practice all three of the soft palate consonants — *K, G,* and *NG.* Read through the following pattern first to make sure you're making the right sound for each consonant. Then listen to the singer demonstrate the sounds for you and join along whenever you're ready.

For each consonant, be sure to touch the back of your tongue to the place right where the hard and soft palates meet. As you touch the back of the tongue to this spot, allow the tip of your tongue to continue touching your bottom front teeth and keep the space behind your tongue (at the back of your mouth) open.

TRACK 15

Co - vet Ga - ga's bling.   Sing o' bling-a - ling.

Can___ Gary___ sing?   Sing o'kling-a - ling.

Co - vet Ga - ga's bling.   Sing o' bling-a - ling.

Can___ Gary___ sing?   Sing o'kling-a - ling.

Working on Lip Consonants

Not surprisingly, the lips play a big role in the coordination of the *lip consonants.* In this section, you explore two groups of consonants, the consonants made with both lips and the consonants made with just the bottom lip.

✔ For the consonants that use both lips — *B, M, P,* and *W* — you want the teeth to be slightly open and both lips to move to touch each other momentarily.

Watch in the mirror as you say *Wah, Mah, Pah,* and *Bah.* The lips move out more for the *W* than they do for the other three because the *W* sounds like the vowel *ooh* and the lips don't close for that sound. Make sure that you don't close your teeth as you make the sounds of these consonants. Allow the lips to touch momentarily for *M, P,* and *B,* but don't let them press closed.

✏ For the consonants that move only one lip — *F* and *V* — the teeth are apart and the bottom lip lifts to touch the bottom edge of the upper front teeth.

Moving the lips to make these consonants in the middle or lower part of your range is pretty easy; you just have to know how to shape the tongue and lips. On the other hand, moving the lips for the consonants with your jaw open while singing a high note takes some practice. If your lips aren't used to moving to create the sounds of these consonants, then your jaw will try to close to make the sounds. But you don't want to close your jaw to make a consonant while you're singing a high note. Rather, you want your jaw to stay open and your lips to move so you can continue to open the space in the back of your mouth to make a glorious sound.

Get your mirror out to check out the movement of your lips. Open your teeth about an inch and leave them open while touching both of your lips together. If one of your lips doesn't move, then practice just moving that lip up and down. Figuring out how to move that particular lip may take a few tries, especially if your top lip is the one that doesn't want to move. But keep practicing; you need to know how to move your lips before you can successfully make the sounds of the lip consonants.

Practicing voiced consonants W and M

You articulate *W* and *M* in a similar way, except that the lips close to touch for the *M* but not for the *W*. Pairing the *W* and *M* together helps you feel the lips moving to articulate the two consonants and compare how they sound. *W* and *M* are both voiced consonants. Close your lips and say *Mmmm* as if you were tasting something yummy. You want the sound of your voice to start at the same time that your lips close for the *M*. Notice the buzzing sensation you feel on your lips when you make the *M* sound.

The *W* sounds like the *ooh* vowel, which I explain how to shape in Chapter 3, and the lips move farther out or away from the teeth than they do for the *M*. The lips come close together to shape for the *W*, but they don't completely close as they do for the *M*.

Note: The only time the *W* may be unvoiced is when it combines with *H* to form *WH*. Otherwise, the *W* is voiced.

To get some practice with singing the voiced *M* and *W*, play Track 16 and sing along with the piano as you make your way through the following exercise. Start by singing just the sounds in the first line. When you feel comfortable making both the *M* and *W* sounds, give the words in the second line a try.

TRACK 16

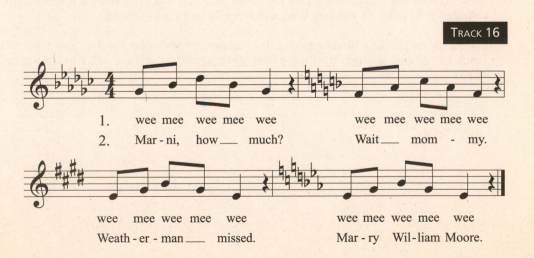

Alternating between voiced B and unvoiced P

You produce *B* and *P* the same way, except that the *P* is unvoiced and the *B* is voiced. Making that distinction when you sing is important because it's what allows your audience to understand your words. To create the sounds of these consonants, your lips need to touch momentarily to stop the airflow, but you don't want to push your lips together. What's the difference? Momentarily stopping the flow of air feels like the consonant is moving out of your mouth, being propelled by the airflow. For the *B*, you want to propel the consonant forward while also making a sound with your voice. Holding or pressing your lips together makes a grunt rather than a voiced consonant. As you touch your lips together to make the *B* and *P* sounds, be sure to keep your teeth apart.

Play Track 16 and sing along with the piano as you make your way through the first and second lines of the following exercise.

TRACK 16

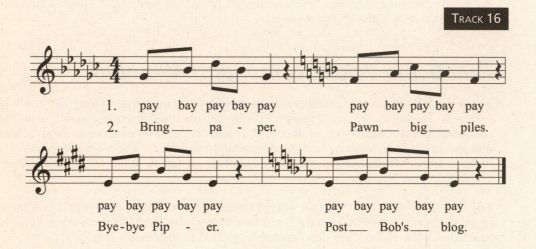

1. pay bay pay bay pay   pay bay pay bay pay
2. Bring___ pa - per.   Pawn___ big___ piles.

pay bay pay bay pay   pay bay pay bay pay
Bye-bye Pip - er.   Post___ Bob's___ blog.

Moving only the bottom lip for F and V

The consonants *F* and *V* are unique because the top lip stays steady while the bottom lip does the work of lifting to reach the upper teeth. You may be tempted to close the teeth as you make these two consonants, but don't give in! Open your teeth slightly and lift your bottom lip to touch your top teeth. As your bottom lip touches your top teeth, blow air between your teeth and lip to make the unvoiced *F*. To make the voiced *V*, simply add the sound of your voice as you touch your bottom lip to your top teeth.

The following exercise helps you practice making the unvoiced *F* and voiced *V* sounds. Play Track 16 and sing along first with the first line of sounds and then with the second line of words.

TRACK 16

1. fah vah fah vah fah   fah vah fah vah fah
2. Five— vot-ing friends.   Ver-i-fy— fines.

fah vah fah vah fah   fah vah fah vah fah
Find a-loof— folks.   Vin-tage fish-ing vest.

Singing through W, M, P, B, F, and V

Here's your chance to sing all the lip consonants. Speak through the text of the following exercise first while watching yourself in the mirror. Keep your teeth parted about an inch and pay close attention to the movement of your lips. Notice that the lips have to pucker just slightly when you get to the W because the sound of the W is the sound of the *ooh* vowel.

After you've familiarized yourself with the words, listen to the singer on Track 17 perform the exercise. Then sing along. Remember that as you sing the exercise, you need to keep your teeth apart while the lips move to create the consonants, and you need to keep the space in the back of your mouth open while the lips move. The lips can move independently and don't need the teeth to close for them to make the sounds of the lip consonants.

TRACK 17

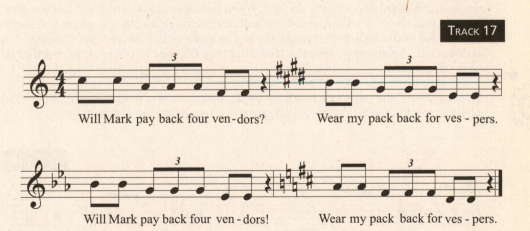

Will Mark pay back four ven-dors?   Wear my pack back for ves-pers.

Will Mark pay back four ven-dors!   Wear my pack back for ves-pers.

Consonant Combos: Moving the Lips and Tongue

The *combination consonants* — J, CH, SH, and ZH — require you to move your lips *and* your tongue. For these consonants, the teeth have to come closer together than they do for the other consonants we talk about in this chapter. Even though the teeth move closer together for these consonants, you still need to practice keeping the space in the back of your mouth and throat open while singing through the consonants. You don't want that space to close just because your teeth are moving closer together.

Singing the voiced *J* and unvoiced *CH* requires you to pucker your lips, place the tongue on the roof of your mouth to create a seal, and then release that seal to allow air to flow over the tip of your tongue. Specifically, for the voiced *J*, you pucker the lips and shape the tongue for a *D* consonant (by creating a seal with the edge of your tongue on the roof of your mouth and the tip of your tongue touching the alveolar ridge). You then use the voice to say a *D* consonant sound and blow air over the tip of the tongue to finish the *J*. The tongue near the roof of your mouth makes a small space that creates the sound of friction when the air moves through. For the *CH*, you do the same thing with your lips and tongue, but you don't use your voice.

You have to momentarily stop the airflow when articulating *J* and *Ch*, but you keep the airflow moving steadily through the small opening between your tongue and the roof of your mouth when you sing the unvoiced *SH* and voiced *ZH*. You also bring your teeth close together for the *SH* and *ZH*. The big difference between these two combination consonants is that you use your voice to sound *ZH* (as in *genre*) but not for *SH* (as in *shin*).

Puckering for voiced J and unvoiced CH

In this exercise, you practice singing through the consonants *J* and *CH*. The *J* consonant uses the spellings *j* (as in *June*), *g* (as in *germ*), and *dg* (as in *grudge*). *CH* uses the spellings *ch* (as in *choose*), *c* (as in *cello*), *tch* (as in *clutch*), and *t* (as in *culture*).

Before performing this exercise, practice speaking through the sounds *jaw* (the sound of the *J* consonant followed by the *aw* vowel as in *claw*) and *chaw* to make sure you're accurately shaping and sounding the consonants. The *aw* vowel requires an arch in the back of the tongue and a slight rounding of the lips. When you're ready to sing the exercise, play Track 16 and sing the following pattern with the piano. Remember to bring your teeth close together for both consonant sounds and not to let too much air escape, creating a big puff of air. You don't completely close the teeth, but they do have to come close together to make these consonants.

Consider recording your practice session to make sure you're making the right sounds and watching yourself in a mirror to make sure you're making the right shapes.

TRACK 16

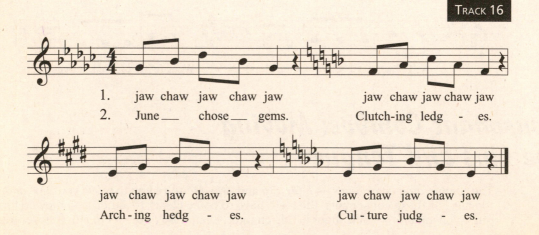

Moving air through SH and ZH

In this exercise, you alter between the voiced *ZH* and the unvoiced *SH*. *SH* is the sound you hear in the words *shirt, vicious,* and *cash*. *SH* uses these spelling combinations: *sh* (as in *shirt*), *s* (as in *sugar*), *ch* (as in *chef* or *machine*), *x* (as in *anxious*), *ss* (as in *mission*), *sc* (as in *conscience*), *t* (as in *partial*), and *sch* (as in *schnapps*). *ZH* uses these spelling combinations: *z* (as in *azure*), *s* (as in *casual*), and *g* (as in *genre*).

The piano plays the melody of the exercise for you on Track 16 so you can sing along. Remember to pucker your lips and position the tip of your tongue at the alveolar ridge — not the teeth — and don't let your tongue touch the teeth.

TRACK 16

1. sheh zheh sheh zheh sheh   sheh zheh sheh zheh sheh
2. A - zure anx - ious chefs.   Ca - sual mis - sion.

sheh zheh sheh zheh sheh   sheh zheh sheh zheh sheh
Spe - cial vi - sion.   Par - tial trea - sure.

Singing through the consonants J, CH, SH, and ZH

This exercise lets you practice making the sounds and shapes of all the combination consonants covered in the previous sections. Listen to the singer perform the exercise for you on Track 18 and then give it a shot yourself. Even as you bring the teeth close together for these consonant combinations, remember to keep the space in the back of the mouth (behind the tongue) open, especially for higher notes.

Joe chose the cas - u - al shirt.

Jump chop shop Zsa Zsa mi - rage.

Joe chose the cas - u - al shirt.

Jump chop shop Zsa Zsa mi - rage.

Songs for Singing Various Consonants

Songs that use a lot of fast-moving text are called *patter songs*. The following list includes patter songs from various styles that require easy movement of the tongue and lips to accurately articulate the text.

Whenever you want to sing a patter song, speak through the text slowly before taking the song at the speed you hear in recordings. Doing so gives you a chance to shape the consonants accurately before having to worry about how quickly you can sing.

- ✔ "The Nightmare Song" from *Iolanthe* by W. S. Gilbert and Arthur Sullivan (male)
- ✔ "Ya Got Trouble" from *The Music Man* by Meredith Willson (male)
- ✔ "A Trip to the Library" from *She Loves Me* by Sheldon Harnick and Jerry Bock (female)
- ✔ "One Week" by Barenaked Ladies (either)
- ✔ "Court of King Caractacus" by Rolf Harris (either)
- ✔ "Life Is a Rock (But the Radio Rolled Me)" by Reunion (either)
- ✔ "The Name Game" by Shirley Ellis and Lincoln Chase (either)

Part II
Making Your Music Magical with Variety

"Very impressive. I've never had anyone belch a C major scale for me before."

In this part . . .

The information in this part helps you discover what to do to make your songs musically diverse. It starts by exploring intervals and rhythm to help you read what's on the page. After you know how to read the notations on the page, you can learn new songs faster and decide whether you want to sing those songs exactly as written or you want to make changes.

This part also helps you with the symbols that tell you about sounds you can make in your song. Knowing the symbols for the various dynamic and articulation markings allows you to follow the road map of musical sounds created by a song's composer. Of course, you can always change that road map slightly with some careful planning; this part shows you how to do that, too.

Chapter 5

Singing Precise Intervals for Musical Accuracy

Technically speaking, when you sing a song, you're singing a group of pitches. Precisely singing the *interval* (or distance) between two pitches helps you sing in tune. (If you don't quite make it to the next note, you may sound flat or out of tune.) This chapter fills you in on the most common intervals found in music. It shows you what they look like and gives you opportunities to practice singing them so you can perform all the common intervals accurately. And because singing a particular interval seems much easier when you can connect a familiar tune with it, I also give you several examples of songs that include the intervals featured in this chapter.

Recognizing the Most Common Intervals

An interval may go up (or *ascend*) in pitch, or it may go down (or *descend*) in pitch. Being able to recognize intervals when you sing a song helps you know the distance between the pitches and tells you how high or low you need to sing.

Every interval name has two parts:

✔ **A word:** The word tells you about the quality of the sound. The three types of intervals are *major, minor,* and *perfect.* (The rest of this section offers details on each type.)

✔ **A number:** The number tells you the distance between the two notes on the musical staff (how many lines or spaces are between the two notes on the staff and how many half steps are between the two notes on a piano). The most common intervals are second, third, fourth, fifth, sixth, seventh, and octave; they can also be written as numbers: 2, 3, 4, 5, 6, 7, and 8.

To figure out the number for an interval, simply count up through the letter names from the first note to the second note. For example, to figure out the interval from C to G, count the letters starting with C and going to G (CDEFG) to get five. So you know C to G is a fifth. You can also count the lines and spaces between the notes on the staff or count the steps on the piano.

Note: The word *staff* (or *stave*) refers to the five horizontal lines and four spaces you see in Figure 5-1. Each line and space on the musical staff represents a musical pitch. When I say that an interval is a certain number of lines and spaces apart, I'm talking about the lines and spaces on the staff. From bottom to top, the treble clef lines represent the pitches E, G, B, D, and F and the spaces F, A, C, and E. The lines in the bass clef from bottom to top are G, B, D, F, and A, and the spaces are A, C, E, and G. For more information on reading music notation, check out the most recent edition of *Music Theory For Dummies* by Holly Day and Michael Pilhofer (Wiley).

Use the keyboard in Figure 5-1 to help you count the number of steps between pitches to identify intervals. The W and H on the musical staff in Figure 5-1 show you the whole and half steps in the scale.

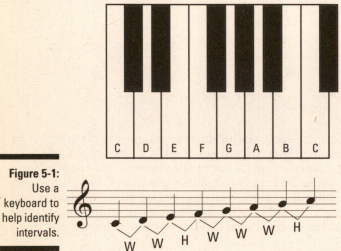

Figure 5-1:
Use a keyboard to help identify intervals.

Singing perfectly in tune on every note of a song is tricky even for professional singers because you have to know the exact distance between two pitches so that you can accurately land right in the center of the pitch. After all, if you land slightly under the pitch, you may sound flat; on the other hand, if you land slightly over the pitch, you may sound sharp or higher than the actual pitch. Don't give up if you miss a few notes here and there in a song. If you work through the exercises in this chapter and keep practicing accurately singing intervals, you'll be well on your way to singing right in tune most of the time.

If you're confused about how to recognize intervals after you read the following sections, you can conquer that confusion by taking a two-pronged approach:

✔ Develop your eye to start noticing the distance between pitches and eventually associate the name of the interval with what you see printed on the page of music.

✔ Develop your ear to hear the difference between intervals so that you can become more accurate in your songs.

Major intervals

Major intervals are a half step larger and sound brighter than the minor intervals, which I cover in the next section. Every major interval has a capital *M* next to the number. The major intervals you may encounter in a song are

✔ Major second (M2)

✔ Major third (M3)

✔ Major sixth (M6)

✔ Major seventh (M7)

The following figure shows you what each of these major intervals looks like.

Minor intervals

Minor intervals are one half step lower than their corresponding major intervals, and they aren't as bright as the major intervals. (In other words, they're more plaintive, melancholy, or subdued than their major counterparts.) The following figure shows you the minor intervals that you may encounter in a song, which I list here:

✔ Minor second (m2)

✔ Minor third (m3)

✔ Minor sixth (m6)

✔ Minor seventh (m7)

Singing minor intervals requires skill because they're closer in distance than the major intervals. You may sound flat if you underestimate the distance between two pitches, but you may sound sharp if you overestimate the distance. Be sure to take the time to work on your minor intervals.

Perfect intervals

Perfect intervals are called *perfect* because they have only one form (perfect), whereas the other intervals have two forms: major and minor. The three perfect intervals are

- ✔ Perfect fourth (P4)
- ✔ Perfect fifth (P5)
- ✔ Perfect octave (P8 or unison)

The following figure shows you what the perfect intervals look like; I help you figure out how to sing them in the later section "Finding Perfect Intervals."

P4 _____ P5 _____ P8 _____

Hearing the Small Intervals

Sometimes the smaller intervals — seconds (m2 and M2) and thirds (m3 and M3) — are harder to hear because the notes sound so close together. For this reason, the smaller intervals require you to use both your ear and your voice to sing right in tune. To help you tune the smaller intervals, you need to know each interval by sound and feeling. In other words, you need to develop muscle memory by practicing singing the intervals. I get you practicing the smaller intervals in the next sections.

Seconds and thirds are the intervals you use most often in *riffs,* short pieces of music that move quickly in a specific pattern and are often improvised. Developing your *sense of pitch* — a sense of awareness of the relationship between pitches — can help you be spot on in your riffs.

Minor and major seconds: m2 and M2

The *minor second* (m2) and *major second* (M2) are the smallest of the intervals in Western music. An m2 consists of two notes that are one half step apart, and an M2 consists of two notes that are two half steps, or one whole step, apart.

The most popular m2 you may know is in the theme from the movie *Jaws* with music by John Williams. The first two notes of the theme song are an m2 interval. Who knew how creepy the m2 interval could sound? A few other songs that you may know with an m2 are

- ✔ **"A Hard Day's Night" by the Beatles:** The m2 is between the words *It's* and *been* and *been* and *a* in the phrase "It's been a hard day's night" in the opening of the song.

- ✔ **"White Christmas" by Irving Berlin:** The first m2 is between the first two words *I'm* and *dreaming,* and the next m2 is between the syllables *dream* and *ing* in the word *dreaming.*

- ✔ **"Isn't She Lovely" by Stevie Wonder:** The m2 is between the two syllables of *isn't.*

If you can sing any of these songs, then you can sing an m2. If you're more of a visual learner, check out the following depiction of m2s on the musical staff.

As for the M2, you know lots of songs that use this interval. Here are just a few of them, the first one being the most famous:

- **"Happy Birthday":** The M2 is between the second syllable of *happy* and the first syllable of *birthday*.

- **The nursery rhyme "Mary Had a Little Lamb":** The M2s are between the two syllables in the word *Mary* and between the second syllable of *Mary* and *had*.

- **"Do-Re-Mi" from the movie *The Sound of Music* by Richard Rodgers and Oscar Hammerstein II:** This song has an M2 between the three words *do, re,* and *mi*.

To see what different M2 intervals look like, check out the following figure.

Minor and major thirds: m3 and M3

The two types of thirds you see are *minor third* (m3) and *major third* (M3). The m3 is two notes that are three half steps apart. The M3 is one half step larger than the m3. Knowing the difference between the two types of thirds helps you sing triads accurately (I fill you in on triads in the later section "Building scales with triads").

Some songs you may know that use an m3 include the following:

- **The nursery rhyme "Rock a Bye Baby":** The first two notes of the song *(rock a)* use an m3. The first two notes of the nursery rhyme "This Old Man" also use an m3.

- **"Hey Jude" by the Beatles:** The first two words of the song, *Hey Jude,* use an m3.

- **"So Long, Farewell" from the movie *Sound of Music* by Richard Rodgers and Oscar Hammerstein II:** This song uses an m3 for the words *so long*.

The following figure shows you several m3 intervals as you might find them on the musical staff.

An M3 is the distance of four half steps on the piano (refer to Figure 5-1), and it's brighter than the m3. When you sing an M3 interval, you need to aim higher, knowing that you're tuning your voice to a brighter interval. When you listen to the intervals and can distinguish between the m3 and the M3, you'll know what I mean when I say *tuning to a brighter interval*.

A few songs you may know with an M3 interval include

- **"It's a Small World" by Robert B. Sherman and Richard M. Sherman:** The M3 is between the words *a* and *small* in the phrase "It's a small world after all."

- **"Summertime" from *Porgy and Bess* by George Gershwin:** The M3 is between the two syllables in the word *summer*.

- **The Gaelic tune "Morning Has Broken":** The M3 is between the syllables of the word *morning*.

You can see examples of the M3 in the figure that follows.

Seconds and thirds in action

After you know how to recognize seconds and thirds, you're ready to practice singing them. Because the two notes of these intervals are so close together, you need to pay particular attention to pitch accuracy if you want to sound in tune.

The following pattern, featured on Track 19, gets you working on seconds and thirds. Notice that the first line covers the M2, the second line covers the m2, the third line covers the M3, and the fourth line covers the m3. The last two lines mix up the intervals to challenge you to distinguish between them. As you sing this pattern, keep your breath moving, listen to the sound of your voice match the sounds you hear the piano playing on the track, and sing precise vowels.

Note: To help you sing the pattern on Track 19, I've included both the scale degree numbers and the solfège syllables in the figure. (You can check out the song "Do-Re-Mi" from the movie *The Sound of Music* to familiarize yourself with solfège syllables.) These two systems are very common for singing intervals and scales. You can sing the pattern on something else if you prefer, but try out the solfège syllables or the numbers to discover the benefit.

Speak through the vowels in your song so you can create the right shape and sound. If your vowels are muddy and imprecise, you may sing out of tune. For instance, vowels that are too dark or swallowed sound flat. If you aren't sure about the shape of your vowels, turn to Chapter 3 for help singing precise vowels.

Finding Perfect Intervals

A perfect interval sounds like it should be gorgeous and used in every song just because it's perfect. But the name *perfect* refers to the sound of consonance (as opposed to dissonance) in this interval. (*Dissonance* is the sound of conflict or tension; think of the music you hear in a movie when the bad guy is doing something evil. When the good guy comes along and beats the bad guy, the music changes to sound happier; that's the *consonance*.) The perfect intervals are *perfect fourth* (P4), *perfect fifth* (P5), and *perfect octave* or *unison* (P8). I help you distinguish between the P4 and P5 intervals and sing an octave in the following sections.

Identifying perfect intervals: P4 and P5

The P4 and P5 are two common intervals that make an appearance in numerous familiar songs. The P4 is the distance of five half steps or four steps on the musical staff. The P5 is the distance of seven half steps or five steps on the musical staff.

A P4 is easy to recognize because it's the interval used in "Here Comes the Bride" (or "Wedding March") by Richard Wagner. In that song, you sing the P4 in the words *here comes*. In case you haven't been to a wedding lately, here are some other tunes that have a P4 (to see what P4 intervals look like on the musical staff, check out the figure that follows this list):

- **The folk song "Auld Lang Syne" with lyrics by Robert Burns:** You sing a P4 on the words *should auld*.

- **"Love Me Tender" by Elvis:** You sing a P4 on the words *love me*.

- **"La Marseillaise" by Claude Joseph Rouget de Lisle:** In the French national anthem, you sing a P4 between the two syllables of the French word *enfant*.

- **"Heigh-Ho" from *Snow White* by Frank Churchill and Larry Morey:** You sing a P4 on the phrase *heigh-ho*.

- **"Taps":** Another famous P4 is the first interval in this song.

To get more familiar with the P5, you may want to practice with the songs in this list:

- **The nursery rhyme "Twinkle, Twinkle, Little Star":** You sing a P5 between the two words *twinkle* and *twinkle*.

- **"Oh-ee-oh" from *The Wizard of Oz:*** The minions of the Wicked Witch of the West sing a P5 in the phrase *oh-ee-oh*.

- **"My Favorite Things" from *The Sound of Music* by Richard Rodgers and Oscar Hammerstein II:** The P5 is between the syllables in the word *raindrops*.

- **"Can't Help Falling in Love" by Hugo Peretti, Luigi Creatore, and George David Weiss as sung by Elvis:** The P5 is between the two words *wise* and *men*.

Now that you have an idea of what a P5 sounds like, check out the examples in the following figure to see what a P5 looks like. You can count the five lines and spaces between the two notes.

Working in unison: P8

A piano has 88 keys. The names of the keys are ABCDEFG, and those seven notes keep repeating in different octaves. If you play one C on the piano and then play another C, those two notes are called *unison*. If the two notes are an octave apart (eight notes apart), the interval is a P8.

Here are a few of the songs you may know that have a P8 interval:

- **"Over The Rainbow" from *The Wizard of Oz* by Harold Arlen:** The P8 is between the syllables of the word *somewhere*.

- **"Singin' in the Rain" from the movie *Singin' in the Rain* by Arthur Freed and Nacio Herb Brown:** The P8 is between the word *I'm* and the first syllable of the word *singing*.

- **"Let it Snow" by Jule Styne:** The P8 in this song is between the word *the* and the first syllable of *weather*.

- **"The Christmas Song" by Mel Tormé and Bob Wells:** The P8 is between the syllables of the word *chestnuts*.

The following figure shows you several examples of the P8 interval.

To sing a perfect octave, you may want to pretend the second note of the interval is right in front of you instead of going up. Thinking of the second note as higher makes the interval seem large and scary. Don't worry if you overshoot the interval the first few times you try. Listen to the sound of the piano and the sound of your voice to help determine whether you're on the right note.

Note: Two guys who are singing the same pitch may have an easier time matching each other than they'd have if they were trying to match a female who's singing an octave higher. So at first, you may find it easier to match the sounds of the same gender on the tracks. However, the more you practice singing, the better you'll get at matching the pitch no matter what the octave is.

Singing perfect intervals

The exercise in this section, featured on Track 20, gives you a chance to work on all three perfect intervals. The first line lets you practice P4 intervals, the second line lets you tackle P5 intervals, the third line gets you singing P8 intervals, and the fourth line challenges you by mixing up all the perfect intervals. As you sing this exercise, be sure to keep your breath moving consistently, open the space in your throat, and leave it open as you leap up the interval to keep your larynx steady. You may also have to change registers as you sing the interval. If you find yourself bumping along, turn to Part III for help with shifting registers in your singing voice.

You may notice some familiar themes in the exercise. The first measure is from "Here Comes the Bride." The second measure is the opening of "Taps." The third measure is from "Love Me Tender." The fifth measure is the opening of the "ABC Song." The sixth measure is from "Raindrops on Roses." The seventh measure is "Twinkle, Twinkle, Little Star." The ninth and tenth measures are from "Over the Rainbow." And the eleventh measure is from "The Christmas Song." As I do for the exercise in the section "Seconds and thirds in action," I list the solfège syllables and the scale degree numbers under the notes in the pattern. Try both of these systems to see which one helps you get just the right intonation on the interval. You can also check out the names of the intervals shown above the notes to help you recognize the intervals you're singing.

Comparing the Larger Intervals

Overshooting larger intervals — sixths (m6 and M6) and sevenths (m7 and M7) — is easy to do because you have to develop your ear and muscle memory to know how far apart the intervals really are. To accurately sing sixths and sevenths, you need to hear the sound of each interval in your ear before you sing it. Knowing just how far apart the two notes are helps you land precisely in the center of the pitch. For those intervals that don't have many song examples to help you out, you'll need to drill them until you recognize them by sound and can sing them easily. I help you recognize sixths and sevenths and perfect your performance of them in the next sections.

Minor and major sixths: m6 and M6

The *minor sixth* (m6), which consists of two notes that are eight half steps apart, is a plaintive-sounding interval that isn't all that common in songs. However, you need to be familiar with it because you may sing the more popular M6 by accident if you aren't sure how far apart the notes really are. The *major sixth* (M6), on the other hand, is bright and cheerful. Because the distance between the two pitches in this interval is one half step larger than an m6, you may have to change registers to sing this interval. If you do, think of the two pitches as being in front of each other so you don't feel like you have to leap up to the top note of the interval.

Two songs that you may know with an m6 are

- **"Where Do I Begin?" from the movie *Love Story* with music by Francis Lai and lyrics by Carl Sigman:** The m6 is between the phrases *where do* and *I begin*.
- **"The Entertainer" by Scott Joplin:** This song uses an m6 between the third and fourth notes of the piece.

The following figure shows you some different m6 intervals.

Some songs that use an M6 include the following:

- **The nursery rhyme "Hush Little Baby":** The M6 is between the words *hush* and *little*.
- **The folksong "My Bonnie Lies over the Ocean":** This song uses an M6 between the words *my* and *Bonnie*.
- **"Surfer Girl" by Brian Wilson as sung by the Beach Boys:** The M6 is between the two syllables of the word *surfer*.
- **"It Came upon a Midnight Clear" by Richard Storrs Willis:** This holiday song uses an M6 between the words *it* and *came*.

To see what the M6 interval looks like in written music, check out the following figure.

Minor and major sevenths: m7 and M7

Two pitches that are ten half steps apart form a *minor seventh* (m7) interval. The m7 isn't on the popular interval list, so you may not be familiar with it. Far more common is the *major seventh* (M7), which is just shy of an octave and one half step higher than the m7. (I cover octaves in the earlier section "Working in unison: P8".) The M7 is an easier interval to hear than the m7 because it sounds like it wants to resolve or move on to another note.

Two songs that incorporate the m7 are

✔ **"Somewhere" from the musical *West Side Story* by Leonard Bernstein:** This song uses an m7 between the words *there's* and *a* in the phrase "There's a place for us."

✔ **The Star Trek theme song by Alexander Courage:** This song uses an m7 in the first two notes of the song.

Look at the examples of the m7 in the following figure to help you visualize the notes you hear in the preceding songs.

Two songs that include an M7 are

✔ **"Take on Me" by A-HA:** The M7 is between the words *take* and *on*.

✔ **"Don't Know Why" by Norah Jones:** This song uses an M7 between the words *I* and *waited* in the opening line.

If neither of these songs is familiar, look at the examples in the following figure and listen to the track in the next section to hear examples of an M7.

The seventh is a large interval that requires a good ear to hear it and land on it accurately. To help you hear the seventh, you may want to compare the sounds of the seventh with the sounds of the octave (see the section "Working in unison: P8). After you know what an octave sounds like, you can hear that the seventh is just slightly smaller.

Singing sixths and sevenths

Telling the difference between sixths and sevenths is tricky, so the measures in the following pattern, which is featured on Track 21, alternate between the intervals. Notice that the first measure has an m6 and the second measure has an M6. The starting note is the same and the top note is different to help you distinguish between the two distances. The m7 and M7 are also side by side so you can see the slight difference between them and so you can practice singing them right after each other. Notice that the M7 resolves to the next half step. In other words, if you stop on the M7, your ear wants to hear the next note as if the melody is left hanging or incomplete. One way to distinguish the M7 is by hearing the resolution to the octave.

These intervals are more complicated than the others in this chapter, so I don't include any solfège syllables or scale degree numbers in the figure. For this pattern, I suggest that you sing the name of the interval. Listen to the singer on Track 21 demonstrate the sounds of the intervals to help you better recognize sixths and sevenths. Then, as you sing along with the track, look at the following figure to help you connect the sounds with what you see on the page.

TRACK 21

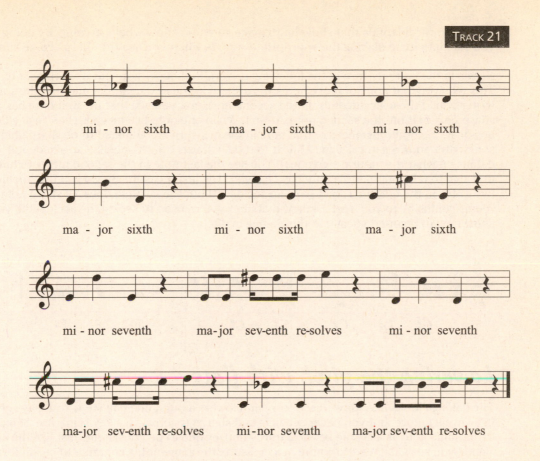

mi - nor sixth   ma - jor sixth   mi - nor sixth

ma - jor sixth   mi - nor sixth   ma - jor sixth

mi - nor seventh   ma - jor sev-enth re-solves   mi - nor seventh

ma-jor sev-enth re-solves   mi - nor seventh   ma-jor sev-enth re-solves

Discovering Chromatics

In a *key signature* (the list at the very beginning of a song that lets you know which notes are always altered in the song), you see a specific number of sharps and flats. Songs normally use just those notes and deviate only sometimes by adding accidentals. An *accidental* is a note that gets changed with a sharp or flat and isn't in the key signature. For example, if you see a song in F major, the key signature will show only one flat — B flat. If you see another note in the song with a flat next to it, that's an accidental. The following sections show you what these accidentals look like and reveal how they change the note they're attached to.

Knowing how to look at music and respond vocally allows you to see music and sing it. You can learn a piece of music quickly if seeing the notation on the page translates to specific sounds and rhythms.

Raising the pitch with sharps

A *sharp* looks like the number sign (♯) and raises a pitch one half step. You often see a grouping of sharps in the key signature of a song. The sharps in the key signature mean that the notes they're next to are always sharp in the song. A sharp beside a note in the song means that it's in addition to the other sharps listed in the key signature. The sharp sign appears to the left of the note and applies to all the notes in that measure.

Sharps tend to make the tone of a song brighter. Although the piano plays the note or chord for you, you have to know the sound before the piano plays it so you can blend your voice to match the right tone. After all, if you think the tone is going to be somber, you'll be out of tune when the piano plays the sharps. Look through your music for the key signature as well as any accidentals that show up to make sure you know what's coming. By doing so, you can anticipate making the appropriate sounds when you see the sharps come along.

Notice in the first measure of the following pattern that every note has a sharp next to it. This tells you that none of those notes were sharp in the key signature and that the songwriter added those accidentals. In the second measure, you see that the first note has a sharp next to it but the second note doesn't. When one note in a measure has an accidental beside it, the other instances of that note in the measure are adjusted to be sharp unless the songwriter adds a natural sign (♮) next to it (see the section "Canceling an accidental" for details on what the natural sign does). You see the last note in the second measure has a natural sign to tell you that this note has changed. The last measure shows you that the first two notes in the measure don't have an accidental but the last one does. (If sharp notation seems confusing to you, rest assured that after you're used to seeing the accidental, you'll know how to respond vocally to the change in pitch.)

G♯ D♯ C♯   C♯ C♯ C   F   F   F♯

Lowering the pitch with flats

The flat sign looks like a lowercase *b* (♭) and lowers a pitch one half step. You may see flats in a key signature, but you never see flats and sharps together in a key signature. Since an F♯ is the same note as a G♭, the key signature chooses one to be consistent. Just like the sharp sign, if you see a flat next to a note in a measure, the same notes continue to be flat for the entire measure.

Although the flat sign lowers the pitch a half step, as a singer, you need to be aware that the difference is *only* a half step. Tuning that half step is important in a song because you don't want to sing flat. You have to listen to the chords played with the flat and make sure your voice tunes with those chords.

The first measure in the following pattern shows that all three notes are flat and that they aren't flat in the key signature. The second measure shows that the first note is flat, so anytime that note repeats in the measure, it'll be flat. The last measure shows that the first two notes aren't flat, but the last one changes and lowers a half step thanks to the flat sign.

A♭ E♭ G♭   B♭ B♭ B♭   D   D   D♭

Canceling an accidental

If a composer decides not to use a sharp or a flat that's in the key signature or that he used earlier in a particular measure, he can add a natural sign next to the note in question to let the singer know that the note has been changed. The natural sign looks like this: ♮. Depending on the change in the note, you may need to think higher or lower to make the right adjustment in pitch.

The first measure in the following pattern shows that the first note and second note are flat. The natural sign cancels out the flat, so the last note in the measure is A natural (or just plain A with no accidental). The second measure shows a sharp on the first note, and that accidental applies to the second note even though it doesn't have a sharp sign next to it. The last note has a natural sign, which cancels out the sharp. The last measure starts with a B natural; the note is natural even though it doesn't have a natural sign next to it because it isn't listed as flat in the key signature. The second note of the measure has a flat sign next to it, and the last one has a natural sign. The natural sign cancels out the flat from the previous note. If there were more B notes in that measure, they would continue to be natural until one had a different accidental next to it.

A♭   A♭   A   G♯   G♯   G   B   B♭   B

Working on Scales

Singing scales is a very popular practice exercise because scales are made up of a specific series of eight notes that are all right next to each other. Singing scales helps you memorize the pattern of half steps and whole steps found in a given key signature. In a musical scale, tones ascend and descend in a particular pattern of whole tones and semitones (whole steps and half steps). The next sections have you work on the building blocks of scales and run through some major and minor scales.

Building scales with triads

The building blocks of scales are *triads.* As you can see in the following figure, triads are the scale degrees 1, 3, and 5 or do, mi, and sol. Triads make for a popular singing exercise; you've probably heard plenty of triads in your choir rehearsals or voice lessons.

For singers, the main thing to know about triads is how to tune the thirds. A *major triad* is built on the intervals of an M3 and then an m3. Because the M3 comes first as you ascend and the m3 comes first as you descend, you need to clearly make the distinction between the two intervals. On the other hand, for a *minor triad,* you sing an m3 and then an M3.

The following figure shows you what triads look like when they appear in a piece of music. Triads can have the three notes stacked on top of each other so that they're played at the same time, as shown in this figure, or they can be played or sung separately, as shown in the next figure.

Practicing triads helps you develop accuracy when you're singing scales because knowing triads helps you confidently recognize notes in the scale. Listen to Track 22, which features the following pattern, a few times so you can hear the difference between the intervals and the difference between the major and minor triads, and then sing along with the pattern. As you sing the triads, listen carefully to the distance between the third and fifth scale degrees. In the major triad, the second note of the major triad (the third scale degree) is higher than the second note in the minor triad. The major third includes a major third (four half steps apart) on the bottom and then a minor third on top (three half steps apart). The minor triad includes a minor third on the bottom and a major third on the top. To confidently tune the notes, sing the vowels listed below the notes precisely and listen carefully to how your voice matches what you hear on the track.

Ultimately, you need to be able to hear the notes before you sing them. If you wait to listen for the piano to play the note, you'll be behind the beat or late landing on your note. Don't worry if you need to practice and listen to the piano play the notes before you start singing along. But as you develop more confidence and skill, you need to let the piano confirm what you're singing instead of waiting for the piano to play the note for you.

Singing major scales

The major scale has all whole steps except between the third and fourth scale degrees and between the seventh and eighth scale degrees. The first note is the first scale degree, or *tonic,* and you count up from there to eight. Before you start singing along with the following pattern, featured on Track 23, I encourage you to really look at the pattern to see the intervals in the major scale and then to listen to the demonstration on Track 23.

As you sing the scales in the following pattern, you need to accurately tune the minor second between scale degrees three and four and between scale degrees seven and eight. Focus on tuning this minor interval both on the way up the scale and on the way down the scale. After all, if your minor second is inaccurate, you may be off pitch for the rest of the scale. Also keep these points in mind as you sing this pattern:

- Sing a precise vowel (see Chapter 3).
- Coordinate your breath (see Chapter 2).
- Allow the resonance to change as you ascend and descend (see Chapter 12).
- Shift registers when necessary (see Chapter 11).

Singing minor scales

Minor scales come in different forms: melodic, harmonic, and natural minor. The natural minor scale is the most common minor scale found in songs. This form includes a half step between the second and third scale degrees as well as the fifth and sixth scale degrees. You can also think of it as this sequence of whole and half steps: W-H-W-W-H-W-W.

Songs can switch from a major key into a minor key, and knowing how the tone color or timbre changes between major and minor can help you sing this switch in tune. After you make the switch into the minor key, your ear has to adjust to the melancholy tone and then switch back to a brighter tone when you go back into the major key.

Get some practice on your minor scales by listening to the following exercise on Track 24 and then singing along. I've added the solfège syllables and scale degree numbers to help you sing the scale in tune. You may notice that the syllables change a bit for the natural minor scale compared to the major scale (see the preceding section). Instead of *mi,* you sing *me,* instead of *la,* you sing *le*, and instead of *ti,* you sing *te*. You can also try singing on the scale degree numbers to see which one helps you stay in tune the most.

Note: If you've already worked on the exercise in the section "Singing major scales," you may notice that the same scales for major are shown in this section in their minor form, allowing you to compare the scales to help reinforce which notes change from major to natural minor.

Practice Piece: "Singing All the Intervals"

The following practice piece, featured on Track 25, combines all the intervals I cover in this chapter. You may want to listen to the track several times to get familiar with the leaping intervals before you sing along. Note that the first few times you perform this practice piece, it may seem quite tricky. But after a while, you'll get the hang of it and have your own song to sing for recognizing intervals.

When you sing the name of a particular interval, be sure to keep your tongue released as you sing the second syllable of the words *major* and *minor*. The sound of the *r* (called *r coloring*) can cause the middle of the tongue to tighten, so focus on making the sound of the *r* without tightening your tongue. The tongue naturally arches for the *r,* but you don't have to tighten the tongue by pushing up or pressing to arch it. It just lifts to arch for the sound.

Songs for Practicing Large Intervals

To help you practice your interval skills, you can try out the songs in the following list. I've chosen mostly songs with larger intervals because they require that you apply several technical skills at one time. (The changes in small intervals are gradual because the notes are so close together, so they're not as difficult to sing as larger intervals.) As you explore these songs, remember to keep the space inside the back of your mouth open as you leap up these large intervals. Allow your tongue and lips to make the right shape for the consonant in the front of the mouth as you open the space in the back. (See Chapter 4 for details on moving the tongue and lips the right way for consonants.)

You may have to switch registers when you sing the large intervals in these songs. I recommend that you look through the music before you start singing so that you can figure out ahead of time where you may need to switch. (I help you coordinate register transitions in Chapter 11.) Then practice singing that section of the song on a vowel (without the lyrics) to practice making the register shift smoothly. When you can sing it smoothly on a vowel, you can add the words and be more confident on how to sing words and shift registers.

- "Over the Rainbow" by Harold Arlen (either)

- "And I Love You So" by Don McLean (either)

- "Greensleeves," an English folk song (either)

- "Songs My Mother Taught Me" by Antonín Dvořák (either)

- "Ich liebe dich" ("I Love You") by Ludwig van Beethoven (either)

- "Can't Help Lovin' Dat Man" from *Show Boat* by Jerome Kern and Oscar Hammerstein II (female)

- "You Needed Me" by Randy Goodrum as sung by Anne Murray (either)

- "Star-Spangled Banner" by Francis Scott Key and John Stafford Smith (either)

- "Bali Ha'i" from *South Pacific* by Richard Rodgers and Oscar Hammerstein II (either)

- "All by Myself" written and performed by Eric Carmen and based on music by Sergei Rachmaninoff (either)

Chapter 6

You've Got Rhythm: Conquering Rhythmic Notation and Tempo

In This Chapter

▶ Recognizing rhythmic notation

▶ Taking your rhythm up a notch with more complex rhythms

▶ Setting the right pace for your songs with tempo

Recognizing *rhythmic notation* — in other words, knowing about note values, flags, stems, dots, and rests — and understanding tempo markings allow you to sight-read new songs. Being able to sight-read can help you choose the right songs for you to sing because by recognizing the notes on the page, you can easily determine whether the range is right for you and whether the song's rhythms are easy or difficult. This chapter walks you through the basics of rhythmic notation so you can improve your sight-reading skills and gives you two practice songs to try out.

Rhythm Basics: Notes and Rests

The different types of notes — whole, half, quarter, eighth, and sixteenth — combined with the time signature determine the basic rhythm of any song. The *time signature* appears at the beginning of the first measure of a song just after the clef and key signature. Usually, it looks like a fraction. The most common time signature is 4/4. In fact, it's so common that it's often referred to as *common time* and is sometimes represented by a C in place of the 4/4. (You can see both representations of 4/4 time in the following figure.) The top number of the time signature tells you the number of beats per measure, and the bottom number tells you what kind of note gets one beat. For example, when the top number of the time signature is four and the bottom number is also four, each measure gets four beats and a quarter note gets one beat.

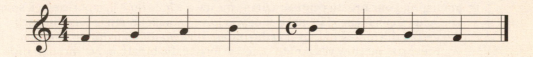

The *melody* of a song is the arrangement of the notes you sing in a particular rhythm. When you first work on a song, you want to figure out the melody (the intervals you sing) and figure out the rhythm so that you know how long to hold each note in the melody.

Trying to figure out a song's rhythm and its melody at the same time can be overwhelming. Layering the work by taking it in steps can help you get a song down much faster:

1. **Write out the text of the song.**

   When you write out the text, pay close attention to the punctuation. The punctuation not only helps you be specific with the meaning of the text but also helps you figure out where to breathe. You can breathe after any punctuation in a song as long as the breath also makes sense with the melody and rhythm.

   Notice where you breathe as you speak through the text and then compare these places to where you'd breathe while singing the song. Mark on the music where you plan to breathe in the song.

2. **Count the beats aloud to figure out the rhythm.**

   In 4/4 time, a whole note or rest gets four beats, a half note or rest gets two beats, a quarter note or rest gets one beat, an eighth note or rest gets half of a beat, and a sixteenth note or rest gets one-fourth of a beat. One system to count out eighth notes is using 1 & 2 & 3 & 4 &. For the sixteenth note, you can use 1 e & a (sounded out as one *ee* and *uh*) to count out the four notes per beat.

3. **Repeat the rhythm on a syllable such as *la*.**

   You can also clap out the beats for each *la* as you go.

4. **Speak through the words in rhythm and make sure the syllables of the words last just the right number of counts.**

5. **Sing through the melody on a vowel.**

   You can choose any vowel that's comfortable for you to sing, or you can sing the melody on *la*. Don't add the text yet because in this step you need to focus on getting the intervals precise. After you practice on the single vowel, then go back and sing through the melody on the words. Make sure to breathe at the places you marked in Step 1.

The following sections explain how to recognize the different types of notes and their associated rests and give you practice playing around with rhythms that include them. ***Note:*** I break down the counts of the notes for you in each figure.

The whole note

A *whole note* (o) looks like a hollow circle (this circle is called the *note head*). It doesn't have a stem. A whole note gets four beats in 4/4 time.

Singing whole notes well always involves the following:

✔ **Managing your breath control:** When you see a whole note in a phrase in a song, you need to plan ahead to make sure you have enough breath to sing through the end of the note. You can sing the phrase on a *lip trill* (moving air through your lips so that they vibrate) to practice feeling the breath move through the phrase. Practicing first with the lip trill can help you figure out how to move the air to sing through to the end of the note when you sing the words in the song. (See Chapter 2 for more on breathing while singing and practicing lip trills.)

✔ **Releasing the note properly:** After sustaining for the duration of a whole note, you may be tempted to squeeze your throat to release the note. Instead, just inhale so the note releases without any effort.

The amount of *vibrato* (the fluctuation of tone in singing) you use on a whole note depends on the type of piece you're singing. Songs that have more of a traditional feel need vibrato, but more contemporary songs require just a glimmer of vibrato. Turn to Chapter 12 for more information on using vibrato.

As you sustain the vowel for the duration of the whole note, you need to keep a consistent shape to the vowel through the end of the note when singing classical songs. Pop songs tend to be more conversational and don't require sustaining a sound for very long. So if you happen to find a whole note in a pop song, feel free to change the vowel midstream. If you find two vowels together (in a diphthong) in a pop song, you can sustain the second vowel. But if you find a diphthong in a classical song, you need to sustain the first vowel sound and then sound out the second vowel at the end of the note. **Note:** A *diphthong* is a combination of two vowels in one syllable sounded one after another (for example, *guy, boy, now,* and so on); I cover diphthongs in more detail in Chapter 3.

The following pattern gives you a chance to practice reading whole notes while plotting out your singing technique. Note that the word *are* has a vowel followed by the consonant *R*. The sound you sustain on the whole note is the first vowel in the word *are*. On the last beat of the whole note, you create the sound of the *R* by arching your tongue and then moving the tip to the alveolar ridge to make the sound of the *t* in *toys*. The words *toys* and *now* each contain a diphthong (two vowel sounds in one syllable). Your goal is to hold out the first vowel sound until the last beat of the note, at which point you change to the second vowel of the diphthong. You then sing through the last consonant of the word and the first consonant of the next word.

Before you dive into this pattern, take some time to sound out the words in it to make sure you know the vowel sounds you need to sustain as well as the shape and sound of the ending consonant of one note connecting to the next note.

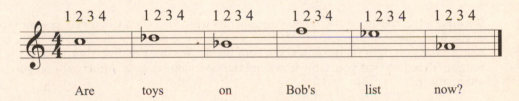

The half note

A *half note* has a hollow note head and a stem (♩). In 4/4 time signature, the half note gets two beats.

Your breath control for a half note depends on what happens before and after the note. For example, if the half note is at the end of a very long phrase, then you need to prepare your breath coordination for a long phrase. In other words, don't expel too much air at the beginning of the phrase; instead, try to evenly move the breath for the duration of the phrase. If the half note is at the beginning of the phrase, move the breath slowly as you sustain the half note, keeping in mind that you have several more notes to sing in the phrase. Check out Chapter 2 to help you establish good breath coordination for singing.

The following pattern has you sustaining vowels on half notes. Because you want the vowel sound to remain consistent throughout the duration of the note, you need to maintain the shape of the vowel until it's time to sing the next note. Extend the vowel sound and wait until the last beat of the note to articulate the ending consonant. Moving your lips or tongue too soon may cause you to change vowel sounds in the middle of the note. (Of course, if you're going for a pop, country, or rock vibe, you may actually want the vowel to change in the middle of the note; see Chapter 12 for more on this.)

Notice that the following pattern incorporates four different meters. The first measure has the time signature 4/4, which means it has four beats per measure and the quarter note gets one beat and the half note gets two. The next measure, labeled 3/4, has three beats in the measure, and the quarter note gets one beat while the half note gets two. The next time signature you see, 2/2, isn't that common, but you sometimes see it in classical music. It means that each measure has two beats and the half note gets one beat. The last measure, which has 6/8 time, has six beats per measure, and the eighth note gets one beat while the half note gets four beats.

The quarter note

A *quarter note* has a head that's filled in and a stem (♩). In the 4/4 time signature, the quarter note gets one beat out of four beats per measure.

Because a quarter note often receives only one beat, you need to quickly prepare the shape of the next vowel or consonant. After all, you want the sound of the next vowel or consonant to happen right on the downbeat (not before or after the note should start). So be sure to read ahead so that you know how long the upcoming note is and how soon you have to shape for it.

In the following pattern, the meter changes, but the quarter note continues to get one beat in each measure. The lyrics give you an opportunity to practice making specific shapes on each beat and challenge you to figure out where you would breathe if this were a real song. You can either practice all six measures in one breath or breathe where it make sense with the words or music.

The eighth note

An *eighth note* (♪) is filled in and has a flagged stem. The flag tells you that the note duration is shorter than that of a quarter note. Specifically, in 4/4 time, an eighth note receives half of a beat.

As you can see in the following pattern, eighth notes can be grouped together with a beam above them, or they can be separate. The composer decides how to group the notes based on the text or the phrasing in the song. In the first measure of the pattern, the first two notes are beamed together, and the last two notes aren't. The curve coming off the stem on those last two notes is the flag. In the last measure, groups of four notes are beamed together, but in the other measures, the notes are either beamed with one other note or separate. As you can see in the pattern, the words may be separated by syllable, or they may be broken out over several notes. When each syllable of a word has its own note, you see a hyphen between the syllables. But when one word or syllable is drawn out over the entire measure, you see a solid line to help you know how long to hold out the syllable.

To practice counting the eighth notes in this figure, get out your *metronome* (a device that can help you count beats and that usually has the most common tempo terms with a number or range of numbers for that tempo) or a clock with a second hand. With each tick of the clock or metronome, count one beat. When you're confident you can count in time with the clock ticking, then count two beats per tick. To count two notes per beat (or tick of your clock), you can say 1 & 2 &. Notice that the numbers above the line in the pattern show you exactly where the beats are. As you count the beats, the number sounds right with the tick of the clock, and the & sounds between the ticks. The first line has two beats per measure, and the second line has three. The fourth line has four beats per measure. When you're confident you can count the numbers in time, then speak the words in time with the tick of the clock.

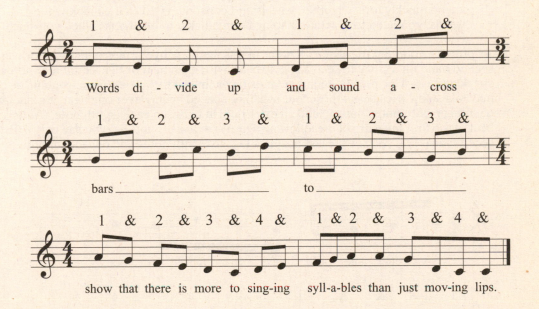

Because eighth notes move quickly, pay attention to the direction of the melody so you can quickly prepare to change registers. The melody may move in stepwise motion (all the notes right next to each other; see Chapter 13), or it may have leaps of large intervals (I fill you in on intervals in Chapter 5). If the melody you're singing requires you to leap through larger intervals on eighth notes, you have to prepare in advance to change registers, change the resonance higher or lower, and sing the right vowels. If you prepare for the quick change of notes in advance, you're more likely to sing the next note in tune. Waiting too long to change the shape for the next vowel may cause you to sing out of tune.

The sixteenth note

A *sixteenth note* has a filled-in note head and a stem with two flags (♪). It receives one-fourth of a beat in 4/4 time; in other words, you need four sixteenth notes to equal one beat.

Like eighth notes, sixteenth notes can be grouped together with other sixteenth notes, or they can be separate, depending on the words in the song. As you can see in the figure later in this section, when a composer groups sixteenth notes together, she uses two beams rather than one. The two beams tell you that you're working with sixteenth notes rather than eighth notes.

Sixteenth notes can look scary on paper because so many of them make up one beat, but they can also be a lot of fun. Plan ahead so you understand where the melody is moving. After you know the melody, singing sixteenth notes can feel like skiing down a hill. If you prepare your body (by opening your body to inhale and opening the space inside your mouth and throat) and then let go and just enjoy the quick speed, you can have a lot of fun moving fast. Find out more about singing quickly in Chapter 13.

Whenever you sing sixteenth notes, keep the following points in mind:

✔ Sing sixteenth notes *legato* (smooth and connected) unless you see markings that tell you otherwise. Chapter 7 contains examples of markings that tell you when to sing the notes short and detached and when to sing them smooth and legato.

✔ Try not to allow an *H* or puff of air to come out between the notes. Instead, connect them so that you can create a phrase rather than just individual notes.

✔ Be sure to sing a specific vowel on each sixteenth note so that your listeners can better understand you when you sing. Whenever you're dealing with a piece with a lot of sixteenth notes, start by speaking through the text to make sure you can shape quickly for each of the vowels and consonants. Even if you know the words, you need to practice shaping them quickly to be precise when you sing.

To practice counting the sixteenth notes in this figure, get your metronome out or use the second hand on a clock to keep a steady beat. With each beat or tick, count four notes by speaking 1 e & a 2 e & a. The number lands on each beat or tick of the metronome or clock. It may take a few tries to get those four syllables spaced evenly over one beat. It's similar to counting eighth notes but you add an extra note in between each eighth note. (***Note:*** The last beat of the first measure of the following figure is a quarter note, so you say only 3. In the second measure, you see the last beat has two sixteenth notes and one eighth note.)

The corresponding rests

Each type of note has a specific type of rest associated with it. These rests tell you how much time you have to breathe before the next phrase. Here's a quick summary of what the different rests look like:

- A *whole note rest* (⁻) looks like a black rectangle, and it falls below the fourth line on the staff.
- A *half note rest* (⁻) also looks like a black rectangle, but it appears above the third line.
- A *quarter note rest* (𝄽) looks like a slanted lowercase *z* with a *c* below it.
- An *eighth note rest* (𝄾) has a stem and one flag.
- A *sixteenth note rest* (𝄿) has a stem and two flags.

The following pattern shows you what all these rests look like and helps you incorporate them into a simple melody. Use the numbers above the staff to help you count out the rhythms in the pattern. Use your clock with a second hand or your metronome to help you count the rhythms in time. Practice counting one count per beat or one count per tick of the clock; doing so is the equivalent of counting one quarter note per beat. You can then practice counting out two counts per beat to count eighth notes. Then count out four notes per beat for sixteenth notes. Use the text that appears above the pattern (the number plus *e & a*) to help you count it out. There are four sixteenth notes per beat in 4/4 time signature.

Practice piece: "The Rhythm Song"

This practice piece helps you put all the note values in one tune. Practice counting the beats aloud by yourself before listening to the singer on Track 26. Continue nailing down the rhythm, following the advice I present in the earlier sections on notes and rests, and then work on the melody. As you do, you'll notice that this tune lies mainly in middle range (for most singers, anyway). To help you get a strong sound in the middle part of your voice, be sure to sing precise vowels. Remember to hold out the sound of the vowel for the duration of the note (don't anticipate the shape of the next vowel or consonant) and sustain the first vowel sound if the syllable has more than one vowel.

TRACK 26

Exploring Advanced Rhythms

Rhythm in popular music can look a little odd — think bracketed notes below (or above) the number 3, random dots added to notes, and emphasis on weaker beats. The good news is that after you know the basic note values (which I fill you in on in the earlier section "Rhythm Basics: Notes and Rests"), mastering these more complex rhythms is a piece of cake. The following sections introduce you to commonly encountered advanced rhythms to help you develop your rhythm skills so you can easily read popular music. These advanced rhythms are also used in classical music.

Joining notes together with triplets

A *triplet* is a set of three notes that divide equally over one or more beats. Visually, they're joined by a bracket or a beam and accompanied by the number 3. Eighth note triplets divide over one beat, quarter note triplets divide over two beats, and half note triplets divide over four beats. You may encounter sixteenth note triplets, which equal one eighth note, but they usually appear in more advanced songs. In a measure of 4/4, two sets of sixteenth note triplets make up one beat. To count out a triplet, most people divide the word *triplet* into three syllables across the three notes — *tri-pl-et*.

Triplets in the vocal line don't always correspond with triplets in the piano line. For example, you may find that the piano plays eighth notes as you sing your triplets. This is called *two against three* and is common in songs. Two against three feels and sounds like a tug of war since your rhythm is different from the accompaniment. This contrast in rhythm can help highlight conflict described in the text of a song, but you'll need quite a bit of practice to get comfortable with singing two against three. Take your time working on your counting skills so that you're ready to handle singing rhythms that contrast with the accompaniment when the time comes.

The first measure of the following pattern has triplets in the vocal line and eighth notes in the piano line for two against three. The second measure moves into 6/8 time. The eighth notes in this measure are grouped into sets of three, but you don't see the 3 over the beam that joins them because the eighth notes in 6/8 get one beat per note instead of being divided over the beat. The vocal line of the third measure has quarter note triplets, which divide over two beats. Notice how the quarter note triplets line up with the quarter notes in the piano part. The vocal line of the last measure has half note triplets, which spread out over four beats. Knowing the duration of each type of triplet helps you figure out how long to sustain each note and how to prepare the articulation.

Adding more notes with dotted rhythms

A dot immediately following a note adds half of the value of the original note. For example, a dot beside a quarter note adds another eighth note to the duration of the quarter note, so in 4/4 time, a dotted quarter note gets one and a half beats. The following pattern, which is in 4/4 time, exposes you to dotted half notes and dotted eighth notes in addition to dotted quarter notes. The dotted half note takes up three beats (two beats for the half note plus one beat for the dot), and the dotted eighth note essentially has a sixteenth note tacked onto it.

Practice this pattern one line at a time. Use your clock or metronome to set a steady beat and count out the first line. When you get that line just right, count out a measure of eighth notes (1 & 2 & 3 & 4 &, which sounds like two counts per beat) to prepare for the next line. Even though there are two eighth notes for every beat in the second line, you only say the & aloud when a note lands right at the &. So in the second line of the figure, you count only the eighth notes (&) aloud after the second and fourth beats. To prepare for the last line — the hardest of the three — count out four notes per beat (1 e & a). The text above the line shows you that the dotted eighth takes up 1 e &, which equals three sixteenth notes. To speak this line aloud, even though you would count the 1 e & a in your head, the only syllables you say aloud are 1 a 2 a 3 a.

Emphasizing the weaker beats with syncopation

The strong beats in a measure commonly have a strong rhythm. For instance, in the 4/4 time signature, the strong beats are one and three; in 3/4 time, the strong beat is one. *Syncopation* switches things up and places the emphasis on the weaker beats in the measure.

The following pattern helps you distinguish between regular rhythms and syncopated ones. In the first measure, the notes land right on the beat or right at the number and you don't have any syncopation. Compare that measure to the syncopated second measure, which has an emphasis on the offbeat. The numbers below the line show you exactly where the beat occurs, whereas the numbers above the line show you both the beat (number) and the off-beat (&). In the first measure, you see the notes land right with the numbers. In the other measures, you see that the numbers don't always line up with the notes. When they don't line up, you're dealing with syncopation.

 To help you really get a handle on syncopation, search for a recording of "The Syncopated Clock" by Leroy Anderson. As you listen to the song, you'll hear the steady ticking of the clock played by the percussion and the fact that the instruments in the orchestra are emphasizing the offbeat.

Practice piece: "Checking Out Rhythm"

This practice piece allows you to combine the skills of counting the right amount of time for dots and singing triplets and syncopated rhythms. The syncopation puts emphasis on the weaker beats of the measure. You can listen to the singer on Track 27 demonstrate the sounds for you, but I encourage you to try to count out the rhythms by yourself before listening to the singer. Write the counts above the line so you know the exact location of each beat. There are four beats per measure in 4/4. When you sing about syncopation in the last three lines, remember that the note may not land right on the beat.

After you're familiar with the complex rhythms of this piece, speak through the text in rhythm to make sure you can combine the rhythm and text. The rhythms are diverse in the song, but you still want to sing the melody line smooth and connected. As you sing, open the space inside your mouth and throat and allow your lips and tongue to make precise consonant and vowel shapes so that your words are easy to understand (see Chapters 3 and 4 for help with singing precise consonants and vowels). Record yourself singing along with the track and listen back to check your rhythm and the sounds you're making. (**Note:** Some of the notes in this piece are tied; a *tie* connects two notes in a measure or across a bar line. See Chapter 7 for more details on tied notes.)

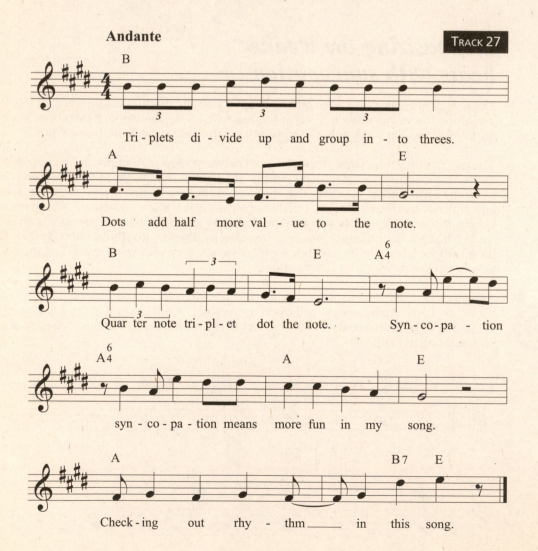

Managing Rhythm at Any Tempo

The speed of a song is called *tempo,* and it's indicated by a *tempo marking* — words or numbers that describe the tempo. The numbers correspond with the number of beats per minute (bpm). For example, a tempo of 60 is easy to keep up with because it matches the ticking of one beat per second on the clock. Grab a clock with a second hand, and you can watch and listen to the ticking of 60 bpm. A tempo of 120 bpm is double 60 bpm, which means you just have to count two ticks per second on the clock.

The words in a tempo marking simply represent the number of beats per minute in that tempo. The following common tempo markings usually appear just above the first measure of a song:

- *Lento* means very slowly (40–60 bpm).
- *Adagio* means slowly or stately (66–76 bpm).
- *Andante* is a walking pace (76–108 bpm).
- *Moderato* indicates a moderate pace (108–120 bpm).
- *Allegro* means quickly and brightly (120–168 bpm).
- *Vivace* is a lively pace that's faster than allegro (140 bpm).

You may also see the following terms combined with a tempo marking. These terms provide additional direction on how to set the pace of a song.

- *Con moto* means with motion. The composer may use *con moto* to tell you to keep the pace moving forward and not labor over each note.
- *Poco a poco* means little by little (*poco* means slightly). For example, you may see *poco a poco allegro,* which means go faster little by little until you're at allegro.
- *Più* means more. You may see *più allegro,* which tells you to be closer to the 168 bpm rather than the slower side of 120 bpm.

You often find terms for changing tempo in the piano part of songs. Even though you're not playing the piano, as a singer, you need to look at the piano part carefully for suggested changes of tempo so that you see the same suggestions for tempo changes that the pianist sees. Common terms for tempo changes are

- *Accelerando (accel.)* means speed up.
- *Meno mosso* means use less movement or go slower.
- *Più mosso* means use more movement.
- *Rallentando (rall.)* means gradually slow down.
- *Ritardando (ritard.* or *rit.)* means slow down more suddenly than you do for *rall.*
- *Rubato* represents a give and take of the tempo or a tempo that's purposely inconsistent.

If a song doesn't have a tempo marking at the beginning, you have to look at the time signature as well as the music and the text to help you figure out the tempo. If the text of the song is sad, the song likely has a fairly slow tempo. A song with text that's happy and joyful is more likely to move faster than a sad song.

To help you with tempo markings, you can use a metronome. The metronome helps you practice at a steady pace so you don't speed up or slow down without realizing it. Most digital pianos have a metronome, as do music writing programs and audio recording programs such as GarageBand. You can also load a metronome app on your smartphone. If you don't have any of these items, you can purchase a metronome to help you in your practice sessions.

Songs for Working on Rhythm

Rhythm is essential in any song, whether you're performing a rap song or a classical aria. The following list includes some rather diverse songs guaranteed to test your rhythm skills. Try to find the sheet music first and spend some time getting the rhythm down before you listen to a recording of the song.

- "Bill of (Your) Rights," an educational rap song by Rhythm, Rhyme, Results (either)
- "Dulcinea" from *Man of La Mancha* by Joe Darion and Mitch Leigh (male)
- "Ye Banks and Braes o'Bonnie Doon" by Wallingford Riegger (male)
- "Stranger to the Rain" from *Children of Eden* by Stephen Schwartz (female)
- "Save the Last Dance for Me" by Doc Pomus and Mort Shuman (either)
- "What a Movie!" from *Trouble in Tahiti* by Leonard Bernstein (female)
- "I Got Rhythm" by George and Ira Gershwin (either)
- "Amor" by William Bolcom (female)
- "Better Than I Know Myself" by Claude Kelly, Cirkut, Ammo, and Dr. Luke as sung by Adam Lambert (either)
- "Old Mother Hubbard" by Victor Hely-Hutchinson (either)
- "hist whist" by John Woods Duke (either)
- "The Silver Swan" by Ned Rorem (either)

Chapter 7

Adding Diversity with Dynamics, Articulation Marks, and More

In This Chapter

▶ Varying the dynamics in your songs based on dynamic markings

▶ Getting familiar with articulation markings and putting them to use with a practice piece

▶ Developing your improvisational skills to add your own twist to songs

A song becomes a work of art when the singer creates a diversity of sounds that highlights the emotional journey of the song's story. Sometimes that diversity of sounds is driven by a song's composer through dynamic markings (directives that tell you how loudly or softly to sing) and articulation marks (directives such as accent marks that tell you how long or short to sing a note, as well as phrasing and breathing directives).

But you can also create a diversity of sound on your own through improvisation. Improvisation is all about making a song your own through techniques such as adding extra words and altering melodies. It's an art form that you can check out whether you're singing classical music or R&B. This chapter explores all of these exciting options for making songs absolutely captivating to listen to.

Singing Dynamically

Composers use *dynamic markings* to tell you how loudly or softly to sing a song and when to vary the volume. You need to be able to recognize these markings so you can scan a song and know when to expect changes to happen. The following sections introduce you to the various dynamic markings and explain where to find them. They also give you practice increasing and decreasing your volume so that you can discover how to use your body to create dynamic contrast in your songs.

Reading the markings

The dynamics in a song can range from really loud to very soft. The following table lists the most common dynamic terms you'll see in a song, along with their abbreviations:

Dynamic Word	Meaning	Abbreviation
Fortissimo	Really loud	*ff*
Forte	Loud	*f*
Mezzo forte	Half loud or medium loud	*mf*
Mezzo piano	Half soft but louder than piano	*mp*
Piano	Soft	*p*
Pianissimo	Really soft	*pp*

Mezzo means *half*, so *mezzo forte* means *half loud* or *softer than forte*. But *mezzo piano* means *half soft but louder than piano*. If you see the word *mezzo* with a loud dynamic level, you have to cut the loud level in half for a softer volume. If you see *mezzo* with a soft dynamic level, you have to raise the soft level to be only half as soft.

Sometimes you must gradually adjust the volume in a piece over the course of a couple of beats or measures. Composers often indicate these adjustments with symbols, although they sometimes use abbreviations of the words instead. The *crescendo* (cresc.) symbol, <, tells you to gradually get louder. The *decrescendo* (decresc.) symbol, >, tells you to gradually get softer.

When you see dynamic markings in a song, you don't see any decibel levels that tell you exactly how loud is loud and how soft is soft. So you need to know your body well enough to know how loudly or softly you can successfully sing. The song you sing may call for the dynamic level of *pp,* but that may be softer than you can sing right now. If singing is relatively new for you, use a moderate version of the dynamic level required in the song. For example, if you're singing a song with a *ff* phrase, you may need to sing the phrase *f* or *mf* for now. After all, singing *ff* requires a lot of body coordination and skill, which leads many singers to push when they sing it. But you don't want to push because pushing makes a really tight sound that your audience doesn't want to hear. Instead, you need to work on singing the different dynamic levels so you can really tell the difference in how your body responds at each level. After you work up to *ff,* you can sing the song as it's written.

Dynamic markings in music usually show up in the piano part because composers know that pianists don't have time to look way up to the top of the vocal line for dynamic levels. So whenever you get a new song, go through the entire piece and look for dynamic markings as well as tempo markings (see Chapter 6). Make a note of these markings by circling them or highlighting them so that you remember to make the necessary changes as you sing your way through the music.

Making a smooth crescendo

The *crescendo* (a gradual increase in volume) usually happens in the climax of a song. To crescendo smoothly, you have to move your breath at a faster rate. In other words, you need to gradually increase the speed of air coming out as you sing. Keep in mind, though, that moving the air faster isn't the same as pushing. Pushing may create a louder tone, but if you push, the tone will undoubtedly sound forced.

Choose a note that's comfortable in your range and crescendo or gradually grow louder over the course of four beats. Notice as the volume increases that you have to make a choice to move the breath faster or push. Always choose to move the breath faster.

If you aren't sure what gradually moving the breath faster to get louder means, try using a lip trill. Start the tone on the lip trill softly and gradually increase the volume. Notice that as you increase the volume, you move your lips faster; moving the lips faster means that the air is moving faster. Also notice that as the tone gets louder, the tone feels like it spins forward at a faster rate. (See Chapter 2 for more on breathing and using lip trills.)

Listen to the singer on Track 28 demonstrate a smooth crescendo. As you follow along with the music in the following exercise, you see a whole note with a crescendo sign over the measure. The dynamic markings say to crescendo from *mf* (half loud) to *f* (loud). You have two beats to rest and breathe, and then you have to crescendo again. The vowels in this exercise change to help you practice singing a crescendo on different vowels.

Singing a crescendo on a lower note is very different from doing so on a higher note, so you need to practice both. After you're confident of your ability to make a crescendo, you can turn off the track and continue to practice making the crescendo on higher or lower notes. I recommend that you try making a crescendo on a few new notes in each practice session. When you get to a note that's challenging for you, then work on making the crescendo smoothly on that note before moving on up the scale.

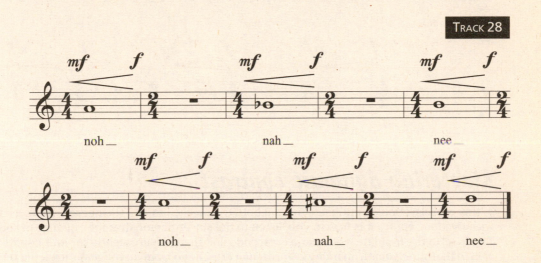

Track 28

Gradually singing softer with a decrescendo

To successfully sing a *decrescendo* (a gradual decrease in volume), you need to visualize the tone getting smaller without closing down the space. At first, you may have a hard time moving from a loud note that feels big inside your head to a soft note that feels so small. To decrescendo to the softer tone, try allowing the tone to gradually float higher. Sing a note loudly in the middle part of your range or on a note that you're comfortable singing and notice the amount of exertion you feel in your body as you sing the loud note. You should feel your breath moving to sustain the note. To gradually sing softer, you don't want the tone to suddenly get softer; instead, you want the change in volume to be gradual. To notice the change in shape from loud to soft, sing the loud note and gradually get softer for a few beats. Start by singing the loud note from *f* to *mf*. Notice that the *mf* sound feels lighter, as though it were floating more. The *f* sound may feel like a laser beam that's speeding out of you. Next, practice singing from *mf* to *p*.

The first few times you try to decrescendo to *p* you may find that you just can't figure out how to sing softer. Try starting a note softly and then making the crescendo. After you know the feeling of starting the note softly, you can look for that same sensation when you decrescendo to the softer sound.

The singer on Track 29 demonstrates a decrescendo for you. When you follow along with the following exercise, you see a whole note with a decrescendo sign over the measure. The dynamic markings say to decrescendo from *f* (or loud) to *mf* (or half loud). If you find that you're confident making the decrescendo from *f* to *mf* after a few practice sessions, you can then practice moving from *f* to *mp*. When you're comfortable doing so, you can practice making the decrescendo from *f* to *p*. You may need to review your crescendo a few times to feel how the tone changes as you grow louder. To find the softer tone, you create the physical sensations of the crescendo but in reverse.

Mastering dynamic contrast

In this exercise, you can practice making both the crescendo and the decrescendo. If singing with dynamic contrast is new to you, listen to the singer demonstrate the change of sound on Track 30. In the first line, you hear a crescendo and then a decrescendo for four counts each. Notice that the dynamic markings represent a crescendo from *mf* to *f* and then a decrescendo from *f* to *mf*. The second line has five counts for the crescendo and five for the decrescendo. The dynamic levels move from *mp* to *f* and back to *mp*. In the third line, you hear the singer move smoothly from the crescendo to the decrescendo without taking a breath between the two whole notes — sustaining for eight counts. Notice how the tone changes as the singer makes the crescendo. The tone becomes more vibrant with the crescendo. During the decrescendo, the tone doesn't fall back, but it does spin lighter. The dynamic markings in this line move from *p* to *ff*. Be sure to count the two beats of rest between the repetitions and allow the muscles in your throat to release with the inhalation. To restart the note softly, pretend that the note starts as a tiny beam of sound just outside of your mouth. The last three lines of this exercise allow you to sing alone with the piano to practice moving from crescendo to decrescendo.

TRACK 30

Articulating What's Written

Various symbols help you communicate the emotion of a song. For example, a piece that's written to express anger may include markings that tell you to sing some notes in a detached fashion, whereas a song that's about true love may have markings that instruct you on how to shape certain phrases and connect various notes. You may even encounter a song with markings in it that tell you when you just need to zip it and let the silence speak for you. In the sections that follow, I walk you through the articulation markings you're most likely to encounter in written music and let you play around with them.

Connecting notes

A *slur* tells you to smoothly connect the notes in a phrase. The symbol for the slur is a curved line above or below the notes. The slur can connect a few notes or a whole phrase. Notice in the following figure that the slur appears above different groups of notes.

When you see a slur in a song, your goal is to smoothly connect from vowel to consonant. To help you do so, think of the phrase as moving forward rather than vertically. The slur also usually implies that you shouldn't take a breath within the phrase covered by the slur. So in the pattern that follows, you'd want to take a breath after the word *mark,* where you see the first slur end and the next slur begin.

The *tie* looks like a small slur. It connects two notes, and the two notes can be in a measure or across a bar line. If you see a tie, you need to sustain the text written under the first note for the duration of the combined notes. Check out the examples of ties in the second line in the following pattern.

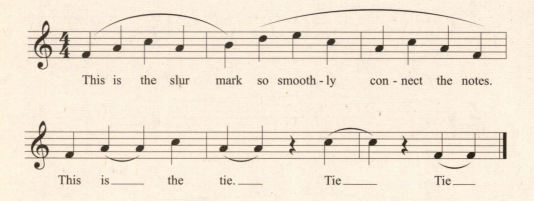

Making a note short and sweet

A dot that appears above or below a note head is your cue to sing the note *staccato* — short and detached. To sing notes staccato, you want to sing the tone but not sustain the note. Singing staccato feels like you just touch the note, not like you push out the note. Your throat is open and your vocal cords close to start the note. (If you press your vocal cords together, the staccato becomes a glottal, which means you're using physical pressure to force the note out.)

If you try to sing fast staccato before you know the proper physical coordination for starting a tone, you'll end up just squeezing out the notes to get them out fast enough. So practice singing staccato notes slowly and then gradually sing them faster.

The following figure shows you what staccato notes look like. Notice that the word *short* has a line that extends for three notes. That means you sing the first vowel in the word *short* on the first note, then repeat the vowel over the next two notes, and then sing through the ending consonants as you cut off the note at the end of that measure. So you don't articulate the *T* until the end of the third note. In the next measure, you see the word *Ah.* The line extending after the word tells you to continue the same sound (the vowel *ah*), but the dots tell you that the notes are short and detached. On the second line, you see more text that has a syllable sustained over several notes. The last word is *singing.* Because it's a two-syllable word, you see a dash between the syllables rather than a long line. Since the second syllable is written under the last note in the last measure, you sing the first syllable in the word *singing,* then repeat the vowel on each of the eight staccato sixteenth notes, and then sing the last syllable on the last quarter note.

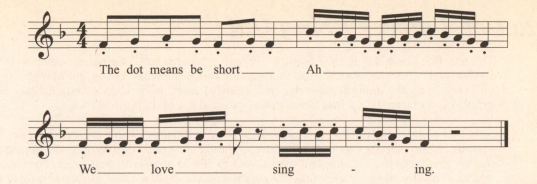

The dot means be short _____ Ah _____

We _____ love _____ sing - ing.

Knowing when to let go

Sometimes composers want certain notes to be longer, and other times they want to manage the pauses in their songs. Following are the four most common markings that composers use to indicate when to sing longer or when to stop singing (you can see what they look like in the following figure):

- ✔ **Breath mark:** The *breath mark* looks like a comma above the melody line. Composers or editors often add breath marks to show you good places to take a breath. See an example of a breath mark at the end of the first measure of the following figure.

- ✔ **Caesura:** The two slanted lines in the second measure of the following figure are called a *caesura*. This marking indicates a break or interruption in the phrase. Composers use this pause for dramatic effect to enhance the climax in the music by creating suspension.

- ✔ **Tenuto:** A *tenuto* mark is a horizontal line over a note; it indicates that you should hold the note a little longer than the note value. You see the tenuto marking in the first measure of the second line in the following figure.

- ✔ **Fermata:** The *fermata* looks like a bird's eye. You see the dot with an arch over it in the last measure on the last note of the following figure. This symbol means to sustain the note longer than the rhythmic value. A moment of silence usually comes right after the fermata before you start the next phrase.

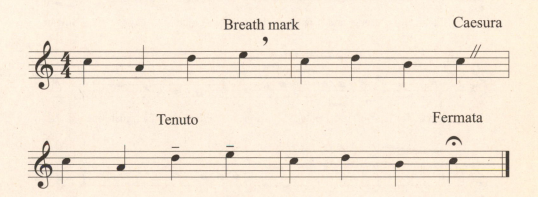

Practice Piece: "I Sing Out!"

The practice piece "I Sing Out!" features dynamic changes and different articulation markings so that you can see how a song can incorporate these elements. Follow along with the singer on Track 31 as she demonstrates dynamic changes, such as crescendo and decrescendo, and articulation markings, such as tenutos, staccatos, slurs, and breath marks.

Note that some of the phrases in this practice piece are marked with a crescendo or decrescendo, but no markings indicate how far you should crescendo or decrescendo. Seeing the marker to change the dynamic and then having to decide how far to go is pretty common. After you work on the piece for a few practice sessions, you can decide how far you should vary the dynamic level based on what happens next in the song. For the first practice session, make a slight change in dynamic level to test your skill. Try singing from *mf* to *f*. Remember that the tone gradually gets louder during the crescendo, the space in your mouth and throat stays open, and your breath gradually moves faster through the change in dynamics. For a decrescendo, you want the tone to gradually get softer as if the tone were spinning higher and lighter.

TRACK 31

Improvising to Give Songs Your Own Unique Stamp

When you hear popular songs sung by famous singers, you often find that the singers engage in a little improvisation. In other words, they put their own stamp on the songs by creating diversity through contrast in dynamics, accents, rhythm, and articulation.

Certain styles of music lend themselves to improvisation more easily than others. For example, in contemporary musical theater (think *Rent, Avenue Q,* or *The Book of Mormon*), you usually sing mostly what's on the page with some variation. Pop music offers more flexibility; you can sing mostly what's on the page but add some extra notes or change the rhythm a little. By comparison, in classical music and traditional musical theater (think *South Pacific, West Side Story,* or *Into the Woods*), you typically sing exactly and only what's on the page. Always know the style of music that you want to sing so you know how much change you can (and should) make to what's printed on the page. The following sections reveal a few common techniques you can use to make a popular song or a song on the radio more of your own.

Adding more words

Adding extra words, either spoken or sung, to a song's lyrics is a common improvisational trick. The extra words are either a reiteration of the text you just sang or a set of new words thrown in for emphasis. They can be anything from *yeah* to *uhuh* to basic pet names, such as *baby, honey,* or *darlin'.* Keep in mind that you don't want to add too many extra words to a song; just add a few for emphasis and add them only a few times in the song.

Changing the rhythm

Singers sometimes play around with rhythm when improvising. They tend to either anticipate a rhythm or delay it. The first time you explore improvising, you can make minor changes to the rhythm by delaying or anticipating a particular note or beat. To *anticipate a beat,* you just come in early or start singing before the designated time. To *delay a beat,* you come in late or later than the original version indicates.

In order to successfully change up a song's rhythm, you first need to be confident of the rhythm as it's written. (Turn to Chapter 6 for practice with reading rhythms.) Rehearse the original rhythm as many times as you need to in order to feel comfortable with it and then start adding your own spin.

Altering the melody

Varying a song's melody is a fun approach to improvisation. When you add short pieces of music that move quickly in a specific pattern and are often improvised, you're changing up the song's melody. You hear this kind of improvisation in many styles of music, but the technique goes by different terms, including *riff, lick, ad lib,* and in classical music, *melisma, coloratura,* or *ornamentation.* The keys to improvising well are to develop your agility (I help you with this in Chapter 13) and to know when to embellish the melody. You can add just enough additional notes to make a song cool without overpowering it by following these general guidelines:

✔ If you're looking at the music for a song, plan to add notes in two to three places per page.

✔ If you don't have any sheet music, plan to add notes in small quantities in the opening section of the song and then at the end for the big finish. After you have the beginning and end planned, you can decide how much more variety you need in the song.

Either way, start with small changes and then work up to bigger changes in the melody. Listening to other singers sing your style of music can help you discover what's typical.

Varying the tone

Great performers often explore variations in tone to tell their story in the song. You can vary your tone in a number of different ways, including the following:

✔ **Singing a breathy tone on purpose:** To sing a breathy tone on purpose, you need to let some air escape without blowing out too much. Intentionally making a breathy tone allows you to lose a little air without running out of air completely. (Think of Norah Jones who adds some breathiness to her songs.)

✔ **Adding a glottal:** A *glottal* is a very slight grunt at the beginning of the tone, usually heard on words that start with a vowel. It's the opposite of a breathy tone. Too many glottals become predictable, and glottals that are too harsh create too much tension in your throat.

✔ **Allowing a break between registers:** Many singers feel a change or break when they transition from head voice (see Chapter 9) and chest voice (see Chapter 8). With training, singers discover how to smooth out their register transitions. (I give you a chance to work on your register transitions in Chapter 11.) However, breaks between registers are common in popular music, where more reckless or unpolished sounds are more appropriate.

✔ **Varying vibrato:** Pop singers often vary the *vibrato* (fluctuating pitch on a sustained note) in their songs. In other words, they use *straight tone* (non-fluctuating pitch on a sustained note), move from straight tone into vibrato, or sing with some vibrato. (For more on vibrato, see Chapter 12.)

Songs for Improving Your Musical Diversity

You can choose any song and explore ways to add diversity, but this list helps you get started. After you choose a song to start with, explore the song as written. When you know what the composer wrote, then you can explore adding your own changes.

✔ "Misty" by Erroll Garner and Johnny Burke (either)

✔ "Bridge over Troubled Water" by Paul Simon and Art Garfunkel (either)

✔ "Come Rain or Come Shine" from *St. Louis Woman* by Harold Arlen and Johnny Mercer (either)

✔ "Autumn Leaves" by Joseph Kosma and Johnny Mercer (either)

✔ "My Funny Valentine" from *Babes in Arms* by Richard Rodgers and Lorenz Hart (either)

✔ "What's New?" by Bob Haggart and Johnny Burke (either)

✔ "The Man I Love" by George and Ira Gershwin (female)

✔ "How Great Thou Art" by Stuart K. Hine (either)

✔ "They Can't Take That Away From Me" by George and Ira Gershwin (either)

✔ "Blue Skies" from *Betsy* by Richard Rodgers and Lorenz Hart (either)

Part III
Working Out Your Range

The 5th Wave
By Rich Tennant

"My vocal range? Well, I'm a soprano in the shower, a coloratura calling my son for dinner, and a real contralto arguing with my husband."

In this part . . .

The word *registers* refers to the different areas of your singing voice. In this part, you explore the three registers — chest voice, middle voice, and head voice — individually and work on creating smooth transitions between them. I recommend getting a solid grasp on the individual registers so you know exactly what each part of your singing voice feels like and sounds like and then practicing creating smooth transitions. Being able to smoothly transition between registers makes all those tough songs more manageable.

This part also explores how to blend registers together to mix. The word *mix* is pretty common in singing, and it can have several different meanings. Lucky for you, this part helps you figure out what mix means for you and what it sounds like and feels like.

Chapter 8

Checking Out Chest Voice

In This Chapter
▶ Recognizing the sounds and sensations of chest voice
▶ Developing strength in your chest voice with a practice piece

Chest voice is the lowest register of the singing voice. Working out your chest voice is important because you need to know its limits so you don't expect the same heavy sensation when you sing in other parts of your voice. In this chapter, I help you discover your chest voice and present a song that you can practice entirely in this register. In case you find that your chest voice is on the weaker side, I give you an exercise for strengthening it. For those of you who discover that it's already the heaviest it can possibly be, I show you that chest voice doesn't have to be huge every time you use it.

Getting Familiar with Chest Voice

Chest voice is the heavier sound in the lower part of your voice. The notes in chest voice feel thick and heavy compared to the notes you sing in head voice and middle voice (see Chapters 9 and 10, respectively, to get practice in these registers). When you sing in chest voice, the vibrations of sound buzz in your throat and chest. See for yourself by singing some low notes and putting your hand on your chest. Feel the vibrations?

Most men take chest voice up to around Middle C, and women usually transition out of chest voice around the E or F just above Middle C. (You can check out *Singing For Dummies*, 2nd Edition [Wiley], for more details about the specific range of each voice type and the normal places for making transitions out of chest voice.) Using a heavy chest voice higher than these transitions may cause an imbalance in your singing voice; for example, your chest voice may become much stronger than your head voice.

The exercises in the following sections help you discover the sensations of chest voice, vary the heaviness of it, strengthen it, and get comfortable singing certain vowels in this register.

Chest voice and belting aren't the same thing. You do use chest voice when you belt, but you don't use full (or 100 percent) chest voice. For the full scoop on belting, turn to Chapter 14.

Exploring the sounds of chest voice

If you haven't tried singing lower in your chest voice, this exercise has your name on it. It sits entirely in your chest voice range, and the pattern is descending so that you can experience going lower into your chest voice. Listen to the singer on Track 32 demonstrate the sounds of the exercise and chest voice. You can hear that the vibrations of resonance are low. Then practice singing along.

As you sing in chest voice, imagine the sound coming out of your chest rather than your mouth to help you sing the lower notes. If you have trouble singing this low, you can slide up to the note. Pretend the note you're about to sing is actually lower and slide between all the pitches until you get up to the note. By pretending that the actual note is lower, you'll likely add more chest voice or more thickness to the tone instead of encouraging more head voice or a lighter sound, which is what happens when you pretend you're going down to the note. You can also try speaking really low to see if you can speak on the low pitch. Many singers don't think they can sing a particularly low note, but when they try to speak it, they realize that they can speak quite low. For example, say *nah* on a low pitch and notice the sensation. If you can speak the low sound, you can sing it, too.

Varying the heaviness in your chest voice

Singers often assume that chest voice is supposed to be ultra heavy. Although many singers do have a heavy chest voice, you don't have to use all that weight or fullness every time you sing in chest voice. You can choose to use a heavy chest voice to sing certain phrases and a lighter chest voice to sing others, as you can see in the following exercise.

Listen to the exercise on Track 33. You hear a singer demonstrate four sounds for you, and then you hear the rest of the repetitions of the exercise with only the piano. The first example from the singer demonstrates 100 percent chest voice, the second demonstrates 75 percent chest voice, the third demonstrates 50 percent chest voice, and the fourth demonstrates a head voice–dominated mix. (*Mix* is how much head voice and chest voice you use on a particular note; see Chapter 10 for more details.) Each of these variations is on the same notes so you can hear the many different sounds that the same notes can have.

TRACK 33

When you're confident you know the pattern for this exercise, use the following steps to help you discover how to vary the sounds you make in chest voice:

1. **Sing the pattern, using the fullest, heaviest chest voice sound you can make — that sound and sensation make up your 100 percent chest voice.**

   I like to use a percentage to describe the chest voice sensation so you can feel the layers of thickness involved in this register. Notice that as you sing higher in pitch you feel a tightening sensation in your throat from the pressure of the heavy chest voice.

2. **Sing the pattern again and aim to use just 75 percent chest voice by allowing the vibrations of resonance to shift higher and by opening the space in your throat to create less pressure or weight.**

   Don't worry about exactly how much is 75 percent; just try to make a lighter sound than you made for 100 percent chest voice. The difference between 100 percent chest voice and 75 percent chest voice is that 75 percent feels lighter; in other words, the sensation is of less weight and pressure in your throat. Sing a few repetitions of the pattern again and compare singing with 100 percent chest voice to singing with 75 percent chest voice.

3. **Sing the pattern a third time and use 50 percent chest voice.**

   Be careful not to flip out of chest voice; instead concentrate on using only half of the weight of your heaviest chest voice sounds. To sing with 50 percent chest voice, open up your throat more and allow the vibrations of resonance to move higher. If you compare the sensation of singing with 100 percent chest voice to the sensation of singing with 50 percent chest voice, you should notice that the resonance for 50 percent feels taller or has high and low vibrations of resonance. When you sing in 100 percent chest voice, on the other hand, the vibrations of resonance are only in your chest, not to mention more pressure is in your throat when you make the sound.

4. **Sing the pattern again, this time using a head voice–dominated mix.**

    If you aren't sure what this sounds like, listen to the singer demonstrate the sound for you on Track 33. Singing with a head voice–dominated mix means singing the same notes you sang in chest voice in Steps 1 through 3 by using more head voice in the mixture. The pattern is low enough that you can't sing it in a pure head voice, but you can take out most of the chest voice. When you sing with the head voice–dominated mix, notice that you feel the vibrations of resonance in your head rather than in your chest.

    Listen to the sequence of sounds the singer makes for you at the beginning of Track 33. Listen carefully to how both the resonance and the weight of the tone change when the percentage of chest voice changes. As the percentage decreases, the vibrations of resonance move higher. You may not need to use a head voice–dominated mix this low in your songs, but you can practice making this sound to make sure you really know the difference between the different layers of thickness you have in your chest voice.

After you explore the differences in the amount of weight in chest voice or the change of percentage, sing the pattern again, using 50 percent chest voice on all the repetitions on the track. When you feel confident about using 50 percent, sing along with the track again and use 25 percent (head voice–dominated mix) on all the repetitions on the track. When you know the sensations of the four percentages, you can choose how you vary the percentage in different phrases in your songs.

While you're singing in chest voice in this exercise, allow your throat to open as you ascend. To help you release some of the pressure in your throat so you can sing with a lighter percentage of weight, imagine your throat getting wider as you ascend. You can also imagine your chest and back (the area between your shoulder blades all the way up to your throat) opening as you ascend; doing so can help you maintain the percentage that you started with in the pattern. If you don't open the throat, you'll feel the space in the throat and chest closing or pressing in with the heavy weight of 100 percent chest voice. If, on the other hand, you do open your throat as you ascend, you won't feel the closing or pressing sensation in your throat.

Note: Figuring out how to vary the layers of thickness in chest voice (what you do in this section) can help you figure out mix. Turn to Chapter 10 for details on how to mix.

Strengthening your chest voice

For most songs, you need to be able to sing a solid C (Middle C for females and the C an octave lower for males); it's even better if you can sing an A just below the C. Many singers can sing much lower than an A, but sopranos and tenors who have really high voices often have very weak sounds below C and, thus, have fairly weak chest voices in general.

If a song you really want to sing has an A or C in it and you just can't sing that note, you either have to choose another song or have the song transposed. Neither option is very fun, which is why I include the following exercise to help you build strength in your chest voice so you can sing the songs you love.

First things first: Listen to the singer perform this exercise on Track 34. After you've listened to the track a few times, you're ready to try the exercise yourself. As you sing the notes, imagine each note coming straight out of your chest (visualize your mouth being right on your chest to help you do so). If you come down to the note instead of letting it come straight out of your chest, you'll encourage more head voice and will create a weaker sound this low in your range. Also, remember that the consonant *M* is voiced and you can use that voiced sound to help you sing the low note.

The notes may seem too low for you the first few times you try this exercise. But don't give up yet. Keep working on it, and you can gradually develop more strength in your chest voice — even if you have to focus on gaining only one note at a time. For example, when you work on developing more strength in the C, you'll slowly gain strength in the B, as well.

Not every voice is designed to sing really low. No matter how many times you practice this exercise, your chest voice may not go to a low A. That's okay. Work on the exercise to develop strength, but know that your voice has a limit to how low you can sing. Instead of getting frustrated, remember that you may not be able to sing really low but you can sing the high notes with ease.

Modifying vowels in chest voice

Two vowels that are difficult to sing in chest voice are *ooh* and *ee*. These vowels encourage head voice, which isn't a good thing when you want to sing in chest voice. To get a fuller sound on these vowels, you need to modify them slightly. Sing *uh* rather than *ooh* or *ee*. For example, if you have to sing *you do*, you can modify it to add more depth and sing *yuh duh*. I know this modification seems silly on paper, but thinking of adding more *uh* to the *ooh* or *ee* sound can help you stay in chest voice. You can modify *we see* to *wuh suh*. If you continue to think about the *ee* even though you shape for *uh*, you'll actually say *we see,* but the phrase itself will have more depth. (You can also apply this suggestion to the other vowels in the following exercise.)

Notice the sequence of the vowels in the following exercise, featured on Track 35. The first vowel *ee* encourages more head voice, and the vibrations of resonance want to sit higher. To help the *ee* be effective in chest voice, you need the vibrations of resonance to happen in your chest, not in your head. You may feel some vibrations in your head, but most of the vibrations should happen in your chest. Pretending that your mouth is right at your chest helps you get the resonance or vibrations to happen in the right place and allows you to create a fuller chest voice sound. ***Note:*** You can apply this suggestion to all the other vowels listed in this exercise.

If you need help with the vowels, listen to the singer on Track 35 demonstrate them for you. You can also check out Chapter 3 for help with vowel sounds.

 The following words have the sequence of vowels from the exercise: *me, miss, may, met, move, no, ought,* and *father*. If you want to add more specific sounds to this exercise, you can practice saying these words to hear the vowel sounds and then apply those same sounds to this exercise.

TRACK 35

Practice Piece: "Finding My Chest Voice"

The following practice piece, featured on Track 36, is your chance to sing a short song entirely in chest voice. I recommend tackling it after you practice the exercises in the preceding sections, especially if you know you have a weaker or overly heavy chest voice. If you've been working to strengthen your chest voice, imagine that you're coming up to the note and that your mouth is right at your chest to help you get a fuller sound. Coming down to the note adds more head voice and creates a lighter sound. If you've been working to lighten up your really heavy chest voice, use the suggestions from earlier in the chapter to open the space as you sing the phrases. Opening the space helps prevent the extra pressure and weight you feel when your chest voice is really heavy.

If you have a really low voice, the range of this piece may be easy for you. But don't toss it by the wayside just yet. Use it as an opportunity to work on specific vowels so that your low notes are right in tune. Lower voices often have a darker tone quality or timbre. Singing really precise vowels can help a darker or heavier voice sing in tune.

Songs That Work Out Your Chest Voice

Songs usually move between registers, so you need to be able to move along with them. The following songs, which vary from country to classical, require you not only to sing low in your chest voice but also to smoothly maneuver in and out of chest voice.

- "I Wouldn't Be a Man" by Rory Michael Bourke and Michael Barry Reid as sung by Josh Turner (male)

- "The Apparition" by Ned Rorem (female)

- "Swing Low, Sweet Chariot," African American spiritual (either)

- "Ol' Man River" from *Show Boat* by Jerome Kern and Oscar Hammerstein II (male)

- "'Tis Nature's Voice" from *Ode on St. Cecilia's Day* by Henry Purcell (female)

- "Scintille, diamant" ("Oh, diamond shine") from *Les Contes d'Hoffmann* (The Tales of Hoffmann) by Jacques Offenbach (male)

- "What Do I Do Now?" from *The Grass Harp* by Kenward Elmslie and Claibe Richardson (female)

- "Would You Go with Me" by Shawn Camp and John Scott Sherrill as sung by Josh Turner (male)

- "Maybe This Time" from *Cabaret* (movie) by John Kander and Fred Ebb (female)

- "The Music of the Night" from *The Phantom of the Opera* by Andrew Lloyd Webber and Charles Hart (male)

Chapter 9

Soaring into Head Voice and Falsetto

In This Chapter

▶ Figuring out how to sing in falsetto

▶ Recognizing and developing your head voice

▶ Trying out your head voice with a practice piece

*H*ead voice, the higher part of your singing voice, is the register that most singers want to work on because the most thrilling notes in many songs are the high ones. If your voice is naturally low, you may need to work slowly and steadily on expanding your range into head voice. For example, you may find that you gain one half step at a time on your range in head voice as you work on the exercises in this chapter. If your voice is naturally high, these exercises can help you refine your skills in singing high notes. Since you already have high notes, you can really focus your attention on how you articulate the vowels and consonants.

Falsetto is the lightest sound of the male voice. The notes you male singers sing in falsetto are the same notes that you can sing in head voice. If your head voice is weak, you can work on falsetto to help strengthen the notes. After all, the lightness of falsetto helps you discover height in the resonance and a much lighter tone. When the notes grow stronger, you can choose whether to sing those same notes in head voice or in falsetto. ***Note:*** I cover falsetto before head voice in this chapter because most males really need to work on their falsetto before they're ready to move on to head voice.

If the patterns in this chapter are too high for you at first, don't strain to sing the notes. Instead, sing them down an octave or, if you're of the male persuasion, sing them in falsetto. Then gradually work up to singing the notes as they're written.

Figuring Out Falsetto

As I mention in this chapter's introduction, *falsetto* is the lightest sound the male singer makes. It sounds feminine and feels lighter or higher than head voice. Men can often take their falsetto down to the A below Middle C and up to the C one octave above Middle C. For comparison purposes, the male head voice usually starts around the E or F just above Middle C, but some change a little earlier, around the D. The ranges for falsetto and head voice overlap, so you need to distinguish between the two so that you can choose which sound you want to make.

Ladies, the exercises in this section can give you a good workout even though you don't have a falsetto. Singing them as they're written gives you a chance to work on your middle voice (see Chapter 10 for the skinny on middle voice). I share how to practice these exercises at the end of each section.

Working out your falsetto

Working out in falsetto helps you develop the muscles of your singing voice so you can easily transition from falsetto to head voice and on to chest voice. Granted, your falsetto may really wiggle the first few times you work it out. Try to see the humor in this and continue working on your falsetto to develop stability and consistency. (Not to mention, you definitely want to know how to sing in falsetto because a lot of fun songs use falsetto sounds.)

Before tackling the following exercise, listen to the male singer on Track 37 demonstrate falsetto for you. Notice how the sound is light and a little bit fuzzy? Falsetto is often a little bit fuzzy compared to your head voice or chest voice, which is usually crystal clear.

This exercise starts with the voiced consonant *V*. As you sing the *V*, sing the consonant on the same note that you sing the *ee* vowel. In other words, don't sing the *V* lower and then scoop up to the note. Even though you're singing in falsetto, you want your throat to stay open and your breath to move consistently. If your throat isn't open, your falsetto will feel tight and may even crack. Don't freak out if the sound cracks. Just try singing the pattern again and be more aware of opening the space and moving the air.

Ladies, you have a couple of options for how to use this exercise:

✔ You can sing this pattern as it's written to work on your mix (see Chapter 10).

✔ If your chest voice tends to be really heavy, you can use this exercise to develop your head voice–dominated mix. Use the *ee* vowel to help you find higher resonance even though you could start the pattern in chest voice.

✔ If you want to sing lighter notes with the guys, sing along with the pattern, but sing an octave higher so you can work on a light head voice. As you ascend, allow the sound to be light rather than full and strong.

TRACK 37

Taking falsetto down

Working on falsetto not only helps your falsetto grow stronger so you can use it in your songs but also helps you develop your head voice. Overlapping falsetto with chest voice allows you to explore singing with a lighter sound, and developing that lighter sound enables you to sing notes in chest voice, falsetto, or a combination for a mix (see Chapter 8 to practice your chest voice and Chapter 10 to practice your mix).

This exercise gives you a chance to practice taking falsetto lower than you normally sing in falsetto (down into chest voice territory) to help you develop specific muscle groups. After all, sometimes the muscles that control chest voice get really strong while the muscles that control head voice get weak. Taking falsetto down into your chest voice range helps you strengthen the muscles that control head voice. As the muscles that control head voice grow stronger, you can start to develop your head voice range.

Listen to the singer on Track 38 demonstrate how to descend and stay in falsetto. Then try singing along. If you find that you suddenly flip out of falsetto into chest voice when you descend in this exercise, try singing the exercise again and notice the sensation you have right before the sound breaks. You can feel the muscles change suddenly when you quickly shift into chest voice. Your goal is to open the space in the back of your mouth and throat and keep the vibrations of resonance high to stay in falsetto. As you sing the exercise, lift the tip of your tongue to the alveolar ridge on the roof of the mouth to articulate the *N* and then round your lips to sing the *ooh* vowel. Be sure to keep your breath moving steadily throughout the exercise. Remember that the muscles you open in your torso on the inhale slowly move back to their normal resting position as you sing the exercise.

Ladies, the *ooh* vowel encourages head voice and higher resonance, so you can use this exercise to work on a higher resonance, which you need for a head voice–dominated mix (see Chapter 10 for details). The exercise starts in middle voice and then descends into chest voice. You can choose to continue singing in a head voice–dominated sound for the entire track to help you practice overlapping registers, or you can gradually transition into chest voice as you descend. To stay in the head voice–dominated mix, keep the vibrations of resonance high as you descend.

TRACK 38

nooh ___   nooh ___   nooh ___

nooh ___   nooh ___   nooh ___

nooh ___   nooh ___   nooh ___

Exploring various vowels in falsetto

The vowels most often used for singing in falsetto are *ooh* and *ee,* but you need to practice singing various vowels in this range because you'll likely have to sing other vowels when you use falsetto in your songs. The *ooh* and *ee* you sing in the previous exercises help you start strengthening your falsetto. This exercise, which you can hear performed on Track 39, helps you develop that same strength on other vowels.

The trick to successfully singing different vowels in falsetto is maintaining the same high resonance and light sound that you have when you sing the *ooh* vowel in falsetto (see the preceding section for details). You may find that different vowels encourage you to add too much weight in the tone and to flip out of falsetto into chest voice. Finding the same light sound in all the vowels in this exercise helps you figure out how to sing any vowel and maintain just the right falsetto sound. As you work through this exercise, be very specific when you shape your lips and tongue for the vowels. The vowels move from being the most rounded on your lips for the *oh* to being more relaxed on your lips for the *ah*. The arch in the tongue changes from having a higher arch on the *oh* to dropping for the *ah* to raising again for the *ih* to lowering for the *ay* and *eh*.

Ladies, you can use this exercise to develop more strength and clarity in your middle voice. Keep in mind that strength in your middle voice isn't about weight or heavy sounds; it's about creating clarity in the tone from specific vowels and resonance. (See Chapter 10 for details on middle voice.)

TRACK 39

Songs for singing in falsetto

Falsetto songs tend to have some notes in falsetto, while most of the notes are in the rest of your range. You can use these songs or portions of these songs to practice your falsetto skills. Numerous songs have been recorded by groups singing in falsetto, but the following diverse list offers some great choices for solo singing.

Ladies, these songs either have gender-specific lyrics or they require sounds that the female voice doesn't make. So take a look at some of the other song lists in this book (and the one I include later in this chapter in the section on head voice) instead of exploring these particular songs.

- ✔ "Pretty Wings" by Maxwell and Hod David
- ✔ "Maria" from *West Side Story* by Leonard Bernstein and Stephen Sondheim
- ✔ "The Most Beautiful Girl in the World" by Prince
- ✔ "The Music of the Night" from *The Phantom of the Opera* by Andrew Lloyd Webber and Charles Hart
- ✔ "My Love" by Justin Timberlake, Timbaland, Nate Hills, and T.I.
- ✔ "Tracks of My Tears" by Smokey Robinson, Pete Moore, and Marv Tarplin as sung by Adam Lambert on American Idol
- ✔ "Lost without U" by Robin Thicke
- ✔ "If You Leave Me Now" by Peter Cetera
- ✔ "Goodbye Yellow Brick Road" by Elton John and Bernie Taupin as sung by Elton John

Discovering Your Head Voice

Head voice gets its name from the vibrations you feel in your head when you sing high notes. You may feel that your voice sounds less powerful and narrower in this register than when you sing in chest voice, but I assure you that notes sung in head voice sound much bigger to your audience than they do in your head.

Most females change into head voice around the E or F an octave above Middle C. Male singers change into head voice anywhere from the D to F above Middle C. Either way, to sing in head voice, you need to open up the space in the back of your mouth and throat. Creating such an opening helps the larynx stay steady so you can produce a rich, full sound. (For tips on keeping your larynx steady, see the later section "Stabilizing the larynx.") You also need to be aware that your breath moves faster and that your vocal cords open and close more quickly when you sing high notes.

To move into head voice, you need to change the weight of your tone so that it gets lighter as you ascend in pitch. After all, the vibrations of resonance need to move higher in your head as you move higher in pitch. You may feel the vibrations of resonance changing and moving up the front of your face or climbing up the back of your head. Either sensation is fine as long as you feel the vibrations shifting higher as you ascend.

Getting a feel for head voice

Give the following exercise a whirl to get a feel for your head voice. As you sing the exercise, which is featured on Track 40, remember that you want the vibrations of resonance to move higher in your head. As you sing the lip trill in the first line of text, allow the vibrations of resonance to move higher in your head as you ascend to the second note in the pattern, which is in your head voice.

The lip trill can be really helpful when you're exploring the vibrations of resonance. You can use a lip trill to discover the high vibrations of resonance you need for head voice even if a note is normally too high for you to sing. Use the lip trill to discover the sensations of resonance and then sing the pattern with a vowel (the *wee* in the second line of text) so you can find the same kind of vibrations of resonance on the vowel. Keep your breath moving consistently throughout the exercise.

If your lips stop vibrating on the lip trill, your breath isn't moving consistently. Place your hands on your sides to feel the opening of your ribs, sides, and abs as you take the breath. As you sing the exercise, you want the muscles that just stretched open on the inhale to gradually move back in.

If some of the notes feel too high for you, sing what feels comfortable for now. As you explore the exercises in the chapter, you can gradually extend your head voice range.

Men, sing this pattern an octave down from where it's written.

TRACK 40

Exploring high resonance in head voice

Singing in head voice requires high resonance. If you aren't sure what that high resonance feels like, this exercise can help you figure it out. Listen to the singer on Track 41 say *wee* and then sing the five-note pattern on *wee*. Then do the same. Where you say *wee* — with a really high sensation of vibrations bouncing around in your forehead — is the same place you want to feel the vibrations when you sing it. Sing the *wee* as if it were coming right out of your forehead at the same place you felt the vibrations when you said the word.

To help move your vibrations of resonance higher into your head, try using your hands to choreograph the movement of the vibrations of resonance. When you say *wee*, use your hand to help you visualize tossing the sound right out of your forehead. Imagine that you have a mouth way up high on your forehead and that you're flicking the sound off of your forehead when you say *wee*. You need to flick the sound out of the same place when you sing *wee*. Singers often try to start lower than the note and then scoop up to the note. This scooping up causes them to pull up weight and not find the height they need in the resonance. Be aware of the difference between the resonance you feel in your head and the resonance you feel in your mouth. For this exercise, you want the high resonance you feel in your head.

This exercise moves pretty high in head voice, so be sure to check your breath coordination before you sing it. Put your hands on your ribs, abs, and back to feel the movement of your body when you say the *wee*. Notice that your body expands out and you feel an exertion in your body when you make the sound. You want that same kind of exertion to happen when you sing the high notes. The exertion may happen in your sides or your back. Either place is great for singing. What you don't want to do is to shove the muscles back into their normal resting position. Just make sure you don't push out or press the notes; if you do, the tone will be tight or strained.

Men, sing this exercise down an octave from where it's written. The exercise moves high into head voice, so sing the notes that feel comfortable for now and gradually work to expand your range to sing the entire exercise. Listen to the singer demonstrate the sounds of singing high in head voice so you know what you're striving for.

TRACK 41

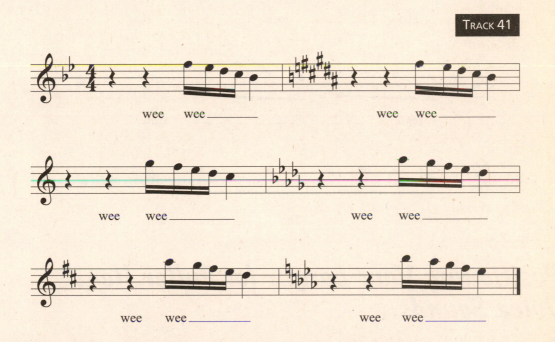

Singing through consonants in head voice

When you sing consonants really high up in your head voice, making those consonants specific enough to be understood can be difficult. To ensure your audience can understand what you're singing, keep the space at the back of your mouth and throat open. Use your articulators (your lips and tongue) to precisely shape each consonant so you aren't tempted to close the space in the back of your mouth and throat. The following exercise, featured on Track 42, gives you a chance to practice making various consonants while singing higher in your head voice. (For help shaping consonants, flip to Chapter 4.)

The singer on Track 42 demonstrates all the consonant sounds in this exercise. Listen to the singer and notice how the sound moves from the consonant right to the vowel. After you listen to the singer demonstrate the sounds, try singing along with the track. Remember to keep the space open in the back of your mouth as your lips and tongue articulate the consonants. You can bring the teeth close enough together to make the correct sound for the consonant, but you should still have some space between the teeth. Make sure to move your breath consistently throughout the exercise; doing so helps you keep the space open in the back of the mouth and throat. If the breath isn't moving, you have to close the space to squeeze to sing the note.

Men, sing this exercise down an octave.

TRACK 42

Positioning Your Larynx for Fuller Head Voice Sounds

Your *larynx,* the home of your vocal cords, is designed to move around. This mobility can be a bit of a problem when you want to sing high notes because when your larynx flies up, the resulting tone is often tight or constricted. Thus, when you're singing a high note, you want a larynx that stays in a neutral position. The next sections reveal how to position your larynx to create full sounds in head voice.

Stabilizing the larynx

The larynx is designed to sit high in the throat, but when you sing, you want to position it lower. When the larynx lowers, the tone changes to a warmer sound because the tone has more room to resonate. A really high larynx creates a tight tone because the tone has less space to resonate. Many teachers talk about maintaining a *low* larynx, but *low* can mean many things. For example, positioning the larynx really low makes the dark sound singers often use in classical music. To make the appropriate sound for your song (which likely isn't a really dark sound), you need to position your larynx low but not too low at the same time that you engage the muscles that stabilize the larynx. The following sections explain how to do so.

Getting acquainted with your larynx

Before you can consciously stabilize your larynx, you need to know how it moves and where it sits. Figuring out how it moves is easy: Just place your hand on your throat and swallow. Notice how the larynx moved up and down?

Men can easily locate their larynx because of their Adam's apple. Women have a tougher time because the female larynx doesn't protrude. If you're a female singer, swallow and notice where your larynx moves to at the end of the swallow. Don't worry if it takes you several times before you know what you're feeling.

For drawings or diagrams of the larynx, search online, using the keywords *larynx diagram Netter.* Frank Netter made some very helpful drawings of the larynx. These drawings can be particularly helpful for women who are having trouble figuring out what they're feeling in their throat.

Lowering your larynx

You subconsciously lower your larynx whenever you yawn. Place your hand on the front of your throat, pretend you're yawning, and notice how your larynx moves lower. The problem with subconsciously lowering your larynx during a yawn is that you probably lower your larynx by pushing your tongue down. Try consciously lowering your larynx during a yawn by releasing your tongue forward to move the tip of the tongue outside of your mouth as you yawn. You may notice that the larynx dropped down but you didn't feel the pressing-down sensation in the back of your tongue. Try this trick several times until you're confident you can inhale and drop your larynx at the same time without pressing down your tongue.

If making a controlled yawn doesn't help you lower your larynx, try taking a surprised breath. Pretend that you're really surprised by something and notice what happens as you breathe. For most people, the surprise causes them to inhale quickly and deeply and release the larynx down. Keep your hand on the outside of your throat to feel where your larynx moves. If you aren't sure where it moves, repeat this trick several times. You may need a little time before you're sure you're making the right movement.

Inhaling, dropping, and singing

When you're confident that you can simultaneously inhale and consciously drop your larynx, leave your larynx in its lower position and say *ah.* When you say *ah,* you want the larynx to stay in the dropped position and not rise. If you aren't sure whether you're dropping the larynx enough, inhale again and see whether you can drop the larynx any lower. You don't want the larynx to drop all the way down as far as it can go, but you do want it to drop lower than its normal high resting position. You may need to practice dropping the larynx and saying *ah* for several days to develop the coordination you need for this movement.

After you master dropping the larynx and saying *ah,* try dropping the larynx and singing *ah* on a note that's lower in your range. If the larynx drops or lowers just the right amount, the tone you sing will be fuller or rounder than it was when the larynx was higher. You'll likely need to experiment with dropping the larynx and singing notes for several days before you can determine whether you're on the right track. Get out your recording device and record the sounds you make. The first few times you try, expect to hear a hooty sound or a sound that isn't similar to how you normally sing. This sound may not be your final product, so don't give up too soon. You need some time to develop just the right coordination to make the full or round sound and to drop your larynx the right way.

After you develop the coordination, you have to decide how to use that coordination to make just the right sound. The right sound depends on the style of music you want to sing. You probably want to drop your larynx low for classical songs, drop it some for musical theater, and release and open it just enough to stabilize the larynx for contemporary sounds, such as rock, pop, and R&B. When you're familiar with the sounds you make as a result of dropping your larynx, you can decide how much dropping is appropriate for your style of singing. After practicing dropping the larynx and singing a note, you can move on to the next section to master the next part of stabilizing the larynx.

Opening your throat

Opening the space below the larynx engages the muscles that keep the larynx from rising when you sing higher notes. To figure out the space I'm talking about here, place your hand on your collarbone in the middle of your throat and feel the indentation. The space you want to open is the place in your throat just above that indentation of the collarbone.

To practice opening this space, try out these helpful techniques:

✔ Pretend you smell something really yummy and notice the sensations that happen in your throat. You may feel an opening sensation really low in your throat as if the area just above the collarbone and below the larynx were opening. That's the opening you want.

✔ Pay attention to the sensations you feel at the very beginning of a yawn. Most people feel the opening you want below the larynx really low in the throat right at the beginning of a yawn.

✔ Open the space behind your tongue. Visualize your tongue from the tip all the way down to where the tongue attaches at the top of the larynx. Place the tip of your tongue on your bottom teeth and inhale. As you inhale, open the space behind the tongue (where the tongue curves to go down your throat). Opening this space all the way down your throat helps you feel the opening really low in your throat below the larynx.

Monitoring your larynx while singing

This section gives you a chance to practice the skills necessary for keeping your larynx steady. I recommend waiting to tackle this exercise until *after* you've mastered stabilizing your larynx (I outline how to do that in the previous sections). When you're confident that you can feel the opening sensation in your throat, you're ready to apply that skill to the following exercise. The singer on Track 43 demonstrates the sounds for you. Listen to the track a few times before practicing the pattern yourself.

Begin the exercise by opening the space in your throat all the way down to your collarbone as you inhale. Leave the space open to articulate the *N* with your tongue and then sing the first note. As you approach the second note, you want to open the space more. Whatever you do, don't let the space close down. The first few times you sing this exercise with the space open this far, you'll probably make a dark and hooty sound. After you get accustomed to the open space, you can change the resonance and move it forward again so the sound isn't so dark.

Monitoring both the space and the resonance is difficult, so I suggest that you focus on allowing the space to open and not worrying about the sound right now. When you know you're opening the space right, then you can work on changing the resonance. Remember to shift the resonance by noticing sensations and not by closing down the space to push the resonance forward.

Men, sing this exercise an octave lower than where it's written.

Managing many high phrases

When you sing a high phrase, the muscles in your throat engage to sing that phrase. If you try to sing several high phrases in a row without releasing those muscles between the phrases, you can tire easily. By releasing the muscles in the throat after each high phrase you sing, you encourage them to momentarily relax and then work again. The following exercise has you singing several high phrases in a row to help you practice managing the phrases so that you ultimately sound something like the singer on Track 44. This exercise is also great for helping you practice stabilizing the larynx as you sing the phrases (see the earlier section "Stabilizing the larynx" for details).

To practice releasing the muscles in your throat, try allowing every muscle in your face, throat, and neck to release. You may not be able to feel the muscles releasing until after 30 seconds or so. When your muscles do release, you should feel a dropping or releasing sensation as if the muscles were contracted and then released or softened.

To sing this exercise successfully, release the muscles in your throat as you inhale so they have a moment of rest before you dive into the next phrase. Also be sure to open the space below the larynx to help stabilize the larynx so that it doesn't rise too much as you ascend in pitch.

When you first start working on the release between high phrases, you'll need about a measure between repetitions to coordinate the release with the inhalation. You may need to hit pause at the end of each repetition to get the release and then hit play to sing along with the next repetition. You may need to work on this exercise for several weeks before you can successfully release in one beat.

Men, sing this exercise an octave lower than where it's written.

Developing Your Head Voice Range

When choosing a song to sing to practice your head voice, you need to look at the overall range of the song as well as the tessitura to see whether it fits your voice at this point in your training. The *range* of a song refers to the highest and lowest notes in it. (The *range of your voice,* on the other hand, refers to the highest and lowest notes you can sing.) The *tessitura of a song* is where most of the notes lie. For example, a song that has one high note mixed in with lots of low notes may have a tessitura that's a perfect match for you. On the other hand, a song that has 15 high notes may have a tessitura that's too high for you even though you're capable of singing one or two of the high notes. (The *tessitura of your singing voice* is where you're most comfortable singing.)

At this point, your range in head voice may not seem very big. For example, near the High C, the notes may feel impossibly high. If they do, you may be trying to sing the highest notes in your head voice the same way you sing the lower head voice notes. But the higher you move in pitch, the higher the vibrations of resonance need to shift and the lighter your tone should feel. Around the High A, you start to transition to another sensation in head voice. To help you sing the higher notes in head voice, keep the following points in mind:

- ✔ **Stabilize the larynx so that it doesn't go flying up as you ascend in pitch.** Open the space in the back of the mouth, the throat, and all the way down below the larynx. See the earlier section for the specifics on how to stabilize the larynx.

- ✔ **Shift the resonance higher.** Allow the vibrations of resonance to move higher in your head. You may feel the sensations in the front of your face on your forehead or on the top of your head. Find out more about resonance in Chapter 12.

- ✔ **Release in between each phrase.** As you take a breath, release the muscles in the larynx for a quick moment of rest between phrases.

- ✔ **Make sure your body really helps you sing the patterns.** You want to feel the entire body engaged in making the sounds and feel your breath moving to help you sing the notes.

Creating spinning tone

Singing high notes in head voice can be easy and fun. When you get the technique just right, the tone may seem as though it comes spinning out of your mouth and into the room. Listen to the singer on Track 45 to hear what spinning tone sounds like. Notice that the notes are moving quickly and seem to be really easy. The singer makes that easy tone happen by trusting his ear to evaluate the sound, opening the space inside the throat and mouth, tracking the vibrations of resonance, and moving the breath throughout the exercise.

Keep in mind that many classical songs require that you sing fast patterns in head voice. Listen to Track 45 again to get familiar with the pattern in this exercise. After you know what the pattern is supposed to sound like, you're ready to start singing it. Men, sing this exercise down an octave. If the pattern is too high for you right now, you can sing in falsetto or sing down two octaves in the sections that are too high.

The following four techniques can help you get more comfortable with spinning your tone as you work through this exercise. Be patient with this exercise. You may need to practice it for several weeks before you can combine all four techniques to successfully sing this pattern.

- ✔ **Trust your ear to tell you when you're on or off pitch.** If you trust your ear, you don't have to try to control the muscles in your throat. You can just let them do their job. By trusting that you can hear the note and then sing it (rather than trying to control the muscles to make the note happen), you can create a tone that's tension-free and spins out of you. In other words, you want to allow the notes to happen instead of making them happen. You can record yourself singing along with the track and then listen back to hear whether you were exactly on pitch. Or you can sing the pattern slowly and gradually speed up so you know that you're singing exactly the right notes.

- ✔ **Open the space in the back of your mouth and throat.** To sing the consonant *F* in the pattern, you need to keep your jaw open (or your teeth apart) and lift your bottom lip to touch your top teeth. Then when you make the *ee* vowel, the space in your throat is already open. Opening the space in the mouth and throat helps you keep the tone tension-free and spinning.

✔ **Track the vibrations of resonance as they move higher in your head.** You should feel the sensations inside your head in the back, on the top, or in the front, or maybe all of the above. But don't picture the notes getting bigger and wider as you ascend; if you do, you'll encourage too much weight in the tone. Instead, visualize the tone getting narrower inside your head as you ascend. The high vibrations help you use just the right amount of weight for head voice. When the vibrations are high, the tone feels like it spins out of your mouth instead of being pushed out. The higher you go up the scale, the smaller the resonance may seem to your own ears. To make sure you're making a full sound in the room even though it seems small inside your head, you can record yourself as you sing and then play it back.

✔ **As you sing higher in pitch, move your breath faster.** Note that you don't want to move more breath; you just want to let the breath you use move at a faster speed. If the breath isn't moving faster as you sing the higher notes, your throat may feel tight. Because the vocal cords are opening and closing faster on the higher notes, you need your breath to be moving faster to keep the tone spinning.

TRACK 45

Sustaining notes in your head voice

To sustain high notes in head voice and make them sound fabulous, you need to keep your larynx steady, which can be tricky considering that the larynx wants to rise on the higher notes. To keep the larynx steady as you sustain the note, you need to open the space in the back of your mouth, the space inside your throat, and even the space below your larynx. Opening all these spaces engages just the right muscles to keep your larynx steady. *Note:* If you don't open these spaces just right, your tone may become thin rather than full and round; turn to Chapter 12 for help opening the space inside your mouth and throat so you can create a consistently beautiful tone.

You also need to release your jaw and maintain a steady flow of air to sustain notes in your head voice. Coordinating the opening of the jaw and the lengthening of the spine can help you easily release the jaw so you can sing higher notes. (If you have trouble with opening your jaw, check out Chapter 12.) To keep your airflow steady, open your body for the inhale (release and expand your ribs, sides, back, and abs) and then make sure the same muscles that just expanded slowly and steadily move back to their normal resting positions as you sing. The body normally collapses quickly on an exhale, but you need to keep the body open longer to sustain a note while singing. Just be careful not to sustain the note by pressing in your throat.

Practice opening the spaces in your mouth, throat, and larynx without singing and then use those same openings to sing the following exercise, featured on Track 46. The first sensation of a yawn (when the muscles stretch and the throat widens) is what you want to remember for opening the throat when singing. Allow the spaces to open more as you ascend in pitch. As you move through the exercise, focus on releasing your jaw and maintaining a steady airflow. You sing an *oh* vowel in this exercise and sustain the vowel on the high note in the pattern. Remember that the *oh* vowel requires your lips to round. You can open the space more and maintain the *oh* vowel if you open your jaw more as you ascend while keeping your lips rounded for the *oh*.

Men, sing this exercise down an octave from where it's written.

Songs for broadening your head voice range

Songs that have an extensive head voice range can be both fun and challenging. The songs in this list are quite high and require that you know your voice well. Listen to them or find the sheet music to determine whether the range seems appropriate for your voice type.

- ✔ "It's Over" by Roy Orbison and Bill Dees (male)
- ✔ "I Love All Graceful Things" by Eric H. Thiman (female)
- ✔ "Softly, As in a Morning Sunrise" from *The New Moon* by Sigmund Romberg and Oscar Hammerstein II (male)
- ✔ "O Holy Night" by Adolphe Adam (either)
- ✔ "I Have Dreamed" from *The King and I* by Richard Rodgers and Oscar Hammerstein II (either)
- ✔ "When I Am Laid in Earth" from *Dido and Aeneas* by Henry Purcell (female)
- ✔ "Must the Winter Come So Soon?" from *Vanessa* by Samuel Barber (female)
- ✔ "M'apparì tutt'amor" ("Soft and pure, fraught with love") from *Marta* by Flotow (male)
- ✔ "Evening Prayer" from *Hansel and Gretel* by Engelbert Humperdinck (female)
- ✔ "Don't Stop Believin'" by Journey as sung by Steve Perry (either)

Practice Piece: "A Bejeweled Love Song"

The range and tessitura of the following practice piece, "A Bejeweled Love Song," are pretty high. The high range challenges you to apply all your head voice skills to successfully sing through the phrases. Singing through the text requires that you keep the space in the back of your mouth open while you allow the tongue and lips to shape the consonants. If you keep the space open in the back of your mouth, your audience will easily understand what you're singing. If you close down the space, the text will be difficult to understand and the notes will feel very high. I recommend that you listen to the singer on Track 47 demonstrate the sounds for you before you dive into this practice piece. You may even want to listen to the track several times to hear the smooth connections from consonant to vowel before you sing along.

Men, sing this practice piece down an octave from what's written.

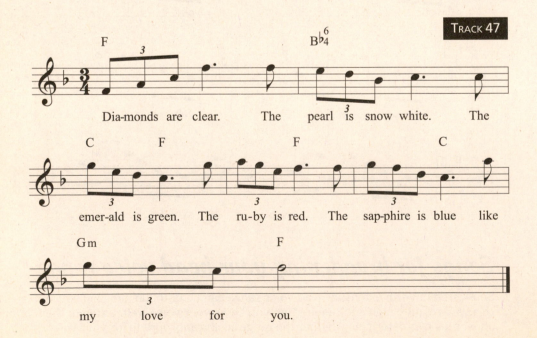

Chapter 10

Mixing Up Your Sound with Middle Voice

. . . .

In This Chapter

▶ Getting familiar with middle voice and strengthening yours with a few exercises

▶ Taking a closer look at mix

▶ Practicing your mix with some gender-specific songs

. . . .

Your *middle voice* is the area of your vocal range that falls between the two main registers (head voice and chest voice); it can sound or feel like either one. *Mix* refers to how much chest voice or head voice you use on a particular note. Middle voice is the best area of the voice to figure out how to mix because it's where your head voice and chest voice registers can overlap. In this chapter, you explore middle voice so you know what it feels like and sounds like. You also practice varying the sounds in middle voice to create a mix.

Note: You need to know what your middle voice feels like before you start overlapping registers with mix, so if you haven't had much practice with middle voice, I recommend tackling the exercises in the first half of this chapter before trying out the ones on mix.

Discovering Your Middle Voice

Middle voice acts like a bridge between head voice and chest voice. This bridge can lead you right into chest voice or right up into head voice. What you need to figure out about middle voice is how to manage resonance and weight to create a strong-sounding bridge between registers. The following sections introduce you to the differences between a man's middle voice and a woman's middle voice, help you discover your particular middle voice sound, and get you singing vowels and consonants clearly in this register.

The middle voice may be an easier concept for mezzos and baritones because they're most comfortable singing in the lower and middle part of the voice. Sopranos and tenors find middle voice a little more difficult; they tend to take chest voice higher to compensate for weakness in the middle voice. If you're a soprano or a tenor, use the exercises in the following sections to help you develop the strength you need to shift in and out of middle voice by choice.

Distinguishing male and female middle voice

Middle voice is different for men and women because of the range of middle voice. (Check out *Singing For Dummies,* 2nd Edition [Wiley], for the specifics on the range for each gender and voice type.)

✔ **For the male singer:** A man's middle voice covers just a handful of notes that transition from chest voice to head voice. These notes are in the vicinity of Middle C to about the E just above Middle C, depending on voice type. That means male chest voice is active until about Middle C and male head voice starts around the F just above Middle C. So if you think of male middle voice as an actual bridge with rungs, the guys have a short bridge with only about five rungs.

As you develop your range and strengthen your registers, you want to use less weight as you sing through middle voice on the way to head voice. If you push too much weight in the middle voice, you'll likely take too much weight or chest voice up the scale toward head voice. Lightening up or using less weight allows you to transition into head voice more easily. If you think of middle voice as the bridge from chest to head, then your bridge is wider in chest voice and narrower and thinner as you move into head voice. (Check out Chapter 8 for an exercise on varying the heaviness in your chest voice to explore the physical sensations of weight in the singing voice.)

✔ **For the female singer:** A woman's middle voice covers a very large portion of her range. For most female singers, middle voice starts around the F just above Middle C and goes to the E one octave higher. So if you picture female middle voice as an old footbridge with rungs, the gals' bridge has at least 12 rungs.

Many female singers have a very weak middle voice if they focus on developing only their head voice and chest voice and don't develop strength in their middle voice. These singers tend to shift into chest voice really high to compensate for their lack of strength in the middle voice.

For both genders, the vibrations of resonance move higher as you ascend in pitch. As a young singer, I couldn't tell the difference between middle voice and head voice until I discovered how the sensations of resonance change. Knowing that the vibrations of resonance should shift higher as I approach head voice helped me build my bridge from middle voice to head voice.

Getting to know your middle voice

In general, middle voice feels easy like head voice but resonates lower than head voice. To get acquainted with the sensations of middle voice, try out the following exercise, featured on Track 48. Here's how to approach the pattern depending on whether you're male or female:

✔ **Guys:** This exercise starts in your chest voice and gradually moves to your middle voice. As you ascend, allow the vibrations of resonance to move higher; think of lightening up the weight of the voice rather than pushing up the weight. The strength of the sound comes from specific resonance, not from pushing the weight. Sing the pattern down an octave from where it's written.

As you develop more confidence in this part of your voice, come back to this exercise and practice making a decrescendo (in other words, gradually get softer) as you ascend on the pattern. The decrescendo helps you feel the sound float and lighten up as you ascend. This lighter sensation can help you when you work on mix (see the sections on mix later in this chapter).

✔ **Gals:** This exercise starts right at the transition out of chest voice into middle voice. You may be tempted to use chest voice when you start, but try to use middle voice instead. Your middle voice feels easy like head voice but has more depth and lower vibrations of resonance. Instead of coming down to start the note, think of the note as coming straight out of your mouth.

Regardless of your gender, use the voiced consonant *M* to help you start a clear tone and then maintain that clear tone as you sing the *ee* vowel. Remember to keep the tip of your tongue touching the bottom front teeth as you sing. If the tongue pulls back in the mouth, the *ee* vowel won't be specific and the tone will be muddy. Allow the tongue to shape (or arch) for the *ee* vowel without pushing up the tongue.

TRACK 48

Strengthening your middle voice

Although many singers associate the sensation of strength in a note with chest voice, you want your middle voice to have strength, as well. You just want that strength to be without weight. After all, the strength in your middle voice is more about the sound than the sensation. Chest voice feels strong because it involves a feeling of weight and pressure. The strength you experience in middle voice feels more like a half chest voice or a stronger head voice.

The exercise on Track 49 helps you develop strength in the middle voice by having you sing a really specific vowel and focus on how the sounds and sensations change as you move down the scale. Gals, the entire pattern is in your middle voice. Guys, the first four repetitions are in your middle voice, and then you descend into your chest voice. Guys, I recommend that you sing this pattern down an octave. Whether you're a guy or a gal, when you first start this exercise, it may feel similar to head voice since you're very close to the head voice transition. As you descend, notice how the vibrations of resonance gradually move lower. Imagine that you have a ladder on your face and the vibrations are climbing down the ladder, or visualize the tone moving down and forward out of your mouth. The top rung of the ladder is around your eyebrows, and the bottom rung is at your mouth. The key is to feel the resonance moving lower without letting it go backward.

Use the voiced consonant *M* to help you start a clear tone. Allow the front of the tongue to arch for the *ay* vowel and keep the tip of the tongue against your bottom front teeth. The tongue can still be flexible as you arch for the vowel; you don't have to tense your tongue to create any vowel. Check out Chapter 3 for more specifics on shaping vowels.

TRACK 49

Finding clear vowels in middle voice

The sound in the middle part of the voice is often weak, but you can sing very specific vowels to help you develop strength in the middle part of your voice. Singing the front vowels (*ee, ih, ay,* and *eh*) often helps singers find the most clarity and strength in middle voice. Singing the back vowels (*ooh, OOH, oh,* and *ah*), on the other hand, is often harder because feeling the vibrations of resonance you should feel in middle voice isn't as easy to do when you sing these vowels.

This exercise, featured on Track 50, lets you practice rolling from a front vowel to a back vowel so you can work on keeping the vibrations of resonance in the same place when you roll from one vowel to the next. The vowel you begin with is *ee* — the easiest vowel to find clarity in the tone because the sensations of resonance are so specific. Use the *ee* as a starting point and roll from the *ee* to the other vowels listed.

Play Track 50 and sing this sequence of vowels to practice making clear sounds in your middle voice. (Guys, you sing this exercise down an octave.) Start the exercise by singing the voiced consonant *M* and then sing the *ee* vowel, which has an arch in the front of the tongue and a neutral shape of the lips. After the *ee* vowel, you change to a back vowel that requires an arch in the back of the tongue and a rounding of the lips. As you move from the neutral shape of the lips for *ee,* you need to round your lips for the shape of the back vowel. The first line moves from *ee* to *ooh*. The *ooh* vowel has the most rounded lip shape of all the back vowels. As you continue through the series of back vowels, the lips continue to round, but the shape opens more. Remember that the back vowels tend to roll backward, so use the *ee* as a spring board to propel the resonance forward. (For more on back vowels, see Chapter 3.) You can listen to the singer demonstrate the clear vowel sounds for you.

If you need words to associate with the vowels, think of the phrase *who took old awful father.* The vowels in these words are the back vowels you're practicing in this exercise.

Songs that work out the middle voice

Understanding the text in songs is a pretty important part of singing (and listening), so songs are often written in a rhythm and note range that are similar to how the text might be spoken. The following list of songs offers you a wide variety of choices to continue to develop your middle voice. Listen to these songs and choose one that you want to use to practice applying the techniques I cover earlier in this chapter.

- ✔ "Precious and Few" by Walter D. Nims as sung by the Lettermen (male)
- ✔ "Blue Moon" from *Sing for Your Supper* by Richard Rodgers and Lorenz Hart (female)
- ✔ "Sometimes I Feel like a Motherless Child," African American spiritual (either)
- ✔ "Spring Is Here" from *I Married An Angel* by Richard Rodgers and Lorenz Hart (female)
- ✔ "The Water Is Wide," folk song (either)
- ✔ "When Did I Fall in Love" from *Fiorello* by Jerry Bock and Sheldon Harnick (either)
- ✔ "Simple Gifts," folk song arranged by Aaron Copland (either)
- ✔ "I'm Old Fashioned" by Jerome Kern (female)
- ✔ "Passing By" by Edward Purcell (male)
- ✔ "I Could Write a Book" from *Pal Joey* by Richard Rodgers and Lorenz Hart (female)

Combining Registers with Mix

For both genders, *mix* is a combination of registers — both head voice and chest voice. If you think of mix as a recipe, imagine using different sized measuring cups for the two registers. Sometimes your mix may be made up of ½ cup of chest voice and ½ cup of head voice; other times it may be ⅔ cup of one and ⅓ cup of the other. After practicing mix exercises, you can feel the difference between the weight you use for each register and estimate the type of mix you're creating. You can't measure exactly how much of each register you're using in your mix at any given time; the only way to tell is by the feeling of what you're singing. The following sections help you figure out when you may want to use a mix, how to roll into one, and then how to change your mix from being dominated by one register to being dominated by another.

Gentlemen, the area of your voice where you most often mix is higher up in your range than it is for the female singer. Specifically, your mix goes from about Middle C and higher. You can mix as high or as low as you want after you know how to vary the amount of weight in the tone. To mix, your goal is to find the happy medium of combining either chest voice and head voice or head voice and falsetto, depending on where you are in your range when you mix. If you put the registers on a scale from left to right, falsetto would be on the left as the lightest of sounds and weight. Head voice would be next in the line with a little more fullness to the resonance and more weight than falsetto (but less than chest voice). Chest voice would be on the far right of the scale with the fuller, heavier sensation. The challenge for the male singer is to find a mix that isn't purely falsetto or chest voice but somewhere in between.

Ladies, the sequence of exercises you need to do to prepare for mix includes the following:

✔ Working on chest voice to discover the layers of thickness and lower vibrations of resonance

✔ Working on head voice to find the higher vibrations of resonance and soaring sensations

✔ Working on middle voice to establish the bridge between head voice and chest voice

If you've worked on each of these areas of the voice separately, blending the registers into a mix will make more sense. (See Chapter 8 for details on chest voice and Chapter 9 for details on head voice; see the first half of this chapter for details on middle voice.)

Knowing when to use a mix

Most singers mix every note they sing. After all, you probably don't spend much time singing with pure head voice. The fullness in your tone comes from adding just a tiny bit of chest voice to the sound.

How you vary the mix (head voice dominated versus chest voice dominated) for any given song depends on the type of music you're singing and the story you're trying to tell. For example, male classical singers work on mix to develop fullness in their tone. Mixing isn't as common for female classical singers, but it is common in other styles of singing, such as musical theater and pop.

Because singing is about storytelling through music and lyrics, you want the sound of your voice to tell a story and use a variety of sounds within the journey of the story. For example, songs that are lighthearted and youthful may work best with a head voice–dominated mix, while songs that are about the hard lessons in life need more of a chest voice–dominated mix. Knowing how to mix allows you to tell the beginning of the story with the appropriate sound and then change the sound when the story gets more exciting.

Rolling into a mix

Your song may require you to change the tone and volume on one note. Working on this exercise, featured on Track 51, helps you practice changing the percentage of weight on a sustained tone so you can make choices of sounds that are appropriate for the story of your song when you sing it. Here's how to approach this exercise depending on whether you're male or female:

✔ **Guys:** Your goal in this exercise is to move from falsetto to a head voice–dominated mix by rolling on one note; be sure to sing this exercise as written and not an octave down. (If you need help with your falsetto, turn to Chapter 9 before tackling this exercise. For practice rolling on one note from falsetto to chest voice, turn to Chapter 11.) Listen to the male singer demonstrate the sounds for you on Track 51. Notice how he smoothly changes the vowels and changes the tone. Singing from the vowel *ooh* to the vowel *oh* helps you move from falsetto on the *ooh* to a more head voice–dominated sound on the *oh*. Gradually open the space more in the throat as you change between the vowels. You want to slowly slide between the two sounds so you can feel a gradual change of weight in the tone. As you sing the *oh* vowel, it should no longer feel like falsetto, but it shouldn't feel like it changes all the way to chest voice, either. Instead, it should feel like you're somewhere in between two sounds — between falsetto and head voice.

The first few times you try to sing along you may accidentally flip out of falsetto and into chest voice. See the humor in it and try again. Remember that your muscles are trying to figure out how to make very specific adjustments; they need to repeat the skill on a regular basis before they can make the transition smoothly.

This exercise may be one you want to practice with no one else around so you can crack or wiggle between notes without an audience. The exercise looks pretty easy on paper, but rolling between the two sounds can be quite a challenge.

✔ **Gals:** This exercise is a great chance for you to roll from middle voice into a light chest voice–dominated mix on one note. Start the sound in middle voice (which means lighter than chest voice with higher vibrations of resonance) and then roll from middle to chest voice. To help you do so, roll from an *ooh* (as in the word *to*) to an *oh* (as in the word *go*). You may flip from middle voice to chest voice the first few times you try, but don't worry. When you get the roll right, you'll feel like you're starting out in a head voice–dominated sound and gradually adding weight in the voice. You aren't rolling into 100 percent chest voice; instead, you're gradually adding thickness as if you were heading toward a heavier sensation in your mix. The change of vowels in this exercise helps you smoothly transition from middle voice into a chest voice–dominated mix.

If you feel a bump or your sound cracks, visualize the throat opening as you move between the vowels. The vocal cords want to get thicker and quickly jump into chest voice, but if you let them do so, you'll undoubtedly hear that bump or crack. If you visualize the throat opening, you can gradually add thickness instead of suddenly changing to a thicker sensation.

Changing around the mix

To make a variety of sounds in your song, you need to know how to create a head voice–dominated mix or a chest voice–dominated mix. This exercise, featured on Track 52, has you alternating between the two sounds to help you figure out exactly what to change to make the quick adjustment between the sounds. Here's how to practice this exercise depending on your gender:

- **Guys:** When you sing along with this exercise, the first mix you want is one that's a hybrid of falsetto and head voice. You want to alternate that sound with a mix that's more chest voice dominated. (If your falsetto needs some strengthening, try singing this exercise in falsetto only for a while.) Sing this exactly where it's written and not an octave down. Doing so gives you the chance to further develop your mix even though the singer on Track 52 is female.

- **Gals:** To help you further define your mix, this exercise allows you to sing the phrase the first time in a head voice–dominated mix and then sing it again in a chest voice–dominated mix. To sing it in a head voice–dominated mix, sing as if you were singing in middle voice or head voice. The notes aren't actually in head voice range, but the vibrations of resonance can be high and the tone has very little chest voice mixed in. To sing it in a chest voice–dominated mix, you can let the resonance drop lower and sing in a light chest voice. The tone should be fuller and thicker because you're adding some weight from chest voice.

You can hear the singer demonstrate the exercise for you on Track 52. Listen carefully to hear the difference between the head voice–dominated mix and the chest voice–dominated mix. For the head voice–dominated sounds, you'll likely feel as though you're coming down to sing the note, and for the chest voice–dominated sounds, you'll likely feel as though you're coming up to sing the note.

TRACK 52

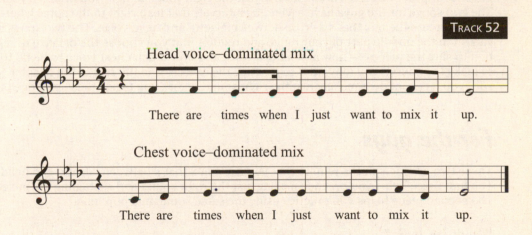

Songs that require a mix

The songs in the following list require that you use a mix, but they vary from head voice–dominated mix to chest voice–dominated mix. You can use the range and *tessitura* (where most of the notes lie on the staff), as well as the lyrics, to help you figure out which type of mix you need to use for each song. Songs that are more lighthearted tend to use a head voice–dominated mix, and songs that are darker or more troubled use a chest voice–dominated mix. You can listen to other singers sing these songs, or you can get the sheet music and decide for yourself what kind of mix you want to use.

- "I Don't Know How to Love Him" from *Jesus Christ Superstar* by Andrew Lloyd Webber (female)

- "Bridge over Troubled Water" by Paul Simon (either)

- "I Don't Know His Name" from *She Loves Me* by Jerry Bock and Sheldon Harnick (female)

- ✔ "Danny Boy" by Frederic Weatherly (either)
- ✔ "Smoke Gets in Your Eyes" from *Roberta* by Jerome Kern (female)
- ✔ "My Own Space" from *The Act* by John Kander and Fred Ebb (female)
- ✔ "Bring Him Home" from *Les Misérables* by Claude-Michel Schönberg and Alain Boublil (male)
- ✔ "Anthem" from *Chess* by Benny Andersson, Björn Ulvaeus, and Tim Rice (male)
- ✔ "Wishing You Were Here" by Peter Cetera as sung by Chicago (male)
- ✔ "She's Always a Woman to Me" by Billy Joel (male)
- ✔ "Sad Eyes" by Robert John Pedrick as sung by Robert John (male)

Exploring Your Mix with a Few Practice Pieces

These four practice pieces are written in just the right range to help you practice your mix. The two songs for the guys have ascending intervals that leap right to the notes where you have to create the mix that's a cross between falsetto and head voice. The two songs for the gals sit in the middle part of your range and require that you choose the balance of registration to sing the pieces — how much head voice and how much chest voice to blend together to make the sound. You may want to practice the exercises in the rest of the chapter to make sure you feel confident making just the right sound before you tackle these practice pieces.

For the guys

These two practice pieces require that you use a mix that's between falsetto and head voice. The first piece helps you practice making just the right sound and sustaining the mixed note. The second piece helps you practice using the same sound in a pop tune.

"Don't Let It Go"

The song "Don't Let It Go," featured on Track 53, is perfect for male singers who want to practice their mix because it sits right on top of their transition into their mix. Sing it as written, not an octave down. Remember that the mix for this piece feels like it's in between falsetto and head voice; it has a spin and the note feels like it's floating. The first few times you sing the following pattern, focus on the amount of weight you put in the tone and the resonance. The weight should be right in between falsetto and head voice. The resonance needs to be moving forward instead of going back into your mouth. **Note:** This practice piece requires that you have a pretty good grasp on transitioning into falsetto and knowing the difference between falsetto and head voice; refer to Chapter 9 for help with head voice and falsetto exercises and Chapter 11 for help making a transition from chest voice to falsetto and back.

Ladies, you're welcome to sing along with this song if you'd like. The tune works your transitions from chest voice into middle voice. Just make sure you use very specific vowels to help you find a clear sound in your middle voice.

TRACK 53

"I'm Dyin'"

"I'm Dyin'," featured on Track 54, is a fast-tempo ditty just for you, guys. Sing it as written, not an octave down. The first note is in chest voice, and the second note leaps up into your mix. Because this mix is right between falsetto and head voice, you may have a hard time landing right on the sound your first few times. To help you figure out where you need to be, listen to the singer on Track 54 demonstrate the sounds for you. You may want to listen to the song several times and work on only portions at a time. The leap up requires you to keep your larynx steady (see Chapter 9). You may be tempted to let your larynx fly up with the ascending pitch, but try not to. Instead, keep the space open in your throat so the larynx stays steady. When you release for the breath, remember to also release your larynx.

If your mix isn't solid enough right now, continue to work on your falsetto sounds (see Chapter 9 for ways to help you do so). By working out your falsetto, you discover how to move from falsetto through a mix into head voice.

Ladies, if you want to sing along with this tune, sing it as written to work on your transitions in and out of chest voice, as well as your mix.

For the gals

The first practice piece for you gals has you repeating a phrase that's chatty and sits in the middle part of your voice. In this part of your voice, you have to balance the amount of chest voice and head voice you use. The second piece starts chatty but moves higher in your range. As you move higher in your range, focus on maintaining the mix instead of turning over into a sound that's totally head voice.

"How Will I Know"

The little tune "How Will I Know," featured on Track 55, gives female singers a chance to work out their mix. The chatty text can help you find an easy flow to your breath so you can just let the sound flow out. Remember that mix can be either head voice or chest voice dominated. For this practice piece, I suggest that you work on a head voice–dominated sound first because that seems to be the trickier sound for a lot of females to master. After your head voice–dominated mix is reliable, you can sing the pattern again, allowing it to be chest voice–dominated, or you can alternate between the two. As the pattern ascends, remember to allow the vibrations of resonance to stay steady or come straight out. If the vibrations of resonance ascend, you'll sound like you're transitioning into head voice.

Guys, when you sing along with this tune an octave down, you're in your chest voice. You start approaching your middle voice range in the last repetition of the pattern. If you've been working on your falsetto and need a challenge, you can sing this pattern in the same octave as the women and sing in your falsetto.

TRACK 55

G   Em7

How will I know   if   (s)he loves me so.

A♭   Fm7

How will I know   if   (s)he loves me so.

A   F#m7

How will I know   if   (s)he loves me so.

B♭   Gm7

How will I know   if   (s)he loves me so.

B   G#m7

How will I know   if   (s)he loves me so.

"My Baby"

"My Baby," featured on Track 56, is a chatty little tune for the female mix. The notes lie right in your middle voice range and give you the chance to show off your mix. The right mix recipe for this pattern is 50 percent head voice and 50 percent chest voice. As you ascend, you may be tempted to belt the tune, but do your best to maintain your mix instead. Continue to mix the registers as you work through this practice piece, but don't roll the resonance forward (as you do when belting). You can listen to the examples of belting from Chapter 14 to hear the difference between the sounds of mixing and belting.

Guys, if you want to sing along with this tune, you can sing in your chest voice by singing it an octave down, or you can sing it as written to work on your falsetto.

Chapter 11

Coordinating Register Transitions

• •

• •

*B*eing able to hear the register transitions a singer makes is pretty common in popular music. But in other styles of music, such as musical theater and classical music, singers want to make smooth transitions so that they move up and down the scale in a seamless line of sound. The good news is that you can work on making smooth transitions between registers and still make the choice to *flip* (allow a sudden change between registers, creating an obvious change in tone) between registers if the style of music you're singing calls for more obvious register flips.

Note: Before you work on register transitions, you really need to have a good sense of the physical sensations associated with each register. Refer to Chapters 8, 9, and 10, respectively, if you need help with chest voice, head voice, or middle voice.

Moving Smoothly between Registers

To make a *smooth transition* — or create a consistent sound so the listener doesn't hear a change between registers — you have to know the sensations for each register. The two sensations that change between registers are resonance and weight. The vibrations of resonance rise as you ascend in pitch and drop lower as you descend. You can feel the sensations from vibrations of resonance in the chest, throat, mouth, and head. As you descend, you want the resonance to lower but not fall. If you feel a sudden shift in your muscles and the resonance suddenly shifts down, you'll hear a big transition between the notes. In contrast, if you allow the resonance and weight to change gradually, you'll be able to make a smooth transition.

Weight in the singing voice is the heavy sensation you have when you sing in chest voice. Taking that same heavy sensation beyond the chest voice range means you're adding too much weight to the tone or using too much weight as you sing up the scale. You don't want the same heavy sensation you feel in chest voice to creep up to your head voice. To transition smoothly, you want to use a chest voice sound that's lighter than your heaviest sound, a strong middle voice sound without any added weight or pressure, and a head voice sound that's lighter than middle voice and resonates higher. If the notes in one part of your voice are weak and you carry one register way beyond the transition point, you'll feel and hear a big transition between the registers. To develop smooth transitions from one register to another, take some time to work on the exercises I present in the following sections.

The key technical ingredients to making smooth register transitions are

- **Opening the space in the throat and back of the mouth, especially as you ascend in pitch:** See Chapter 12 for details.

- **Allowing the resonance to shift higher as you ascend in pitch:** Turn to Chapter 12 for the lowdown on shifting your resonance higher.

- **Gradually changing the amount of weight in the tone:** I cover changing the weight in your chest voice in Chapter 8.

- **Maintaining a consistent breath flow throughout the pattern:** I help you work on breathing in Chapter 2.

Dropping into chest voice

The goal of this section is to help you discover the physical sensations and sounds of flipping into chest voice so you can compare the physical sensations of each register. When you explore the following exercise, featured on Track 57, allow the sound to flip into chest voice. Use the *ooh* vowel (as in the word *shoe*) to help you find a lighter sound on the top of the pattern and the *ah* vowel (as in the word *father*) to help you transition into chest voice. The flipping sensation you feel when you go from one vowel to the other is just the sound your muscles make when they suddenly change registers (because the *ooh* vowel encourages head voice sounds and the *ah* vowel encourages chest voice sounds).

Notice how the resonance also changes suddenly when you allow the sound to flip? Listen to the singer on Track 57 demonstrate the sound of flipping between the two notes and making a sudden change in the sound.

Note: Men, sing the entire pattern as written, not down an octave, and focus on flipping from your falsetto to your chest voice. Ladies, start each repetition of the pattern in middle voice and then flip into chest voice. On the fifth repetition, you may be tempted to sing both notes in chest voice because you're in your chest voice range. Instead, start the first note in middle voice and then flip to chest voice.

TRACK 57

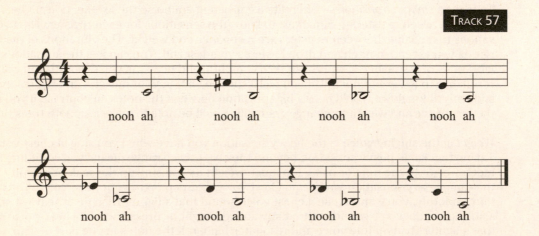

Changing back and forth from chest voice to middle voice

The following exercise, which you can hear on Track 58, offers you the chance to make smooth transitions from chest voice to middle voice and back down to chest voice. The vowels *ooh* and *ah* help you make the transition smoothly. Allow the first note on *ah* to be in chest voice and the second note to be in middle voice. To smoothly transition from the first note in chest voice to the second note in middle voice, allow the space in your throat and the back of your mouth to open as you ascend and slide between the notes. Instead of visualizing the third note as falling down, allow the space to stay open as you descend. Can you feel that the note in chest voice is heavier than the note in middle voice? You want that change in weight or thickness to happen in order to move smoothly between the registers.

If you're having trouble smoothly transitioning from chest voice to middle voice and back again, lighten up on the chest voice note. Singing the note with a very heavy chest voice makes the transition much harder because you create such a difference in the chest voice note and the middle voice note.

Note: Men, the first few repetitions may be a little high for you to comfortably move from chest voice to middle voice. If your voice is lower (bass or baritone), practice the first three repetitions by moving smoothly from chest voice to falsetto. For the rest of the repetitions, move from chest voice to middle voice. Sing the whole pattern as written, not down an octave. Ladies, start each pattern in chest voice and smoothly transition into middle voice. As the repetitions go lower, continue to sing the first note in middle voice and transition into chest voice.

To help you smoothly transition, keep these three guidelines in mind:

- ✔ Gradually open the space more in your throat as you ascend.

- ✔ Allow the breath to move consistently throughout the entire exercise.

- ✔ Gradually allow the vibrations of resonance to shift higher as you ascend and lower (move from your mouth down into your chest) as you sing from the higher note to the lower note.

As you transition in this exercise, visualize the notes in front of each other rather than on top of each other. For example, imagine that the first note is right at your mouth and the next note is a few inches in front of your mouth. In doing so, you feel that the notes are close to each other and easily connected instead of far apart with a large gap between the two notes.

Climbing from middle voice to head voice

The goal when singing this exercise is to create a smooth transition from middle voice into head voice, just as the singer does on Track 59. To ascend into head voice, you need to allow the vibrations of resonance to shift higher and the amount of weight in the tone to lighten up as you sing higher. To help you shift the resonance higher, you can track the resonance as you sing. The shift in vibrations usually feels as though it moves from the front of your mouth to the back of your mouth and up the back of your head. If you feel this shift, then intentionally follow the movement as you ascend on the pattern to make sure the resonance remains consistent each time you sing it. Feeling the vibrations go down your throat or swallowing them isn't the same as allowing the resonance to go up the back of your head, so remember how the vibrations change on the way up so you can reverse that on the way down.

If you find the leap from middle voice to head voice to be difficult, you can leave off the first note in the pattern and start on the second note. Then when you're confident that you know the path of the vibrations of resonance as you descend, you can sing the first note and allow the resonance to shift to where it was when you started on the second note of the pattern. As you descend, keep the lighter sound that you found on the top note in head voice. Notice that starting on the top note helps you feel the height in the resonance. Continue to work through this exercise, focusing on bringing head voice down.

To start this exercise, open the space in the back of your mouth and throat and then lift the tip of your tongue to the ridge on the roof of your mouth to make the sound of the *N* consonant. You don't have to close your teeth; just lift the tip of your tongue so you can keep the space in the back of your mouth open. Your lips round for the *oh* vowel. As you ascend in the pattern, your jaw should drop. When your jaw drops, you can keep the lips rounded for the *oh*. You can try out the text on the second line if you want to explore the sensations of singing the pattern on a front vowel. (*Ay* uses an arch in the front of the tongue so it's called a *front vowel*, and *oh* requires an arch in the back of the tongue so it's called a *back vowel*; see Chapter 3 for details.)

Note: This pattern is designed to help all voice types. Don't worry if the first few repetitions don't move into your head voice because the later repetitions will. Just sing the pattern and move into head voice when it's right for you, but keep in mind that it's better to shift into head voice sooner rather than later in this exercise. Men, you sing this exercise down an octave.

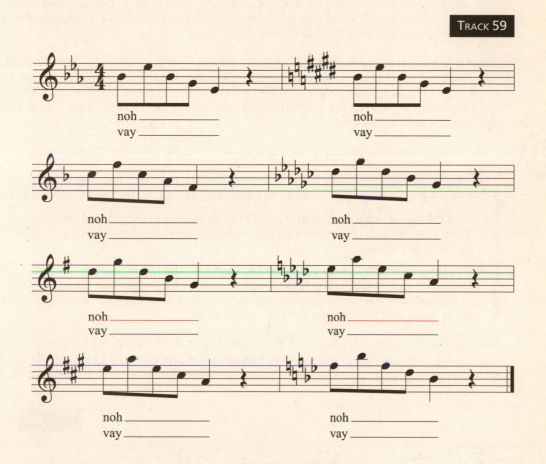

TRACK 59

Leaping to and from Falsetto

Singing exercises that move from falsetto to chest voice helps you develop smooth transitions from the lightest sound in the male voice to the heaviest. In the beginning when you work on the exercises in the following sections, the sounds may flip between falsetto and chest voice. You'll likely notice a cracking sound, but don't worry! That sound doesn't mean something is breaking. It's just the sound from your muscles suddenly changing registers and the resonance suddenly shifting. After you've worked on the exercises a few times and are confident that you know the difference between the weight of the notes and the change in resonance, you can work on the exercises and practice transitioning smoothly from falsetto to chest voice. (If you need a falsetto refresher, check out the falsetto exercises in Chapter 9.)

Singing from falsetto into chest voice

Singing from falsetto to chest voice is a challenge because you have to change from the lightest sound the male voice makes to the heaviest. But you definitely want to practice moving smoothly between these two registers so you can strengthen the muscles you use to move back and forth between registers. When you smoothly transition between falsetto and chest voice, you let the muscles that control falsetto start out in charge and then gradually turn over the reigns to the muscles that control chest voice.

Listen a few times to the male singer on Track 60 demonstrate how to move from falsetto into chest voice, using the following exercise. Then give it a shot yourself. To smoothly transition from falsetto to chest voice, be sure to gradually open the space in the back of your mouth and throat, to keep the breath moving consistently, and to smoothly change the resonance and weight in the tone.

If you have trouble moving smoothly from falsetto to chest voice, try these tips:

- When you drop into chest voice, don't drop to 100 percent chest voice. Drop into a lighter chest voice so that the transition isn't so drastic between registers.

- Sing the notes separately at first to feel the difference in weight and resonance. Then sing the exercise as written, concentrating on making smooth transitions between the notes.

- Use the vowel *ooh* to help you find the falsetto on the top of the pattern and think of the *oh* vowel as the transition into head voice before you move into chest voice on the *ah* vowel. You may not feel the transition into head voice, but head voice is in between falsetto and chest voice.

Note: Ladies, you can sing along with this exercise and practice moving from middle voice to chest voice. Even though you don't have a falsetto, the preceding suggestions can still help you remember what you need to do when you move from middle voice to chest voice.

TRACK 60

Changing from chest voice to falsetto

The challenging part about singing in chest voice and then transitioning to falsetto is that you have to release the weight of chest voice as you ascend into falsetto. You can hear a smooth chest-to-falsetto transition performed by the male singer on Track 61. Listen to this example several times before diving into the following exercise.

When you're ready, focus on smoothly transitioning from the chest voice first note (the *ah*) to the falsetto second note (the *ee*). Allow the space in your throat and the back of your mouth to open as you ascend and allow the resonance to shift higher. Note that you can open the space and still successfully sing an *ee* vowel on the second note.

After you ascend to the *ee* vowel, take a breath, sing the note again, and then descend. Taking the breath allows you to restart the top note in falsetto before you descend. (See the comma above the melody line? That's a breath mark; see Chapter 7 for details.) Instead of picturing the last note falling down, allow the space in the throat and mouth to stay open as you descend and picture the note being right in front of you. If the *ee* vowel wiggles too much and is unsteady, sing an *ooh* vowel until you gain more confidence in your falsetto.

Note: Ladies, you can sing along with this exercise and practice moving from chest voice to middle voice. If you struggle with the transition between these two registers, use the suggestions I offer to men going from chest voice to help you move from chest voice to middle voice.

TRACK 61

mah ee mee ah mah ee mee ah mah ee mee ah

mah ee mee ah mah ee mee ah mah ee mee ah

Rolling back and forth from chest voice to falsetto

This exercise offers you a chance to really distinguish between registers by singing the same note in different registers. The reason you want to practice singing one note in different registers is that you may need to change registers when you crescendo on a single note in a song. For example, songs often have you crescendo from a falsetto to a mix or from a mix to chest voice. Listen to the singer on Track 62 demonstrate moving back and forth from chest voice to falsetto.

To smoothly transition from chest voice to falsetto, you need to lighten up the weight in the tone. Think of the tone as floating up to help lighten the weight. (If you're struggling with this exercise, you can explore the sensations of rolling from a falsetto to a mix in Chapter 10; after doing so, you'll notice that this exercise takes that exercise one step further by rolling all the way from chest voice to falsetto and back again.)

You may find that you need more time than the singer on the track allows to roll between the sounds when you first start working on this exercise. Start by listening to the singer demonstrate the sounds for you. Then turn off the track and take your time rolling from chest voice to falsetto. Work on only the first half of each measure — moving from chest voice (the *vah*) to falsetto (the *ooh*) on one note — until you feel confident doing so. When you know the sensations and can smoothly move from chest voice to falsetto, then work on moving from falsetto (the *ooh*) back to chest voice (the *ah*). Don't be discouraged if you aren't able to make this transition in a matter of hours (or days); successfully achieving this transition may take several weeks of practicing. Take your time and really explore the sounds and sensations to develop your muscular coordination.

Note: Ladies, you can use this exercise to practice rolling from chest voice to middle voice and back again. If you have trouble, use the same suggestions that I offer the guys who are moving from chest voice to falsetto and back again.

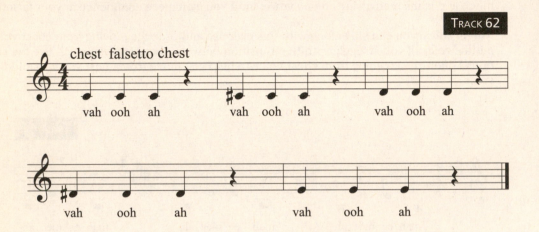

Refining Your Smooth Transitions

The exercises in this section require that you make smooth transitions more than one time in each pattern. To go back and forth between registers, you need to know exactly what to change to transition between registers, and then you need to make those changes several times in a row.

Note: If you're just getting the hang of making smooth transitions, then working on patterns that have only one transition is more ideal for you. You may find that you get the transition perfectly one time but don't quite get it right the next time. Don't worry; you need time to develop the physical coordination to make smooth transitions. After you're confident that you know how to make the transitions successfully, then you can move on to exercises that require you to transition several times in a row.

Shifting from middle voice to chest voice

In this exercise, you practice smoothly transitioning from middle voice into chest voice and back. For the first vowel (the *ooh*), the lips round and the back of the tongue arches. For the second vowel (the *ah*), the lips are relaxed and the back of the tongue has very little arch. (The arch in the tongue for the *ooh* vowel is higher than it is for the *ah* vowel.)

Listen to the singer on Track 63 demonstrate the sounds for you. Practice speaking the two vowels next to each other so you can feel how the shape changes between them. When you're confident that you can change the shape precisely when you speak the vowels, you'll be more likely to shape the vowels precisely when you sing them. If you feel good about moving between registers from *ooh* to *ah,* try the second line of text, which moves from *ee* to *ah,* for a new challenge.

As you sing the first note of the exercise, notice the sensations you feel; you want to feel those same sensations when you return to the same note later in the exercise. Allow the muscles to gradually thicken as you approach chest voice instead of changing suddenly. Also remember to transition into a lighter chest voice rather than your heaviest so that you can get back out of it.

Note: Gentlemen, depending on your voice type, you may transition from head voice through middle voice into chest voice for some of the first few repetitions of this exercise. That's okay. Just be sure to sing the pattern as written, not an octave down. If the first three repetitions are too high for you, start in falsetto and transition down into chest voice.

TRACK 63

Shifting from middle voice to head voice

This exercise, featured on Track 64, allows you to practice shifting from middle voice to head voice and back. The main difference between middle voice and head voice is that head voice has higher resonance and feels a little lighter than middle voice. As you ascend in pitch, allow the resonance to shift higher, and then return to where you started. Allow the space in the back of your mouth and throat to open more as you ascend and let the jaw drop. As the jaw drops, make sure it drops from the back rather than from your chin.

Keep your hands on your sides, back, and abs to monitor your breath flow. The airflow speeds up as you go higher in pitch. The muscles that you move when you open your body for the inhale move back to their resting position as you sing through the exercise. As the pitch rises in the pattern, you feel the muscles moving at a faster rate than when you sang the first note, which is the lowest note in the exercise. You can sing the pattern on a *lip trill* (when air flows between the lips, causing them to vibrate while your voice sings a pitch) to feel the movement of the air. Then sing the pattern again on the *oh* vowel and compare the flow of air as you sing the *oh* with the flow of air you used during the lip trill. Listen to the singer on Track 64 demonstrate the sounds for you.

Note: Gentlemen, depending on your voice type, you may move from chest voice through middle voice to head voice on some of the repetitions of this exercise. Sing the pattern down an octave from where it's written.

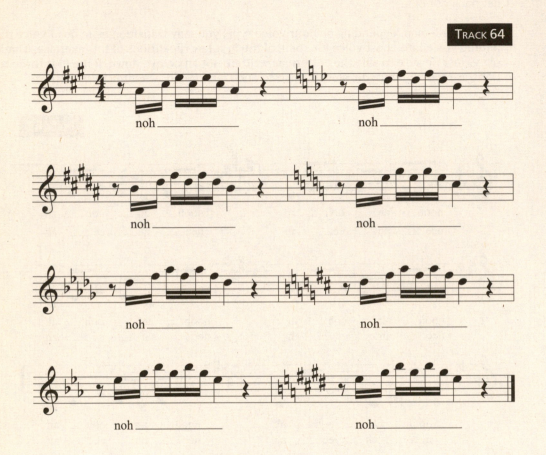

TRACK 64

Practice Piece: "Marching Forth"

The following practice piece, "Marching Forth," which you can hear performed on Track 65, moves between registers so you can practice making smooth register transitions. The tempo is slow enough that you can take your time as you make the transitions. The range of the piece is wide to challenge you to move from a low chest voice all the way up into head voice. As you sing the higher notes, remember to allow the vibrations of resonance to move higher in your head as if the sound were coming out of a hole in your forehead. Keeping the space in the back of your mouth and throat open helps you easily articulate the text while singing in head voice. Right after you sing in head voice, you return down to chest voice. As you descend in pitch, you want to shift the resonance lower and feel the vibrations in your chest.

TRACK 65

Dm G7

Rain-y days and sleep-y af-ter-noons. Days pass

G6 Am Dm

in a peace-ful haze. Time mar-ches forth with-out pause.

G4⁶ Am

I march forth with hope dar-ing to dream.

F Am

What I dream I will be - come.

G4⁶ Am C4⁶

Rain-y days and sleep-y dreams march-ing forth.

Songs That Require Register Transitions

The songs in this list require you to move between registers. The goal in each of these songs is to smoothly transition between the registers. Letting the registers flip is easy to do (and acceptable when you're working with pop songs), but smoothly transitioning (which is what you need to do in the following songs) takes more practice.

Always look at the range of a song to make sure it's right for you. Songs are published in numerous keys; make sure you choose the key that challenges you but isn't too much for you at your current stage of technical development.

- ✔ "Who Can I Turn To?" from *The Roar of the Greasepaint — The Smell of the Crowd* by Leslie Bricusse and Anthony Newley (either)

- ✔ "You Are Loved (Don't Give Up)" by Tawgs Salter as sung by Josh Groban (either)

- ✔ "Mein gläubiges Herze, frohlocke" ("My Heart Ever Faithful, Sing Praises") by Johann Sebastian Bach (either)

- "Gesù Bambino" by Pietro Yon and Frederick H. Martens (either)

- "Places That Belong to You" by James Newton Howard and Alan and Marilyn Bergman (either)

- "When I Fall in Love" by Victor Young and Edward Heyman (either)

- "Oh, quand je dors" ("Oh, While I Sleep") by Franz Liszt (either)

- "He Shall Feed His Flock" from *The Messiah* by George Frideric Handel (female)

- "If with All Your Hearts" from *Elijah* by Felix Mendelssohn (male)

- "He Looked beyond My Fault" by Dottie Rambo as sung by David Phelps (either)

Part IV

Advancing Your Singing Technique

The 5th Wave   By Rich Tennant

"She really knows how to belt out a song."

In this part . . .

This part helps you advance your singing technique to make a variety of sounds. For instance, your tone varies based on how much space you open and how you use resonance. Here, you find out how to vary the resonance to make exactly the kind of tone you need for the style of music you like to sing.

Speaking of music styles, whether you're singing classical music or R&B tunes, you need to be able to sing fast-moving pitches quickly and accurately. In other words, your voice needs to be agile. Lucky for you, this part also helps you develop your agility through a variety of exercises.

The last chapter in this part covers the topic that most singers ask about — belting. Knowing how to belt that high note is what every singer from pop to musical theater wants to know. Here, you explore basic to advanced exercises for belting. You can even apply your newfound belting technique to a practice piece.

Chapter 12

Developing Your Vocal Tone

. . . .

. . . .

Everyone, including all you singers out there, has a unique tone of voice. For instance, you recognize a friend's voice over the phone because you recognize the tone of her voice. So what makes your tone of voice different from someone else's? Tone of voice (in both speaking and singing) involves three key elements: resonance, pitch, and the inflections you add to vary your pitch. In singing, the inflections and pitch are written within the song, but how the sound resonates is up to the singer. In this chapter, I explore different ways to create beautiful tone and then explain how to vary your tone so you can sing different styles of music.

Touching on Tone Basics

In singing, tone varies from you to the next singer in part because of the difference in the shape of your body, especially your head, but also because of what you do physically to create and maintain tone throughout a song. The following sections explore the physical variables that affect tone in order to give you a solid foundation for creating beautiful tone.

Practicing the onset of tone

When you create the onset of tone (in other words, when you start the tone) in a phrase, you may not think about how you make the sound; you may just make it. That approach can work great . . . until you have to start a tone very softly on a high note or sing a staccato (short and detached) note. If you want to start with good tone on every phrase you sing, you need to have an understanding of how your vocal cords operate, and you need to practice coordinating how they open and close.

You can close the vocal cords in two ways: by using muscles and by using breath. Ideally, you use both when you sing.

    ✔ **Using your muscles:** The vocal cords are in your larynx, which is in your throat. For a visual of what your vocal cords look like, hold up your index and middle finger. Point both fingers toward you with your palm facing the floor. Your vocal cords are joined in the front of your neck and open at the back of your neck, and they can open and close just like your fingers can close to touch each other and then separate to form a *V* shape. You can't feel all the muscles that help the vocal cords open and close, but they activate when your brain sends a message to make a particular sound. Opening and closing the cords is what you do in the steps just ahead.

✓ **Using your breath:** Your vocal cords can also close when air blows between them. The air creates suction, which helps close them so they can vibrate as the air passes between the cords. This suction is what happens when you make a lip trill; the air passes between your lips, causing a suction that makes them come together and vibrate.

Exploring the right sensation for closing the cords helps you start the tone with just the right amount of muscular coordination so the breath you move enhances the tone. Moving air without understanding the muscular coordination may lead to a breathy tone.

Use the following sequence to practice the physical coordination for starting a tone for singing. Notice that Steps 3 and 4 describe two things you don't want to do when you start a tone in singing. But practicing these steps now helps you feel the difference between starting a tone the right way (Steps 1 and 2) and starting it the wrong way (Steps 3 and 4).

1. **Pretend that you're about to say something; open the space in your throat and mouth at the same time as you inhale and then stop.**

   When you pretend you're about to speak, your vocal cords close to start the tone. That very slight sensation of closure is what you want to explore for starting a tone in singing. Practice this closure several times to get familiar with the sensations of the vocal cords closing.

2. **Pretend that you're about to say something and then add sound; open the space in your throat and mouth as you inhale and then say *ah*.**

   The vocal folds close gently when you pretend you're about to say something, and then the air moves as you say *ah* to start the tone. Practice starting the tone with *ah* several times to feel the sensation of opening the throat and closing the vocal cords.

3. **Start the tone by blowing too much air; blow the air with an *H* as if you were saying *hhhhhhhhhaaaa*.**

   Blowing too much air out at the start of the tone is something you don't want to do when you sing. But I suggest that you explore the sensation you get by following this step so you can feel the difference between blowing too much air when closing the cords and using just enough air to sing the tone.

4. **Start the tone with a glottal; add a slight grunt as you say the vowel *ah*.**

   A *glottal* is when you press and force out sound. Again, you don't want to use a glottal to start a tone in singing, but I recommend exploring the sound so you can distinguish between the clear and easy onset of sound you do want to make and the forced sound you don't want to make. You can use a closure of the cords that has a slight glottal for emphasis on a vowel, but you don't want to press the cords together or blow too much air when you sing. Just close the cords and then make sound, as you do in Step 2.

Closing the vocal cords and closing the throat are not the same. When you close the vocal cords, the rest of the throat stays open.

The following exercise, which you can hear performed on Track 66, helps you practice creating the onset of tone on individual notes and in small groupings of notes. The dots you see paired with some of the notes are staccato marks, which tell you to sing the notes short and detached (for more on articulation markings, see Chapter 7). Singing short notes allows you to practice starting a tone without worrying about sustaining the tone. The exercise moves slowly enough that you have time to feel the start of each note. However, you may want to listen to the whole pattern and practice the onset of tone at your own speed before you sing along with the singer on the track. You may also want to practice just the first portion of the exercise before you move on to the second portion. Guys, sing this exercise an octave lower than what's written.

The singer on the track demonstrates the sounds for you. She also demonstrates the sounds that go with the markings on the exercise. If you aren't sure what the markings mean, you can either listen to the singer for the demonstration or turn to Chapter 7 for a list of typical markings you see in songs.

Opening the space to change the tone

Changing the amount of open space you have in your throat and mouth greatly affects tone. Classical singers open this space a great deal, whereas pop, rock, R&B, and jazz singers open it only a reasonable amount. Singers striving for a legit (or head voice–dominated) sound use a lot of space, and belters keep the throat tension free but not as wide open (see Chapter 14 for belting exercises).

To get an idea of what opening the space in the mouth and throat feels like, pretend you're yawning and notice the first flexing open of the muscles in the throat and mouth at the start of the yawn. You should feel the space in the back of your mouth open; specifically, you should feel the back of the roof of your mouth lift up as the back wall of the throat expands. The following sections explain how to get the right amount of open space in your mouth and throat so you can create good tone when singing.

Lifting the soft palate

The position of your *soft palate* — the soft tissue in the back on the roof of your mouth — affects the tone of your singing voice. When your soft palate is too low, your tone can be nasal. By lifting the soft palate, you create more space for the tone to resonate.

You can practice lifting your soft palate by pretending you're about to yawn. Don't go through with the yawn, though; just lift the soft palate. After you know what lifting your soft palate feels like, practice lifting it and releasing it down. Practice this yawning technique five times in a row. When you can easily lift and release your soft palate, then lift it and hold it up for five counts before releasing it. Tada! You just lifted your soft palate by choice, which is a skill you need to have to create good tone when singing.

Now try lifting your soft palate and singing a tone on a vowel while keeping your soft palate lifted. For now, don't worry about the tone; just explore the position of the soft palate. Then you can decide whether you like the tone. The goal here is to develop the physical coordination necessary so you can move your soft palate to create the tone you need for any given song. Depending on the vowel you sing, you may need to arch the tongue. For example, singing an *uh* vowel (as in *cup* or *bug*) requires a slight arch in the middle of the tongue. You should still be able to see the back of the mouth and soft palate when you sing an *uh* vowel; after all, you want to be able to sing the tone and keep the soft palate up. You may want to record your practice in this step so you can compare the sounds as the tone changes as you work on opening the space.

Then sing the tone on a different vowel while keeping the soft palate lifted. In the beginning, the soft palate will probably drop when you start to sing. That's okay. Just keep practicing the techniques I cover in this section. When you can consistently feel the physical coordination of lifting the soft palate, you can record yourself singing the tone to notice the change between the tone when the soft palate is lifted and when it isn't lifted. The first time you listen to yourself experimenting with lifting the soft palate, you may not like the sound. Remember that you may need to practice quite a bit before you can really feel the lift in the soft palate and hear the positive changes in the tone. The tone may become warmer or fuller as you continue to practice and create more space for the tone to resonate when you lift the soft palate.

Dropping the jaw

How you drop your jaw has a direct impact on what tone you create when you sing. If you drop just your chin, you open the space in the front of the mouth but close down the space in the back of the mouth. When the space closes in the back of the mouth, the tone is tight and not as free. By dropping the jaw from the back, you open just the right space and give the tone room to resonate.

To practice dropping your jaw the right way, keep your lips closed and yawn as if you were bored at a dinner party and you didn't want to insult your host by letting a huge yawn escape. Feel your teeth opening in the back at the same time that the space inside your mouth opens. This opening of the jaw is what you want for singing.

As you drop your jaw, be sure to lengthen your spine. Think of your jaw dropping as your skull lifts. This lengthening of the spine can really help if you have trouble moving your jaw or if you have problems with stiffness in your jaw joint. As you practice dropping your jaw, watch your jaw movement in the mirror to make sure you see the coordination of movement between the jaw and the lengthening of the spine. You won't see your head push up, but you'll feel a lengthening in your neck.

Releasing tension to enhance tone

Tension anywhere in the body affects the tone of the singing voice. If you're not sure how to recognize tension in the body, intentionally tighten up your whole body and then release it to feel the difference between being tense and being released. You can also go through the body one section at a time and release the muscles in that section. The best part about this systematic check for body tension is that you can do it when sitting in a chair, lying down, or standing up. Simply start at the bottom at your feet and work your way up to your head.

Body alignment also affects how much tension is in your body. I suggest that you review the alignment exercises I cover in Chapter 1 to make sure your body is aligned for maximum singing potential. You can also check for body tension and poor alignment when you practice yoga, meditate, or do any other activities that focus on your breathing and body awareness.

Coordinating breath to improve tone

Breath coordination has a big impact on what your tone sounds like when singing. If you have good breath coordination, you move your breath consistently throughout the phrases in a song. When you don't move your breath consistently, the tone may be tight and constricted because you're pressing muscles together to push out the tone.

To maintain good breath coordination, you need to know how to move your body specifically for any length of phrase. For example, when you know you have to sing for only two measures, you use a different amount of breath flow compared to when you know you have to sing for six measures. If you can control the muscles of exhalation, you can create an open and free-flowing tone. Check out Chapter 2 for exercises designed to help you develop your breath coordination.

To help you coordinate your breath in the songs you're practicing, place breath marks in all the places where you know for sure you plan to breathe (see Chapter 7 for details on these markings). You can breathe anytime you see punctuation or a rest and anytime the musical phrase or lyrics lend themselves to a pause. You can work on shorter phrases when you begin a new practice song and then challenge yourself to sing longer phrases. When you're ready to sing the longer phrases, you need to pay attention to your body coordination so that you can keep the right spaces open to create just the right tone for your song.

Eliminating intonation issues

Intonation problems (issues that affect your ability to stay in tune in any given song) usually stem from how you prepare the tone physically and how you listen to the sounds you make. Part of the physical coordination required to sing in tune (that is, without intonation problems) involves singing precise vowels. Singing precise vowels affects tuning because the tone of the singing voice needs to be a balance of bright and dark. In this case, *bright* means that the tone is forward and high in ping (meaning that it rings with brilliance). *Dark* means that the sound is back in the throat or mouth and is more woofy. Think of the speakers on your sound system; you need both *woofers* (speakers that amplify low bass) and *tweeters* (speakers that amplify high treble). The human body is really just one big speaker, so the singing voice also needs a balance of woofers and tweeters. As you sing vowels, you need to balance the way the vowels resonate. When you sing dark vowels, you use more woofer in the tone, and you may sound more like you're singing *uh* even when you're singing a different vowel.

Experiment with your vowels to feel how the resonance changes and how vowel precision affects your tone.

The other piece to the tuning equation is how you listen to the sounds you make. When you sing, you hear a lot of sounds inside your head. When you only listen to the sounds inside your head, you tune the voice very differently than you do when you listen to the sounds outside your head. Singers who tend to sing out of tune usually only listen to their singing inside their head. If I've just described you, take the time to record your singing sessions so that you can hear how the tone of your singing voice matches (or doesn't match) the pitch of the piano or other instrument playing your song.

If you deal with intonation issues when you sing, try these suggestions to help you fix them:

✔ If your pitch is inconsistent, make sure you listen to your voice out in the room, paying close attention to how your voice matches the tones on the piano.

✔ If you consistently sing flat (meaning that you sing lower than the actual pitch), monitor your vowels to make sure they're precise and resonating throughout your head rather than just in your throat. You want a balance of high ping (tweeter) and rich low resonance (woofers), not just woofers.

✔ If you consistently sing sharp (meaning that you sing higher than the actual pitch), you're likely pushing too much. Try to relax and trust your body and breath coordination instead of pushing out the sound into the room.

✔ If you know you sing out of tune but aren't sure what the problem is, try any of the preceding three suggestions while recording yourself. Or find a friend who has a good sense of pitch and ask him or her to listen to you and tell you if you're sharp or flat.

Creating Echoing Tone with Resonance

Resonance is the echoing of tone inside your body and outside in the room where you're singing. If the room is really lively, you'll hear a lot of resonance bouncing around the room. Rooms with a lot of carpeting or fabric-like material, such as drapes, absorb more sound and keep it from bouncing around, which, in turn, means you'll have a more difficult time hearing resonance. You need to be aware of what resonance feels like and sounds like so that you can sing well to any type of song in any type of room. You explore the sensations of resonance and then discover how to vary resonance in the following sections.

Finding your resonance

You feel the vibrations from resonance both when you speak and when you sing. Place your hand against your throat and say your name. Did you feel the vibrations from your resonating tone? Keep your one hand against your throat and place your other hand on the top and back of your head. Sing a low note and notice where you feel the vibrations. Now sing a high note and notice where you feel the vibrations. You probably felt the vibrations in your throat when you were on the lower note and then in your head when you sang the higher note. Why do you need to know how the vibrations change as you change pitches? Understanding how the vibrations of resonance change as you sing helps you aim the resonance just right for high or low notes. If you don't know where the tone vibrates, you may just try to push sound out instead of allowing it to vibrate and resonate.

The following exercise, which you can hear on Track 67, has you sing specific vowels so you can practice finding your resonance. The vowels are *ee ooh ee* (as in *he too*), *ee oh ee* (as in *we go*), *ay ooh ay* (as in *day two*), and *ay oh ay* (as in *day glow*). Singers typically feel the most vibrations of resonance on these particular vowels. As you work on this exercise, notice where you feel the vibrations. Guys, sing this pattern an octave lower than what's written.

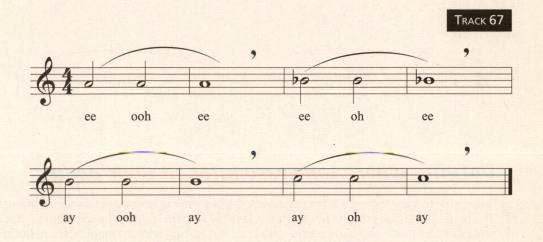

TRACK 67

Using vowels to explore resonance

When you sustain a note in a song, you sustain a vowel. Hence, you can develop your resonance by exploring your vowels. You need to know how to create specific resonance for any vowel, and in this exercise, you explore moving from vowels that you can easily feel the vibrations of resonance with to vowels that you can't feel the vibrations with quite as easily. Specifically, the front vowels are a little easier to feel vibrations than the back vowels (refer to Chapter 3 for the scoop on the different types of vowels). You feel more vibrations in your face and mouth on front vowels like the *ee* vowel, which may be why most singers say that *ee* is their favorite vowel. (If *ee* isn't their favorite, it's usually one of the other front vowels, such as *ay*.) On the other hand, the back vowels usually help you feel more resonance in the back of the head. In any given song, you want to maintain a balance of resonance so that you have vibrations in both the front and the back of the head.

The following exercise, which you can hear on the piano on Track 68, features a series of vowels. As you sing the first *ee*, notice where you feel the vibrations of resonance. You may feel the vibrations in your face, head, mouth, or other areas around the head. As you move from the *ee* to the *oh* (as in the word *go*), allow the resonance to stay in the same place that it was for the *ee*. In other words, you don't want the resonance to fall backward when you sing the *oh*. Again, keep the resonance in the same place as you move on to the *ah* vowel (as in the word *father*). In the second phrase, which starts in the third measure, you have to start on the *ah* vowel. Remember where you felt the vibrations from resonance when you were singing the *ee* vowel and start there for the *ah* vowel. The second line begins with *ay*. Some singers find *ay* to be just as helpful as *ee* in feeling vibrations. As you move from *ay* through *oh* to *ooh* (as in the word *two*), keep that resonance vibrating in a similar location. Guys, sing this exercise an octave lower than what's written.

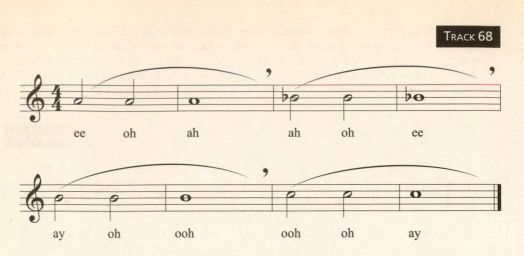

ee   oh   ah   ah   oh   ee

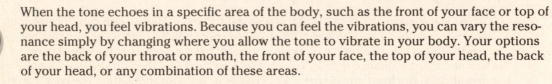

ay   oh   ooh   ooh   oh   ay

Varying where tone resonates in your body

Being able to vary the amount of resonance in your singing is valuable if you're interested in any type of music other than classical. Classical singers require the maximum amount of resonance so their tone carries throughout an auditorium without amplification, but non-classical singers often use mics, so they have more flexibility with the amount of resonance they use. Not knowing how to vary your resonance may encourage you to push too much.

When the tone echoes in a specific area of the body, such as the front of your face or top of your head, you feel vibrations. Because you can feel the vibrations, you can vary the resonance simply by changing where you allow the tone to vibrate in your body. Your options are the back of your throat or mouth, the front of your face, the top of your head, the back of your head, or any combination of these areas.

If you decide that you want the tone to resonate in your throat, just think that thought and the tone will change and vibrate more in your throat. Then if you want to change the resonance to the front of your face, simply change your mind's direction and allow the tone to resonate in the front of your face. Just by thinking about where you want the tone to vibrate helps you change the way your tone resonates.

To get some practice with varying your resonance, try to alter where you allow the tone to resonate by sustaining a tone for at least four counts and doing the following:

✔ **Direct the sound to the very back of your mouth.** Visualize the tone flowing backward and down your throat as if you might swallow it. Directing the tone backward creates a dark and woofy tone.

✔ **Target the sound to the front of your face.** Visualize the tone flowing through your mouth and out through your cheeks or eyes. This tone moves in the opposite direction from the previous step and sounds bright and brilliant.

✔ **Aim the sound to a place of your choosing.** You can pick the inside of your mouth at your teeth, the top of your head, the back of your head, or anywhere within the region of your head and mouth. Record yourself and listen back so you can hear how your tone varies based on where you let the sound resonate.

After you've explored variations of resonance, sing along with the piano on Track 69 and vary how the tone resonates in the following exercise. For the first line, explore your low resonance by allowing the vibrations of resonance to be in your mouth or throat. For the second line, practice your high resonance by allowing the vibrations of resonance to be way up in your head as if they were coming right out of your forehead. For the third line, try out your bright tone by allowing the resonance to move forward. Use the *ee* vowel to help you find the ping or brilliance in the tone so you can create a lot of forward resonance. For the fourth line, explore your dark tone by not moving your resonance forward and by making it feel huge inside your mouth and not out in the room. Guys, sing this exercise an octave lower than what's written.

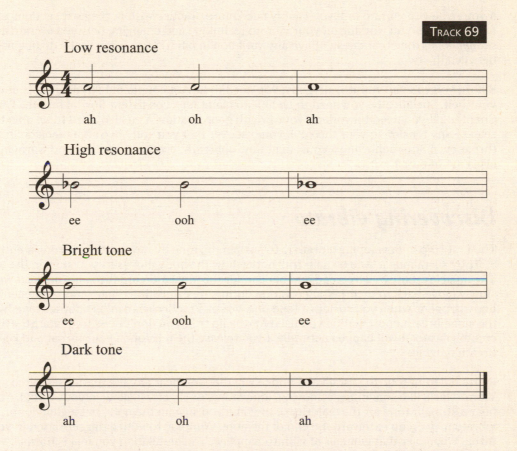

Choosing the right resonance for a song

When you choose a song to sing, you're choosing not only to sing in a particular style but also to use resonance in a certain way. For instance, classical singing and classical songs use a lot of resonance because making a lot of sound is part of the style. Classical singers often sing quite loudly without pushing. They use a lot of resonance, and their tone carries in the room. Popular (non-classical) songs, on the other hand, usually use less resonance. For example, if your song is a popular song about two people falling in love or some other similar topic, the tone will be brighter but less full than most classical pieces, so you'll need to move the resonance forward as opposed to moving it to the back of your mouth. If your piece is about getting mad at your neighbor, then you'll need to use a bright forward resonance that has lots of ping to imitate someone yelling. Songs about lost lovers and heartache use a darker tone, so you need to allow the vibrations of resonance to be lower in your throat and not forward. Changing the tone brings variety to your songs so that you don't have to push too much chest voice.

Varying Tone with Vibrato

Vibrato is the name for the less-than-a-half-step fluctuation of pitch in singing. It happens from the release of tension in the throat, not the creation of tension. If the throat is really tense, the vibrato either doesn't happen or a tremolo occurs. A *tremolo* is a really fast vibrato usually characterized by a very narrow fluctuation in pitch. It can be distracting in a song because the vibrato becomes the focal point of the performance. (The opposite of a tremolo is a *wobble,* a slower rate of vibrato with a wider fluctuation in pitch. Wobbles usually occur from a lack of breath coordination.)

If you're new to vibrato or if you simply need more practice with it, the next sections can help. They get you working on your vibrato technique and changing between vibrato and *straight tone* (tone that doesn't have any variation in pitch) so you can really distinguish between the two.

Before you can use vibrato correctly, you need to have a couple of technical skills under your belt. Specifically, you need to be able to maintain a consistent flow of breath. Turn to Chapter 2 if you need to work on your breath coordination. You also need to be able to release any tension in your throat. If you discover that you still have some tension in your throat even after achieving a consistent flow of breath, try the stretching and warm-up exercises in Chapter 1.

Discovering vibrato

The first step in developing vibrato is to sustain the tone by moving the air consistently. Start by sustaining a tone on a lip trill; notice how the body moves as you sustain the tone. The muscles that you stretched and opened for the inhalation are the same muscles that slowly move back to their resting position during the exhalation. That same movement of the body happens when you sustain a tone on a vowel. Practice sustaining another tone by using the same breath coordination you used for the lip trill. You don't need to bounce the abs to create vibrato; it will happen naturally if you release the tension in your throat and keep the breath moving.

Pick a different tone to sustain and notice whether you hear any fluctuations in pitch. Vibrato feels like something is moving, undulating, or slightly jiggling in your throat. You may hear a straight tone for the majority of the time you sustain the note, but a glimmer of vibrato may creep in toward the end of the note. Continue to notice the sensation in your throat whenever that glimmer of vibrato happens. The undulation you feel is normal, so don't try to stop it from happening.

If this is the first time you're hearing your vibrato, allow it to happen naturally for several practice sessions before you try to change it. Continue to sustain different notes and notice the different sensations you feel for each one.

If your vibrato is wide or wobbles, you may not be moving the air fast enough, or you may be letting your tongue and larynx bounce. Try the following techniques to fix it:

✔ **Change the flow of your breath.** Review the exercises in Chapter 2 on breathing; in particular, work on longer phrases so you can feel the sensations in your body as you sustain a long series of notes. Sustain the tone on a lip trill to feel the movement of air, and then compare that flow of air to what you feel when you sustain the tone on a vowel.

✔ **Make sure your tongue and larynx aren't bouncing.** Try singing a tone with your tongue extended slightly out of your mouth. Releasing the tongue forward just beyond the teeth can help you feel any tension in the base of the tongue as you sing. (The base of the tongue is the part that curves down your throat.) Place your hand underneath your chin to feel whether your tongue is bouncing as you sustain a tone, or look in the mirror and watch your tongue. To keep your larynx from bouncing around, try to stabilize it by continuing to explore the sensations of singing with your tongue extended slightly out of your mouth so you release any tongue tension and work on your breath coordination to make sure your breath is flowing steadily as you sing. You can also explore opening the space very low in the throat to help stabilize the larynx. (See Chapter 9 for specifics on stabilizing your larynx.)

Another technical issue that affects the rate of your vibrato is the balance of registration. If your chest voice gets too heavy, then you may develop a wider vibrato. Work on the exercises in Chapter 8 on chest voice and Chapter 10 on mix to help you find just the right amount of weight in your chest voice.

Changing between vibrato and straight tone

Classical singers use vibrato almost all the time. Although some classical music requires straight tone, vibrato is the norm in that style. Other styles of music use less vibrato in general or some vibrato that's less pronounced. For example, most pop singers use vibrato when they sing longer sustained notes, but they may choose to use straight tone at other times. Think of the classical vibrato as steady and obvious. For other styles of music, think of vibrato as being a normal part of the sound, although singers may choose to use it only for short periods of time and other times choose to sing a straight tone.

No matter what style of music you usually sing, you need to be able to switch between vibrato and straight tone because singers in every style of music use both straight tone and vibrato. Work through the following steps to practice moving from straight tone to vibrato and to experience the difference between the full force of your vibrato and the feeling you get when you use just a little vibrato:

1. **Sustain any note in the middle part of your range that's comfortable for you to sing for at least six beats and allow the vibrato to happen the entire time you sing the tone.**

   As you sustain the tone, notice the sensations you feel in your mouth and throat. You may feel undulations in your throat, or you may just feel waves of sound coming out of your mouth. Both types of undulation are normal for vibrato. Just make sure the undulations you feel aren't actually wobbles (when the vibrato is too wide or unsupported). If you're experiencing wobbles or if you didn't feel any vibrato at all, flip to the preceding section for help.

2. **Sustain the same note for at least six beats, this time using straight tone the entire time you sing the tone.**

   Straight tone feels as though the vibrato almost happens but doesn't. The tone seems to be suspended as you sing compared to vibrato, in which the tone seems to move forward with the undulations. Don't squeeze in your throat for the straight tone. Instead, just sustain the tone without letting the vibrato start.

3. **Sustain the same note by starting with straight tone and then moving into vibrato.**

   In this step, you may feel as if you allowed the vibrato to start — as if you released something so that the vibrato could happen. You may also feel something release in your throat for the undulation of the pitch.

4. **Sustain the same note by starting with vibrato and then moving into straight tone.**

   Don't squeeze your throat to stop the vibrato. You may feel the undulations suspend as if the vibrato could happen at any moment. The muscles in your throat do activate to make the tone, but they don't tense up. Squeezing in your throat may prevent the vibrato from sounding. Likewise, you don't want to force the vibrato to happen or squeeze to create a straight tone. The movement of the breath helps you sustain the tone so you don't have to squeeze in the throat.

5. **Sustain a note by moving from straight tone to vibrato, but use only a little vibrato.**

   The normal rate of vibrato is five to eight pulses per second. For this step, you can use anything less than the normal rate to slow down the vibrato. If thinking of the number of pulses is confusing, just think of using only a portion of your vibrato; in other words, allow some but not your full vibrato to sound.

6. **Start a tone by allowing just a glimmer of vibrato (the same amount you experienced at the end of Step 5) to happen.**

   If you can start the tone with just a glimmer of vibrato (some vibrato but not your full vibrato), notice the sensations in your throat as you sustain the note. With your breath consistently moving, you should feel the undulation continuing as you sustain the tone; however, the undulations shouldn't feel as wide as they do when you use your full vibrato.

After practicing these steps, turn on Track 70 and try singing along with the following exercise. The first line consists of whole notes, and you have four counts for each note. On the first note, allow the vibrato to happen for the entire duration of the note. Use straight tone for the duration of the second note. For the third note, move from vibrato to straight tone, and on the fourth note, move from straight tone to vibrato. Guys, sing this exercise an octave lower than what's written.

When you change from vibrato to straight tone (or vice versa), make the first sound for at least two counts before you change your tone. If you can't switch that quickly, then turn off the track and practice changing the tone at your own pace. After a few solo practice sessions, you can try singing along with the track again.

The second line of the exercise mimics what you experience in a song. In the first measure of the second line, you use straight tone, and then you allow vibrato to happen in the second measure as you sing the whole note. In the third measure, you use straight tone and then start the whole note in the fourth measure with straight tone and then allow the vibrato to happen. Practice the pattern using the suggestions written. For the vibrato on the second line, use your full vibrato when you sing with the track and then go back and sing it again using only a glimmer of vibrato. When you're confident about moving between straight tone and vibrato, you can make choices to use vibrato (or not) in your song.

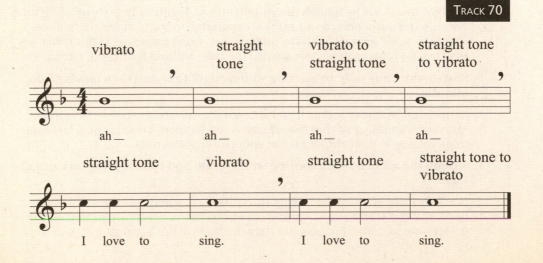

Practice Piece: "Changing Tone"

This practice piece, "Changing Tone," encourages a change in tone by having you imitate a different singer for each line. For the first line, sing as if you were a pop singer and use a more speech-like tone without vibrato or full resonance. As you sing the second line, sing as if you were a classical singer whose voice you love. Sing with vibrato and use a lot of resonance. As you approach the higher notes, open the space in your throat and the back of your mouth so the tone has a lot of room to resonate. In the third and fourth lines, sing like your favorite pop singer. After the fermata (the bird's-eye symbol, which indicates that you should sustain the note longer than its value) on the fourth line, go back to using a very full resonating tone for the fifth line. For the last line, just sing like you. The singer demonstrates the changes in tone for you on Track 71. Listen to the track several times to get used to the melody, rhythm, and changes of tone and then play the track again and sing along to create your own diverse tones. Guys, sing this piece an octave lower than what's written.

TRACK 71

I love her/his voice. I wish I could_____ sing like her/him.

Those glo-ri-ous, glor-ious notes._____

But if she/he sang_____ like me she'd/he'd have to_____ change her/his tone.

Chang-in' chang-in' change her/his tone.

Her/his tone. Ah_____

But_____ for now I'll just be me.

Songs for Developing Your Tone

Singers create a specific tone based on the kind of music they sing. The variety of tone ranges from the opera singer who creates a full, round tone to the folk singer who creates a very simple tone with a speech-like quality. When you choose a style of music to explore, the best way to work on your tone is to choose a ballad within that style of music because ballads are slower songs that allow you to sustain tone.

The following list contains a diverse group of songs from different styles of music to help you start developing your tone. You can work on any of the songs in the list; note that I've organized them according to which specific aspect of tone they work on. The word *either* in parentheses after a song lets you know that it's appropriate for male or female singers. I also include a note specifying what style of music the song is in.

- Vibrato
  - "Ave Maria" by Charles Gounod (either; classical song)
  - "Beyond the Sea" by Jack Lawrence and Charles Trenet as sung by Bobby Darin (either; pop song)
  - "I'll Know" from *Guys and Dolls* by Frank Loesser (either; musical theater song)
- Resonance
  - "Wishing You Were Somehow Here Again" from *The Phantom of the Opera* by Andrew Lloyd Webber (either; musical theater song)
  - "Stand by Me" by Ben E. King, Jerry Leiber, and Mike Stoller as sung by Ben E. King (either; soul song)
  - "She's Got a Way" by Billy Joel (either; rock song)
- Space
  - "Shenandoah" (either; American folk song)
  - "Killing Me Softly" by Charles Fox and Norman Gimbel as sung by Roberta Flack (either; soul song)
  - "So in Love" from *Kiss Me Kate* by Cole Porter (either; musical theater song)
  - "Sure on This Shining Night" by Samuel Barber (either; classical song)

Chapter 13

Expanding Your Vocal Agility

In This Chapter

▶ Breathing quickly between fast-moving patterns

▶ Improving your vocal agility by practicing songs in stepwise motion

▶ Developing agility when singing thirds and larger intervals

▶ Putting everything together with a practice piece

Some singers can easily sing a fast song with a lot of notes. Others have a difficult time singing melodies that bounce along and prefer to sing slower songs. Whether you love having all the notes whiz by or you prefer the slow lane, this chapter has some challenges for you because it gets you practicing your agility.

Agility in singing is the ability to sing fast-moving pitches quickly and accurately. Developing agility is especially important if you want to sing classical music, pop music, or R&B. Although classical music usually has all the notes written on the page, early classical composers assumed that the singer would add extra notes called *embellishments.* Similarly, pop and R&B singers often add their own embellishments to the songs they sing. Whether you sing classical music or R&B, the agility exercises in this chapter can help you develop flexibility in your voice, which, in turn, can help you become a more versatile singer. ***Note:*** When you're first starting an exercise, you may need to listen to the pattern a few times simply to get used to hearing all the notes.

You may want to review Chapter 5 on intervals to become more familiar with the types of intervals you sing in a song and then come back to this chapter to put those intervals to the test in agility patterns. You can also review Chapter 6 on rhythm to find out how to look at a song to determine whether you need a lot of agility to sing it.

Exploring the Art of the Quick Breath

Being able to inhale quickly gives you enough air to sing a phrase with a lot of fast-moving notes. Not inhaling quickly enough in a fast-moving song makes the tone tighter and the song more difficult to sing freely. When you don't have enough air as you sing, you feel like you have to press or push to get the notes out. The following sections explain how to breathe quickly so that you can sing fast songs the way they were meant to be sung without losing your breath in the process. If you need help with breathing basics, such as coordinating your muscles and opening up your body, flip to Chapter 2.

Catching your breath quickly in fast songs

Singing fast songs can be really fun, but getting enough air in quickly can be tricky. The following exercise can help you get enough breath between fast-moving patterns:

1. **With your hands on your ribs or sides, open your ribs and abs quickly.**

    When you open the ribs quickly, remember to also keep your throat open so that the inhalation is silent. The opening should feel like you're widening a tube inside your body. If you need to, you can practice opening the ribs slowly and then gradually open them faster. (See Chapter 3 for more on how to open the ribs.)

2. **Sustain the sound of a consonant for eight counts and then take a breath in for one count.**

    Choose a consonant that makes noise, like *Sh, F, Z,* or *S.* Take a breath and then make the sound of the consonant for eight counts. At the end of eight counts, take a breath for one count. You may need to practice Step 1 several times before you can open your ribs quickly enough for this step. Practice Step 2 until you can make the sound even and consistent. If the sound pulses or wiggles, you aren't moving the breath consistently.

3. **Sing a note for eight counts and then take a breath in for one count.**

    This step is similar to taking a breath in a quarter note rest in a song. Repeat this step at least four times in a row to determine whether you're really getting enough air in one count. Repeating the step four or more times simulates what happens in a song: You sing a phrase and then quickly take a breath; you sing another phrase and then quickly take another breath. Managing your breath in the first few phrases of a song is easier than managing your breath after the tenth phrase. To get enough air throughout an entire song, you need to consistently open your body at the end of each phrase.

4. **Sing a note for eight counts and then take a breath in for half a count.**

    Often a half count is the amount of time you have to sneak in a breath in faster songs. Taking a breath in half a count or beat is the same as taking a breath in an eighth note rest in a song. (See Chapter 6 to practice counting out beats.)

Taking a quick breath

The following exercise, featured on Track 72, has a short but quick succession of notes with a quick break in the middle to simulate the timing of a breath in a song. You sing short phrases followed by a quick breath and then long phrases followed by a quick breath. Then you start over when the next repetition begins on the track. First, listen to the track without singing so that you can time the breath. Then play the track again and sing along with the pattern. The goal is to open your body quickly for a silent inhalation in between fast-moving notes. Men, sing this exercise down an octave lower than what's written.

If the exercise on Track 72 sounds too hard to keep up with, spend some time just listening to the piano playing the notes for you. Part of developing your vocal agility is developing your hearing. Your ear may need a little time to get used to all the notes flying by in fast songs. You'll be much more confident singing fast songs when you can hear the patterns in your head even when the piano isn't playing them.

TRACK 72

Howdy, Neighbor! Working on Stepwise Motion

A huge part of developing agility is working on exercises that move in *stepwise motion* (that is, exercises that contain notes that are right next to each other). Singing melodies in stepwise motion is a lot like running because you have to put one foot in front of the other and go! Of course, singing melodies that move slowly is easier. After all, you have plenty of time to get your breath and shape your mouth for words in slower phrases. In contrast, when you sing faster phrases in stepwise motion, you don't have time to think about how to shape your mouth or focus on your breath, so these actions need to become second nature to you. Practicing phrases with notes in stepwise motion, like the ones I include in the following sections, is a great way to improve your vocal agility so that you can keep up with the fastest of the fast.

Giving up control to get a feeling for agility

The melody on Track 73 (shown in the following figure) starts slowly and gradually gets faster. As it speeds up, dare to open your mouth, let go of any control you may have over the notes, let them fly out of your mouth, and just sing. You can listen to the singer on the track demonstrate the sounds for you. Breathe during the allotted rest at the end of each line. Men, sing this exercise an octave lower than what's written.

Stepping up the pace

The exercise in the following figure, featured on Track 74, uses stepwise motion in the melody, but a few of the notes repeat. These repeating notes give you the chance to practice quick repetition of notes without bouncing your jaw. When you sing them right, you should feel like the notes are fluttering out of your body.

You make the *N* by touching the tip of your tongue to the alveolar ridge on the roof of your mouth. As you lift your tongue for the *N* and then round your lips for the *ooh* vowel, be sure to keep the space open in the back of your mouth and throat.

If you keep the space inside your throat and mouth open and allow your ear to tell you whether you're singing the right notes, you can sing the repeated notes without pushing them out. Also, after your ear is used to hearing fast passages, you can trust that your ear will keep you in tune so you don't have to push. Men, sing this exercise an octave lower than what's written. ***Remember:*** Your goal is to maintain a consistent flow of air.

TRACK 74

nooh _____

nooh _____

nooh _____

nooh _____

nooh _____

nooh _____

Turning around on the tonic

In the exercise on Track 75 (shown in the following figure), you sing a familiar stepwise pattern that ascends all the way to the top of the scale. With the turn around the first note, or *tonic* (the first note of a key signature), you can practice your half and whole steps to make your pitch more accurate. To do so, take a breath, allow the front of the tongue to arch for the *ay* vowel and bring up your bottom lip to touch the back of your upper front teeth for the *V*. Try to create the consonant *V* without closing your jaw; in other words, keep the space inside your mouth open after the breath and then sing through the *V*. As you ascend in pitch, open the space in the back of your mouth and throat even wider to allow plenty of room for the tone to resonate. Also, make sure you keep the breath consistently moving throughout the exercise. Men, sing this exercise an octave lower than what's written. If the exercise is too high for you, you can either sing it down another octave or sing the higher notes in falsetto.

If you get lost in all the notes, tap your hand on your leg with each note.

Running to the top of the scale

This exercise (shown in the following figure and featured on Track 76) allows you to do two things at one time: work on your agility and practice getting a fast breath in the middle of a pattern. You have one quick beat to take a breath in the middle of the pattern and then one quick beat to breathe before the pattern starts over. (I help you open your body quickly to make sure you're ready for the quick breath in the middle of the pattern in the earlier section "Catching your breath quickly in fast songs.")

To form the *L* consonant in this exercise, lift your tongue to the alveolar ridge on the roof of your mouth. As the pattern moves higher, you may need to transition into head voice (see Chapter 9 for details). If the high notes feel stuck, sing the pattern slowly and pay close attention to your transition into head voice. You can feel the resonance vibrating higher when you're in head voice. After you smooth out the transition to head voice, you can gradually speed up the pattern. Men, sing this exercise an octave lower than what's written. If the exercise is still too high for you, you can either sing it down another octave or sing the higher notes in falsetto.

If you're feeling rushed with the breath, sing only half of the pattern and use the second half of the pattern to practice your breathing. When you feel like you can manage the quick breath, put all the pieces together and sing the whole pattern.

If your *ah* doesn't sound like an *ah* when you listen to the recording of your practice session, sing the exercise using a word that has *ah* in it, such as *father*. After you're confident that you're singing the vowel in *father* accurately, sing the *ah* alone but continue to sing as though you were singing the full word *father*.

You can continue to add more layers of skill with each practice session. After you feel confident about this exercise as it's written, you can add different consonants to each note to practice moving your tongue for the right shape and sound. Consonants such as *N, D, M,* and *B* are all good ones to start with; consonants that require air with the sound, such as *Ch, J, Sh,* and *H,* are more difficult to manage. Practice the exercise on Track 76 with different consonant and vowel pairs to continue to develop your vocal agility.

Mastering Thirds

Music doesn't just move from one set of neighboring notes to the next. Songs often feature intervals of a *third* (the distance of three lines and spaces on the musical staff). The exercises in the following sections allow you to practice jumping around on the interval of a third. For a refresher on *intervals* — the distance between two pitches — turn to Chapter 5.

Singing every other step of the scale

Singing thirds isn't hard, but mastering this skill will probably take a little bit of practice. When you listen to Track 77, which is shown in the following figure, you can hear that the exercise starts slowly and then gradually moves faster. When you sing the exercise slowly, listen to the notes of the exercise and notice what you feel in your throat. You want the notes to feel like they're right next to each other; you don't want a big bump between them. (If this exercise lies at a *register break* for you, meaning that it lies at the place where you shift from one register to another, such as from chest voice to head voice, head on over to Chapters 8, 9, and 10 for help with individual registers and Chapter 11 for help with moving smoothly between registers.) Men, sing this exercise an octave lower than what's written.

When you sing thirds, imagine that the notes are right out in front of each other rather than up and down on top of each other. If you think of the notes as being up and down, you may encourage your larynx to bob around. You want your larynx to stay steady (see Chapter 9).

Be sure that your bottom lip touches your upper teeth as you make the *F* sound. Keep the teeth open and move just the bottom lip. Then make the *ee* vowel sound by allowing the front of the tongue to arch. Even though the front of the tongue arches for the *ee* vowel, you need to leave some space open in the back of your mouth and throat for the tone to resonate. The tongue doesn't tense when it arches for the vowel.

Gaining momentum

The exercise shown in the following figure (and featured on Track 78) moves in thirds all the way up the scale. Use the consonants *B* and *P* to help you stay in rhythm and land accurately on each note. Consonants can help move the sound forward if you think of the consonant itself as a springboard — as though the consonant springs you forward to the next note in the pattern. (If you think of the consonant or pattern as being vertical — as in, the notes and consonants are up and down — the pattern can feel heavier and more difficult.)

As you ascend in pitch, open the space inside your throat more and maintain that amount of space when you restart the top note of the pattern after the breath. The higher notes of the pattern may be in head voice, so allow the vibrations of resonance to shift higher so that you can soar into head voice (see Chapter 9 for an introduction to head voice). Open the body for each breath and allow the air to flow consistently throughout the exercise. Men, sing this exercise an octave lower than what's written.

Notice that you have a rest in the middle of the pattern; this rest allows you a chance for a quick breath. Aim to take this breath quietly instead of sucking in air. A quiet inhalation requires that you open your body and your throat. The noisy inhalation or gasp, which can be heard very easily if you're singing with a microphone, means you tried to pull in air without opening up first. For help catching your breath quietly yet quickly between phrases, check out the earlier section "Exploring the Art of the Quick Breath."

Taking Musical Leaps with Larger Intervals

Larger intervals, such as fourths, fifths, sixths, and octaves, require more skill to maintain a steady tone, move smoothly between vocal registers (head voice and chest voice), and keep your breath moving consistently as you sing all the notes. Hence, keeping your larynx steady is extremely important when you sing these larger intervals. (If your larynx bobs up and down when you sing larger intervals, flip to Chapter 9 for tips on how to keep the larynx steady.)

Practicing exercises that have larger intervals is kind of like jumping hurdles: You need to be confident that you can land on your feet after you leap over the larger intervals. Leaping through a melody may feel a little bit out of control, as though the notes are just leaping out of your mouth, but that's okay. What you don't want is to push out the notes or bounce your jaw for each note. Your audience may be distracted watching your jaw bounce around instead of listening to your beautiful singing.

The exercises in the next sections feature a wide variety of intervals so that you can experiment with mixing up intervals in faster-moving patterns. I recommend following along with the music so that you can hear and see the patterns at the same time. Knowing what the intervals look like and sound like will help you become more accurate in your singing. (If you need a refresher on intervals before tackling these exercises, turn to Chapter 5.)

Starting on the top

The exercise shown in the following figure (and featured on Track 79) introduces intervals of a *sixth* (two notes that are the distance of six lines and spaces on the musical staff). But it also uses a tempo that's a little slower to give you a chance to adjust to the larger leap. Remember, the first note and the fourth note in the pattern are the same, so they should feel and sound the same. To easily sing the fourth note in the pattern, pretend that you're starting the exercise over again with the same amount of open space that you used to start the pattern. Smoothly connect from note to note; in other words, sing *legato* by creating a continuous sound as you change between the pitches. When the sound isn't legato, it sounds as if you're adding an *H* or puff of air between the notes. (***Note:*** The *3* over the top of the group of notes means *triplet.* All the triplets in the figure consist of three eighth notes spaced over one beat.)

This exercise begins with a *D* consonant to help you start the tone. The consonant helps you feel something specific when you sing the interval. You can sing the pattern as written with the *D* only on the first note, or you can add a *D* to each note until you're confident that you're accurately singing each note. Men, sing this exercise an octave lower than what's written.

When you know the sound and sensation of the distance between the pitches, you can make this exercise more challenging by singing it without the consonant. Sing the vowel without creating a *glottal* (pressing the vocal folds together to start the tone). If you can't start the tone without a glottal, use the consonant until you're confident you know how to start the tone. When you're ready, go back to starting with just the *eh* with an easy onset. You may feel yourself changing into a different register as you descend (see Chapter 11 for exercises related to register transition). Singing legato — smooth and connected — helps make the transition between registers flow more easily.

Jumping up (or down) an octave

An *octave* is a large interval that's often made up of two notes in two different registers. Hence, octaves often require you to leap from chest voice to head voice. Great singers are able to make such a leap smoothly and with finesse. The following exercise (featured on Track 80) helps you work on that leap. As the notes ascend, you can feel the higher resonance. Although the higher notes may sound full in the room, they may sound narrower in your head. (If you need more practice with octaves before you get started on this exercise, check out the interval exercises in Chapter 5 and the register transition exercises in Chapter 11.)

To make the *G* in this exercise, touch the back of your tongue to the roof of your mouth. Keep the space behind the tongue (the space in the throat) open even as you make the *G* sound in order to create an open and vibrant tone. The *oh* vowel sound requires the lips to round. Watch yourself in a mirror to make sure your lips are rounded and the space in the back of your mouth is open. As you inhale, open the space for the *oh* and then make the sound of the *G* as you begin the tone. Men, sing this exercise an octave lower than what's written.

TRACK 80

Practice Piece: "A Joyful Noise"

This practice piece challenges you to sing a short song filled with lots of moving notes. Before you practice singing the right notes, you may want to listen to the singer on Track 81 demonstrate the sounds for you. Notice that the fast notes are very precise and sound easy. The singer is monitoring the airflow to make sure the muscles that opened for the inhalation are gradually moving through the entire phrase. You have to trust your voice to sing the right notes because you don't want to control notes moving this fast. You have to listen to the phrase enough times to get all the notes in your ear and then trust your voice to sing those notes.

The singer also demonstrates how to sing through the consonants. You need to make the right shape to sound the consonant and then allow a continuous flow of sound to happen as you sing. In other words, you don't want the sound to stop when you articulate consonants. Remember that your lips and tongue shape for the consonants, allowing you to keep the space open in the back of your mouth and throat. Men, sing this practice piece an octave lower than what's written.

TRACK 81

A joy - ful noise rings ___ all ___ a-round.

Sing - ing forth a ___ migh - ty sound.

Joy - ous sing-ing. Joy - ous sounds ___ fill the air.

Joy - ous. Joy - ous sounds.

Joy - ous songs to fill the air.

Songs for Flaunting Your Agility

Because R&B songwriters write their songs, assuming that you'll add your own touch, the songs in this section are from other styles of music that have the notes written right on the page for you. In these classical pieces, you can add more notes of your own after you become familiar with what's customary in the particular style of music you're singing. The songs in the beginning of the list have some phrases that require agile movement of the voice but aren't especially complicated. The *Messiah* pieces at the end of the list are difficult and require some agility skills to successfully sing them. So you may want to check out these pieces when your technique is solid and you're ready for a challenge.

Each publisher decides how much information they put in a song. Look for sheet music or books with songs that include a lot of helpful information, such as the embellishments written out, a translation of the song if it's in a foreign language, the pronunciation of the words, and extra information about the time period.

✔ "If Florinda Is Faithful" ("Se Florinda é fedele") by Alessandro Scarlatti (male)

✔ "Victorious, My Heart!" ("Vittoria, mio core!") by Giacomo Carissimi (either)

✔ "Dance, Dance Gentle Maiden" ("Danza, danza fanciulla gentile") by Francesco Durante (male)

✔ "My Heart Ever Faithful" by Bach (either)

✔ "I'll Sail upon the Dog Star" by Henry Purcell (male)

✔ "Think of Me" from *The Phantom of the Opera* by Andrew Lloyd Webber (female)

✔ "Every Valley Shall Be Exalted" from *Messiah* by G.F. Handel (male)

✔ "O Thou That Tellest Good Tidings to Zion" from *Messiah* by G.F. Handel (female)

✔ "Rejoice Greatly, O Daughter of Zion" from *Messiah* by G.F. Handel (female)

✔ "Thus Saith the Lord" from *Messiah* by G.F. Handel (male)

Chapter 14

Belting It Out with Exercises from Beginner to Advanced

*B*elt (also known as *belting*) is a combination of forward resonance and a mix of registers — some chest voice and some head voice. Singers often wrongly assume that belting is just using full chest voice all the way up the scale. But chest voice has multiple layers of thickness, and the heaviest chest voice sounds aren't what you want for belting. Check out Chapter 8 on chest voice to find more information about the thickness and weight of chest voice and Chapter 10 for details on mixing registers. After you're comfortable with your chest voice and head voice, you can begin to explore belting, knowing that you use a lighter chest voice.

A big question that I hear from students is about the difference between belting for musical theater versus belting for a pop or rock song. Because musical theater written in the past 20 years has a lot of influence from pop and rock, the lines between the styles are starting to blur. Consequently, the basics of belting are the same for any style, just as the basics of singing apply no matter what style of music you sing. The exercises in this chapter help you with your belt sound whether you're performing a solo from *Wicked,* groovin' to Lady Gaga, or rocking out with Rod Stewart.

If you're not yet a belter, I suggest you work through this chapter slowly. If belting is a new sport for you, I recommend that you work on the singing techniques that I describe in other chapters and then return to this chapter later. Skills from other chapters — breath coordination, knowledge of tone, familiarity with shapes and sounds of vowels, and the ability to use different vocal registers — are necessary to make great belt sounds. You can certainly learn to belt, but you need to make sure your singing technique is solid before you turn your attention to this chapter.

Guys, keep in mind that belting is a term for sounds that the female voice makes. You won't hear it called belt for the male voice even though you can make the same sounds. That being said, you can certainly get a good vocal workout by singing along with the exercises in this chapter. Just sing everything down an octave to work on resonance in your chest voice.

Note: When you're first starting an exercise in this chapter, I recommend that you listen to the whole exercise a few times to get used to the sounds. Then you can sing along to practice making those sounds yourself.

Getting Started with Belting Basics

To start practicing belting, you first need to work on your speaking voice to discover the sensations of speaking on pitch and exploring forward resonance. Then you can move on to working on your belt range and sustaining belt sounds. To begin your journey, keep reading to find out what it feels like to belt in different parts of your range and how you can start making your first belt sounds.

Don't start out your practice session with belt sounds. Make sure you do a thorough warm-up; warming up gets your voice ready for the big sounds of belting. Without that warm-up, you may end up pushing. (Turn to Chapter 1 for details on warming up the voice.)

Feeling belt transitions in the voice

Many singers believe that belting should feel the same throughout their range, but lower belt notes actually feel very different from the higher notes. The lower notes feel fuller and stronger, whereas the higher notes feel a little lighter and have more forward resonance (see Chapter 12 for details on resonance). But even though higher belt notes don't feel as strong as the lower notes, the higher notes aren't weak; they just don't feel as heavy.

Belt transitions work differently depending on whether you're female or male:

- **For the women:** Women often belt up to an A above Middle C. A transition happens around that A because that's about how high women can take full chest voice. After you understand the layers of thickness of chest voice and can lighten up your chest voice, you can belt well beyond that A. You may need to practice for a good six months before you can belt an octave above Middle C, but most females can eventually extend their belt to the D and E an octave above Middle C. And after you understand that belting isn't just pure chest voice and you know how to mix the sound, you can belt even higher.

  Ladies, if you're a beginner belter, you may want to sing only belt songs that go to the A just above Middle C until you develop the skills I describe in the rest of this chapter. If you sing songs that go higher than that, you may have to push too much, and you may end up forcing a heavy chest voice, which isn't the goal. *Remember:* When done right, belting beyond the A above Middle C should feel easy. This easiness is the result of using *some* chest voice but not *full* chest voice. The goal here is to belt without feeling like you're pushing a huge weight around in your throat.

  Because finding contemporary songs that go only to an A can be tricky, I list several songs for beginner belters later in the section "Songs for Beginner Belters Looking to Try Out Their Technique." Most of these songs go to about a C an octave above Middle C; they have a narrow range and don't go as high as the more contemporary songs. You can work on these songs until you develop more notes in your belt.

- **For the men:** You don't have to worry so much about transitions in belting because belting isn't that different from how you normally sing. (After all, male singers often take fuller chest voice sounds into head voice territory.) Instead, male singers need to focus on how to adjust their resonance for the brassy sound of belt. (I help you work on adjusting your resonance for belting in the later section "Resonating All the Way to the Back Row.") Working on your transitions into head voice and strengthening your mix help you create the right balance of registers so you can focus your attention on creating just the right kind of resonance when you belt.

The exercises in this chapter are in your chest voice range if you sing them an octave lower than written. By singing along with the tracks, you can practice finding the perfect balance of resonance as well as just the right amount of chest voice. If you haven't explored head voice or mix, you may want to turn to Chapters 8, 9, and 10 before exploring this chapter.

Making a plan to develop your belt

Before you take on the belting exercises I outline in this chapter, you need to make a plan for how you're going to develop your belt. If you're new to belting, I suggest that you work on the exercises in the order listed in the chapter and that you work on each one for at least a week before moving on to the next exercise. Nine or so weeks may seem like forever, but if you take your time and really develop your belting skills now, then you can become a great belter later. If you have more experience belting, then you can start anywhere you like in the chapter. However, most belters use too much weight in the tone, so starting with the exercises just ahead on resonance may help you figure out how to use resonance to make a big sound rather than a heavy chest voice.

You also need to consider your voice type. Belting may be harder for a mezzo than a soprano or for a baritone than a tenor. Mezzos and baritones tend to have a heavier chest voice and tend to pull weight up into head voice. As a result, they often use this same kind of weight when belting. If I've just described you, take your time and work on the exercises in this chapter. Mezzos especially need to work on the speaking voice exercises to discover how to make chatty sounds without adding too much chest voice. For more information about the range of each voice type, check out the latest edition of my book *Singing For Dummies* (Wiley).

As you practice belting, record your sessions so that you not only feel the sensations as you're singing but also hear the sounds when you listen to the recording. Those fabulous belters you hear in recordings probably did 50 takes of the song to get it perfect. Plus, they can make heavier sounds for their recordings than singers who need to make belt sounds every day in performances. Bottom line: Don't try to be perfect or imitate someone else with your belting and don't be fooled into thinking singers can use really heavy chest voice every day.

Resonating All the Way to the Back Row

Resonance is the echoing of tone. When you belt, you want to move resonance forward — or aim the vibrations of resonance in your face at your cheeks or beside your nose. Why? Because forward resonance allows you to keep a brilliance in your tone while belting without using too much heavy chest voice. Think about how the sound of your voice changes when you get excited. (If you don't know what I'm talking about, think about a time when one of your friends got excited about something. Do you remember hearing a change in your friend's voice?) The pitch gets higher, and you hear more zing in the sound. That's the kind of sound you want to explore to help you with belting.

Here are a couple of tactics you can use to help you bring resonance forward:

- **Speak phrases using an accent.** You can use an accent from Brooklyn, Boston, Chicago, or some other fabulous city with a specific accent. Think of America Ferrera when she starred in the TV series *Ugly Betty* or Kristin Chenoweth in any of her character roles. Allow the accent to inspire you to bring the resonance forward.

- **Imitate someone you know who has a bright and forward tone in his or her speaking voice.** One of my students imitated the bright sounds her boss made in staff meetings, and another student imitated her Italian grandmother. Just talk to yourself, imagining the sound coming out of your cheeks at the top of your cheekbone rather than out of your mouth. You may feel a lot of sound behind your nose, but you don't want to put the sound in your nose. (You know the sound is nasal if, when you hold your nose and say the words aloud, all the sound gets trapped inside your nose.) You should feel a lot of vibrations in your face and nasal passages when you belt, but the sound shouldn't live in your nose and be nasal. It should live in your face beside your nose and on your cheeks.

After you find the forward resonance, you need to discover how resonance changes as you move up the scale or ascend in pitch. When you speak at a lower pitch, you can feel the vibrations from the resonance in and around your chest. As you ascend in pitch, you can feel the vibrations move higher as if the resonance were climbing a ladder on the outside of your face. The ladder starts at about your mouth and moves up beside your nose to the bridge of the nose and then up to your forehead. You may feel a widening at Middle C and a narrowing from about the A above Middle C to the octave above Middle C. In other words, resonance feels like it starts wide and then narrows as you ascend.

As you climb higher in pitch to the C an octave above Middle C, you can feel the vibrations of resonance in the bridge of the nose. (For men, the notes are an octave lower — the octave below Middle C to Middle C.) The tone narrows, but the space doesn't. You can use this resonance ladder as you work through the exercise I include in the later section "Buzzing your words on various pitches."

Although you may be tempted to change the resonance based on which vowels you're singing (the *a* in the word *cat* and the *ay* in the word *day* are the easiest vowels to belt), try to keep the resonance in the same place even when you change vowels. For example, the *ooh* vowel in the word *move* encourages more head voice as compared to the *a* in *cat*. If you have to belt an *ooh* vowel, simply pretend that you're singing the *a* vowel or modify toward the *a* vowel to help you find the same or similar resonance. After you feel that the resonance is similar — when you feel other vowels buzzing in the same place as the *a* — you can try singing the actual vowels.

Chatting It Up

Great belters make belting seem so easy. The sound comes flooding out of their mouths as if it takes no effort at all. One trick to getting that easy sound is to work on speaking sounds. If you think about the belt songs that you like, most of them have a chatty feeling in the melody. After all, belt songs don't usually have long, sustained lines like their classical counterparts do. The text is conversational and sounds like the person is talking on pitch. The following sections give you practice incorporating resonance as you speak on pitch and build your speaking range. The exercises in them help you practice making the chatty sounds often found in belt songs and then applying them to specific pitches.

Buzzing your words on various pitches

After you feel comfortable bringing resonance forward (as I describe in the earlier section "Resonating All the Way to the Back Row"), you're ready to combine that forward resonance with a chatty sound. To do so, practice saying the phrases in the following list, using a *mix* (use of chest voice and head voice at the same time) or light chest voice. Try to use no more than 50 percent chest voice at Middle C and less and less as you ascend. (Great belters make it sound as if they use 100 percent chest voice when they belt, but they don't.)

- ✔ Yeah! That's what I thought.
- ✔ Hey! Cut it out.
- ✔ Oh, my gosh!
- ✔ Ma! Dad! Where are you?
- ✔ What! No way!
- ✔ Ow! That hurts!

Notice the exclamation point after some of the words in the phrases. That punctuation helps you remember that you need some attitude behind the words. After all, belters aren't wallflowers. Belt songs are written for the characters who have so much to say it comes bursting out. They're not for the shy, quiet type.

When you say the preceding words, elongate the vowel sound to feel the buzzing of the resonance. After you feel the buzzing, you can say the word for as long as you want to say it and still maintain the buzzing sensation. If you feel as if you're pushing up, focus on using a mix rather than a heavy chest voice. The mix feels like the sound comes straight out, while heavy chest voice feels like you're pushing up (see Chapters 8 and 10 for details on chest voice versus mix).

Note: A guy's chest voice range is wide, while his middle voice range is narrow. Hence, guys normally speak in chest voice. In contrast, a woman's middle voice range is wide, while her chest voice range is narrow. Women usually speak right between chest voice and middle voice. Whether you're a guy or gal, anytime you speak, your speaking voice has pitch and registration just like your singing voice. Women have to pay special attention to their speaking voice so they can decide which pitch they speak and how they use registration.

You can practice speaking the phrases in the preceding list on a low pitch to feel the sensations of speaking in chest voice and then speak them again on a higher pitch to practice your mix. Remember that you can mix on any pitch by using a combination of head voice and chest voice (see Chapter 10 for details). As you speak the words in the preceding list, remember that you're looking to create forward resonance while monitoring how much chest voice you use on a variety of pitches. Using a chest voice sound that's really heavy when you speak makes it harder for you to generate the forward resonance.

Speaking chatty sounds on specific pitches

In addition to finding chatty sounds on any pitch, you can find those same sounds on specific pitches. The following exercise (featured on Track 82) has you speak the phrase "I wanna know," which allows you to start the tone with a vowel and a clean onset, as opposed to a glottal. (You get to decide what it is that you know — like whether you'll win the lottery or whether your date will show up tonight — so you feel more inspired to liven up the phrase.)

As you ascend, try to gradually release more chest voice. For instance, start at the bottom of the scale with 50 percent chest voice. Ladies, you may feel a pulling sensation at about the F just above Middle C, which means you need to start lightening up the chest voice. The pitch where you feel the pulling sensation may be slightly higher or lower than the F since voices vary on where they feel the transitions. Guys, you may feel this pulling sensation anywhere from the D to F just above Middle C. Remember that you don't want to go all the way into head voice. Your goal is to maintain some chest voice but to use a lighter percentage of chest voice as you go up the scale. As you ascend, the vibrations of resonance move forward and higher to help release some of the weight of chest voice. Then as you descend, the sensation reverses as you gradually add chest voice.

Listen to Track 82 to hear the singer demonstrate the sound for you. Notice that the singer uses a mix (chest voice and head voice). As she speaks up the scale, notice how the sound stays in a mix and doesn't fall into a heavy chest voice. You can also hear how the resonance moves higher as she ascends. Now it's your turn. Listen as the piano plays the pitch two times; as you listen, take your breath and get your body ready to make the sound. As the piano plays the pitch the third time, speak the text "I wanna know" on that pitch. The lower pitches may feel heavier. You can allow a little more chest voice when you're speaking lower in your range, but don't use 100 percent chest voice.

You're speaking on pitch for this exercise, not singing. *Speaking on pitch* means you don't need to sustain the tone as you do when you sing.

TRACK 82

I wan-na know.   I wan-na know.

Working on your speaking range

The text of a belt song is often chatty or conversational. Working on your speaking range helps you practice making chatty sounds in a wider range than you normally speak. The following exercise (featured on Track 83) has you speaking the phrase "that fat man," which uses a bright vowel in each word and encourages a little more thickness (chest voice) in your sound (although you can also use the phrase "I wanna know" if you need to work on lightening up the sound). Be prepared to use your breath and keep it flowing consistently while you're moving up and down the scale and remember to climb the resonance ladder as I describe in the section "Resonating All the Way to the Back Row." *Tip:* To get the resonance forward, pretend that the really fat man in the exercise is crowded next to you on an airplane.

Listen to the singer demonstrate the sound for you on Track 83. Notice that the sound is chatty and that the resonance changes as the pitches descend. After you listen to the singer demonstrate the sounds, play the track again and speak the phrase "That fat man" on the variations in pitch you hear on the track. Because this exercise starts pretty high, try starting in a head voice–dominated mix and then adding 1 percent chest voice with each new pitch. (You can review the percentage exercise in Chapter 8 to discover how to add and take away layers of thickness in chest voice.)

TRACK 83

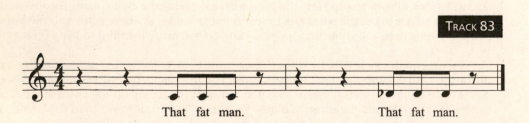

That fat man.   That fat man.

Using different phrases to expand your speaking range

To expand your speaking range — and also discover how to maintain forward resonance on different vowels — give the following exercise on Track 84 a shot. The words you speak are "Not now! Oh, no! Not now!" The first time you say "not now," pay attention to where you feel the resonance. As you sing "oh, no," you need to go back to that same height on the word *no*. You can use the visual of the vibrations of resonance climbing the ladder on your face. The ladder starts at your mouth and moves up beside your nose to the bridge of your nose and even up to your forehead. You want the same buzzing vibrations on the words *not now* and *oh, no*. As you say *not now,* notice the sensations of the vibrations. You want to reverse that sensation when you ascend on the words *oh, no*. What you don't want is for the sensation to be heavier as you ascend on *oh, no*.

Listen to the singer on Track 84 demonstrate the sounds for you and then play the track again and join in. The pattern moves pretty high on purpose. Challenge yourself to figure out how to find just the right resonance and the right balance of chest voice as you speak. You can turn off the track when it gets too high.

TRACK 84

Developing Stamina for Belting

Because belting requires more effort than making lighter sounds, you need to use a lot of physical coordination to connect air to sound and develop stamina. To develop enough stamina to get through a belt song, you need to practice your belt sounds for short periods of time daily. Most beginner belters can work on their belt sounds for 10 to 15 minutes before getting tired.

If you normally speak softly, you may want to practice speaking louder to develop your stamina and endurance. Find a place where no one will worry if you sound like you're yelling. Then practice speaking the following phrases (or any other phrases that inspire you to make loud sounds) loudly:

- Dad, Ma made me mad.
- Hey, man!
- No, I don't care.
- Taxi!

Be sure to take a breath and use your breath to make the loud spoken sound. Focus on using a mix that has some chest voice in it and isn't all head voice.

Practice speaking loudly for several minutes at a time over a few days. Work up to two minutes twice a day. When you feel confident speaking loudly for two minutes, you should notice more strength in your voice and especially in the skills you use in the belting exercises. If you tire easily, check your breath coordination. Place your hands on your sides to check the movement of your ribs, abs, sides, and back while you sing. You need to open all these areas on the inhalation and then slowly allow the muscles to move back to their resting position as you sing. Pushing in or shoving won't help you sustain the note with breath. You need solid breath coordination to help make these fuller sounds or you will press in your throat. Chapter 2 has a lot of exercises for developing breath coordination for singing.

 Never yell without supporting the sound with your body. If you normally speak with a head voice–dominated sound, you can practice adding more chest voice to your speech. Adding more chest voice to your spoken sounds is similar to what you want to do when you belt. You add more chest voice by adding more weight to the tone. Keep in mind, though, that adding weight isn't the same as pressing. Check out Chapter 8 for more information about weight in the chest voice.

Comparing Belt and Mix

Sometimes people use the words *belt* and *mix* interchangeably, so knowing which term means what can be confusing. When I talk about *mix,* I'm referring to a balance of registration, or a mixture of some head and chest voice happening at the same time. I use *belt* to mean that you use that same balance of registration (that is, mix) while using forward resonance. If someone asks you to *mix belt,* that means using a sound that has forward resonance and also a mix of registration. People began using the term *mix belt* so that singers would belt using mix instead of pushing heavy chest voice.

Pay attention to the following characteristics to help you distinguish belt from mix as you listen to songs:

Belt

The sound of belt is really forward and brassy. In other words, belt sounds aren't gentle and delicate. The sounds are bold and daring. Belt also sounds like it's pure chest voice even when it isn't.

Belt feels like a lot of resonance bouncing around in your face.

Because you use some chest voice when you belt, it may also feel more powerful than your head voice.

Mix

The sound of mix can be quite varied, from head voice dominated to chest voice dominated, or it can be a blend of the two. Either way, though, the sound is neither forward nor brassy.

Mix feels like the resonance is more in the middle of your head.

Generally speaking, mix feels like head voice when you use more head voice than chest voice, but it feels like a light chest voice when you use more chest voice than head voice.

 Listen to Chapter 10's mix tracks with this chapter's belt tracks for a side-by-side comparison of the sounds the singer makes. Refer to the appendix to determine which tracks are which.

Changing from mix to belt on one note

Sometimes songs have you sustain a note and change from mix to belt, so you definitely want to get some practice with this particular technique. In the following exercise, featured on Track 85, you work on moving from a mix to a belt. Follow these steps to get the most out of this exercise:

1. **Practice saying the vowels in the words *no* and *cat*.**

   Notice that the resonance of the vowel in *cat* naturally wants to roll farther forward than the vowel in the word *no*. The vowel in *no* is the vowel you need to mix in this exercise, and the vowel in *cat* is the one you need to belt.

2. **Sing the words *no* and *cat* on the same note.**

   As you sing, notice where the vowels vibrate. The *oh* in *no* should vibrate in the middle of your mouth or on your teeth. The *a* in *cat* should vibrate in your face or very forward. If you don't feel it in your face or forward, try out the suggestions listed in the section "Resonating All the Way to the Back Row." After you're confident that the resonance rolls forward on the *a*, sing the two vowels again to feel the change in resonance.

3. **Sing the two vowels on one note without stopping between them.**

   Intentionally roll the resonance forward as you move from the *oh* to the *a*. Be sure you're using a mix and not a heavy chest voice.

   To help you hear what this step should sound like, listen to Track 85, on which the singer demonstrates rolling from a mix to a belt, using the two vowels *a* and *oh*.

TRACK 85

oh__ a__   oh__ a__   oh__ a__

Songs that move from mix to belt

The songs in the following list all begin with a mix and gradually progress to a belt. You may notice that the opening of each song involves the character discovering something or trying to make a decision on how to proceed. As the story (that is, song) progresses and the character gets more specific about circumstances, the sounds move to a belt.

- ✔ "I Don't Know How to Love Him" from *Jesus Christ Superstar* by Andrew Lloyd Webber and Tim Rice
- ✔ "Let Me Come Home" from *The Wedding Singer* by Matthew Sklar and Chad Beguelin
- ✔ "Out of the Blue" from *The Wild Party* by Andrew Lippa
- ✔ "Touch-A-Touch-A-Touch Me" from *Rocky Horror Show* by Richard O'Brien
- ✔ "With One Look" from *Sunset Boulevard* by Andrew Lloyd Webber
- ✔ "I Just Want To Be a Star" from *Nunsense* by Dan Goggin

✔ "What Doesn't Kill You" by Kelly Clarkson

✔ "Cry" by Angie Aparo as sung by Faith Hill

✔ "My Heart Will Go On" from the film *Titanic* by James Horner and Will Jennings as sung by Celine Dion

✔ "Listen" from *Dreamgirls* by Henry Krieger and Tom Eyen as sung by Beyoncé

Belting Your Face Off

In the world of casting directors, agents, and managers, you need to be familiar with the phrase *belting your face off* because people often use it to describe the process of really singing out and making bold belt sounds. Notice that this phrase doesn't mean to push or press and make harsh sounds, and it certainly doesn't mean that your face falls off! When you *belt your face off,* you're simply putting the sound in the room and making sure your audience notices you. And that, after all, is the whole point of belting in the first place!

In the next sections, you get to test out your belting sounds by practicing belt phrases in different keys. The following exercises gradually progress to higher keys so you can practice expanding your belt range. Each pattern starts lower and modulates higher. You don't have to sing all the modulations. Work as high as you feel comfortable doing, knowing that you can continue working on your belt to master the higher keys in future practice sessions.

Applying your belt sounds to a tune

Track 86 features a chatty belt exercise that's good to tackle after you practice the exercises in the earlier section "Chatting It Up." Listen to the track first. Then play it again and sing along (see the following figure for the words and music). As you ascend in pitch, allow your vibrations of resonance to climb the resonance ladder. (I tell you all about this in the earlier section "Resonating All the Way to the Back Row.") You want the highest note of the phrase to resonate higher on your resonance ladder. Although the sound may feel as if it narrows as you go higher in pitch, you don't have to narrow the space in your throat accordingly. The space won't be as large as it is when you sing your classical songs, but it needs to remain open if you want to create a vibrant tone.

If you flip into head voice and the resonance rolls backward, you can modify the vowels in the words to keep the sound forward and belt like. For example, you can make all the vowels in the song similar to the *a* in *cat.* Or, if *a* doesn't work for you, you can make all the vowels like the *ay* in *day.* Although modifying all the vowels sounds funny, doing so can help you get used to applying your belt sounds to a tune. When you can feel where the sound vibrates as you modify the vowels, you can go back to singing the actual vowels in the words and maintain the same sounds and sensations in the resonance.

The exercise on Track 86 changes keys several times. Feel free to sing the first key (shown in the following figure) until you gain confidence. When you feel more confident combining the forward resonance with mix, you can sing all the repetitions along with the track.

TRACK 86

Increasing your belt range

The belt exercise on Track 87 is perfect for helping you increase your belt range. The melody descends, but then you have to leap up a large interval. That interval is in the phrase on purpose. Very often singers get stuck when they have to leap up a large interval in a belt song. They try to hit the leaping interval by pushing up more chest voice to get the note to come out, and they end up with a ceiling on their belt. They can go only so high or can sing the note only a limited number of times because they sing it with so much heavy pressure from too much chest voice.

For this exercise, first listen to the singer demonstrate the sounds for you on Track 87. Then listen to it again and sing along, focusing on the words "that man" in the phrase "that man can't find me." Notice how the top note sounds and feels when you sing the descending pattern. Then sing the notes in a different order. For instance, sing "man that" and notice the height of resonance on the word *man*. Finally, sing the notes in the correct order, paying attention to how high the resonance goes on the ascending interval. If you have a hard time hitting the leaping interval on the words "that man," check out the exercise in the earlier section "Using different phrases to expand your speaking range," where you sing descending and then ascending intervals.

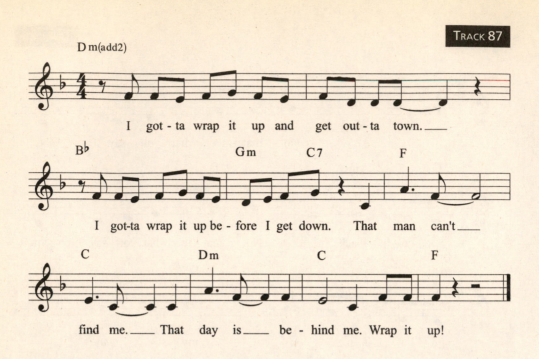

TRACK 87

Developing vocal stamina

Track 88's short belt exercise challenges you to sustain several higher belt notes as well as to sing multiple higher belt notes. Consider this exercise your chance to figure out how not only to belt higher but also to develop the stamina for a song that has more than one or two higher belt notes. The notes in the song stay a little higher than the belt exercises I present earlier in the chapter.

As you sing through this exercise, be sure to take a solid breath and then use your body and the movement of the air to help you sustain the notes. If you feel like the exercise sits a little too high for you right now, you can allow the sound to flip into your head voice until you develop your belt sound enough that you can sing all the notes. You don't want to push to sing this higher belt song if you're not ready. *Tip:* You can sing this song in a mix if you aren't yet a confident belter.

Testing Out Your Belt Sounds with Practice Pieces

Here's your chance for a real belting workout. Guys, the first practice piece is for you. It's a short rock song that I think you'll enjoy singing. Listen to the sounds first so you know what a male voice sounds like when applying the information from this chapter.

Ladies, the second practice piece is all yours. It moves from a mix into a belt. Head straight there or turn to Chapter 10 if you need a little help with your mix.

"Don't You Tell Me No Lie"

Is belting in a rock song different from belting in a pop song? And how does belting in other contemporary styles of singing compare? The answer to these questions depends on the song in question — specifically the tune of that song. For example, if you're singing a song made famous by Tina Turner or Rod Stewart, the sound that you expect to make has more bite in it than a song sung by Barbra Streisand or Elvis Presley.

The specific belting technique used by rock singers may include allowing little or no vibrato (see Chapter 12), sustaining a note for emotional value rather than musical value, and allowing the emotions to dictate the overall sound. In short, unlike classical singers, who sing the whole value of every note, pop and rock singers aren't as concerned with making perfectly correct sounds, and they sustain the note only long enough to make the point in the text. They dare to make a breathy tone or a scratchy tone on purpose because it fits the mood of their song.

To see what I mean, try out this practice piece, which is shown in the following figure and featured on Track 89. In the song "Don't You Tell Me No Lie," you can be a little more laid back with your articulation. Be clear enough that your audience can understand you but not so precise that you pronounce each and every syllable perfectly. Sing the song like you would speak it. Keep the text moving as if you were speaking on pitch. Because most of the notes are chatty, you don't need to use much, if any, vibrato. (Using too much vibrato in this style of music makes it sound like you're "oversinging.") You also want to fall off the notes instead of sustaining a full sound through to the end of each note.

"It's Time"

The short practice piece "It's Time," which you can see in the following figure and hear on Track 90, starts in a mix and moves to a belt. The melody is chatty in the beginning and continues to build toward a belt. As in many songs, the sounds build as the intensity of the story builds. In other words, as a song unfolds, the sounds of the voice should build as the excitement of the story grows and a realization happens. To start in a mix, make the sound chatty and use a balance of registration — some chest voice and some head voice. As you move from mix to belt, change the resonance and gradually move the sound forward.

Listen to the singer demonstrate the sounds for you. You hear her start the song in a mix and then change over to a belt later in the song. Notice how the resonance changes as she moves into the belt. The sound moves forward and the tone has more bite to it. You may need to listen to the track several times to hear the difference in the sounds.

Cooling Down Your Voice after Belting

Belting is a high-energy sport that requires a lot of stamina. Just as you cool down your body after you get really hot and sweaty at the gym, you need to cool down your voice every time you finish belting. Think of belting as an intense vocal workout. After this intense workout, you need to let the muscles cool down gradually and then give them recovery time. Turn to the end of Chapter 1 for a great cool-down exercise. Although it's meant as a warm-up in that chapter, you can use it to cool down your voice, too.

If you don't have the exercises in this book with you and you need to cool down, sing patterns that are in the middle part of your voice and gradually sing softer and softer. You don't have to go all the way down to a whisper; you just need to go down to a softer volume with less pressure.

Keep in mind that after belting hard in a performance or practice session, you may want to be quiet for a while afterward to let the voice rest. Going to the after party, where you have to speak loudly, only continues to tire out your voice. Schedule some time for quiet so that you can rest your voice to get it ready to belt again the next day.

Songs for Beginner Belters Looking to Try Out Their Technique

These songs aren't easy, but they aren't impossible for a beginner belter who has been working on belt exercises. The goal when working on these songs is to develop your belt enough that you're confident you can maintain the resonance and balance the registration. You can break down the songs into sections and gradually work your way up to the higher sections. Mezzos, you can start with lower belt songs until you gradually develop your higher belt. Sopranos, you may find it easier to belt higher songs than lower songs. (Guys, you can find songs in the next list that help you apply the concepts from this chapter.)

- ✔ "You Can't Get a Man with a Gun" from *Annie Get Your Gun* by Irving Berlin
- ✔ "There Are Worse Things I Could Do" from *Grease* by Jim Jacobs and Warren Casey
- ✔ "Good Morning Baltimore" from *Hairspray* by Marc Shaiman and Scott Wittman
- ✔ "The Love of My Life" from *Brigadoon* by Alan Jay Lerner and Frederick Loewe
- ✔ "I Think I May Want to Remember Today" from *Starting Here, Starting Now* by Richard Maltby and David Shire
- ✔ "Ooh! My Feet" from *The Most Happy Fella* by Frank Loesser
- ✔ "One of the Girls" from *Woman of the Year* by John Kander and Fred Ebb
- ✔ "I Cain't Say No" from *Oklahoma!* by Richard Rodgers and Oscar Hammerstein II
- ✔ "Shy" from *Once on This Mattress* by Mary Rodgers and Marshall Barer
- ✔ "What Did I Have That I Don't Have?" from *On a Clear Day You Can See Forever* by Burton Lane and Alan Jay Lerner

Songs for Advanced Belters Looking for a Challenge

This list of songs includes belt songs from musical theater, pop, and rock that are challenging in a variety of ways. The challenges may include a higher range, repeated high notes, or a variety of vowels. (Guys, the songs that are marked either or male allow you to make the sounds described in the chapter, but you won't find them listed anywhere as belt songs for men.)

- "Rags" from *Rags* by Joseph Stein, Stephen Schwartz, and Charles Strouse
- "Oklahoma?" from *Dirty Rotten Scoundrels* by David Yazbek
- "Holding Out for a Hero" by Jim Steinman and Dean Pitchford as sung by Bonnie Tyler in the film *Footloose*
- "What Am I Doin'?" from *Closer Than Ever* by Richard Maltby and David Shire (male)
- "The Edge of Glory" by Lady Gaga
- "Mr. Know It All" by Brian Kennedy, Ester Dean, and Brett James as sung by Kelly Clarkson
- "Cowboy Casanova" by Mike Elizondo and Brett James as sung by Carrie Underwood
- "Crazy" by Steven Tyler, Joe Perry, and Desmond Child as sung by Aerosmith (either)
- "You Give Love a Bad Name" by Jon Bon Jovi, Desmond Child, and Richie Sambora as sung by Bon Jovi (either)
- "One Song Glory" from *Rent* by Jonathan Larson (male)

Part V
The Part of Tens

The 5th Wave   By Rich Tennant

"So you're attempting to learn how to sing, but your wife hates country music... Go on..."

In this part . . .

*W*ant some pointers on developing your practice routine so you can make consistent progress in improving your singing skills? Have burning questions that you want the answers to, right here and right now? This part has what you're looking for.

It's also home to the appendix, which shows you which CD tracks pair up with which exercises so you can find the information you need quickly without having to play through every CD track or flip through every page in the book.

Chapter 15

Ten Tips for Practicing Like a Pro

In This Chapter

▶ Creating a practice routine

▶ Finding the right exercises to practice

▶ Preparing for a performance

Singing practice can be a whole lot of fun, or it can be really boring, depending on what you do during it. If your practices lean more in the boring direction, you've come to the right place. This chapter offers ten tips to make your practice sessions productive and fun. In it, I help you organize your practice sessions so you can make the most progress, and I show you how to use your practice time to prepare for the main event: your performance.

Set Aside Time to Focus on Singing

Try to make some time in your practice schedule to focus all your attention on your singing technique. Being able to multi-task while singing is good when you're on the stage, but trying to work on too many things during practice when you're in the early stages of developing technique can slow down your progress.

Allowing at least 30 minutes for each practice session gives you enough time to make progress without making a huge dent in your daily schedule. Most singers need about 10 minutes just to get physically and vocally warmed up enough that they can start to practice their technique. Think of each practice session as having three parts: the warm-up (physical and vocal), the technique drills, and then the application of those drills to the songs you sing. Knowing you want to have these three components in each practice session helps you figure out how long you need to practice.

After you decide on the length of your practice session, figure out a way to make practicing part of your daily routine. If you have that time marked in your schedule, you're more likely to practice regularly. Repetition from practicing regularly is key to developing muscle memory and becoming a better singer.

Plan What to Practice

Spending time practicing your technique helps you reinforce and refine your skills so that you can continue to make progress as a singer. During every practice session, you want to do all three of the following:

1. **Warm up.**

2. **Practice exercises to reinforce your technique.**

3. **Apply that technique to your songs.**

As you plan each practice session, choose exercises from the chapters in this book and work on the accompanying tracks on the CD. Try to choose exercises that challenge you but aren't too far beyond your current skill level. Look over the topics I cover in this book (the table of contents is a good place to start) and choose exercises that work on skills and techniques that interest you. The exercises in each chapter are progressive, so the exercises at the beginning are easier than the ones near the end.

You can choose to do all the exercises from one chapter in one practice session, but you may prefer to choose a variety of exercises from several different chapters to keep your interest up. Whatever exercises you decide to do, make sure you work on multiple skills over the course of several practices. After all, you don't want to be great at one skill and terrible at another.

Don't give in to the temptation to practice just your song. Doing so helps your song sound great but doesn't help you advance your technique. Instead, continue developing your technique so that each new song starts at a higher level of skill.

After you decide what to practice, gather the equipment you need so you can get to practicing right away. Get your electronic equipment for playing the CD tracks ready. You need a glass of water, your music, and a recording device so you can listen back to the differences in the sounds you make during the session. You may want to have two devices, one to play the tracks and one to record you singing along.

Use the Exercises in This Book

The exercises in this book have accompanying tracks where singers demonstrate the sounds for you. Their singing helps you connect the description in the chapter with a specific sound. The first time you hear a track, you may want to just listen to the singer and follow along with the pattern in the chapter. After you know the pattern and the sounds you want to make, you can sing along with the track and practice making the sounds yourself.

Be sure to read the in-text descriptions for each exercise because some of the tracks don't have a singer to demonstrate sounds; they just have the piano playing the pattern. These exercises give you an opportunity to really listen to yourself making the sounds.

Try not to give in to the temptation to go through all the book's tracks right away. The exercises range from easy to hard and are designed to keep you challenged for a long time. Take your time working on each exercise. You may find that the first few repetitions are easy and in just the right range for you, but the range may get more challenging as the track progresses. Work on the portion of the track that's comfortable for you first; then gradually work your way up to the harder segments.

Record Your Practice Sessions

You can record your practice sessions in a couple of ways, depending on how you plan to use the recording. Making an audio recording of your practice sessions allows you to listen to your singing to hear your progress and to take note of areas that you still need to work on. Making a video recording allows you to both listen and see yourself practicing. You can even watch without listening to the sound so you can objectively watch how your body moves when you sing. As you watch or listen to the recordings of your practice sessions, you may want to keep track of the exercises you practice and the improvement you make in a journal.

Use a good-quality digital recording device so you can hear the most realistic sound of your voice as possible. The sounds you're exploring during your practice sessions can be subtle, so just make sure your device is good enough to really hear the quality of your voice and the different sounds you're making with very little static.

Track Your Progress

Looking back over your progress helps you set future goals and feel good about your accomplishments. The best way to keep track of your progress is by keeping a journal of what you practiced and when. Use the following categories to help you get started on your journal:

- **Date of practice session:** The date just helps you keep track of when you did a particular practice session.

- **Time of day:** Noting the time of day helps you discover which time of day is best for your practice sessions.

- **Length of session:** Keeping track of the length of your sessions is particularly important if you're preparing for a performance and want to test your endurance.

- **Stretches for the physical warm-up:** You may note over time that you refine your physical warm-up to a very specific series of movements that get you physically warm in a short period of time.

- **Exercises for the vocal warm-up:** You may find that you develop a specific series of exercises that you do at the beginning of every practice to get your voice warmed up. You may even be able to combine the physical and vocal warm-ups to save time.

- **Exercises for developing technique:** The exercises you practice for developing technique are extremely important. If you're monitoring your progress on your own without a teacher, you have to monitor your progress and decide when you're ready to move on to the next lesson. Be patient and don't rush through exercises, and try to find ways to test your skills to determine when you're ready to move on. Keep track of your thoughts on what you hear from your practice recordings.

- **Songs you sing to apply the technique:** Make a list of songs you really want to work on and put them in order of difficulty. Make a note of what you need to accomplish before you can tackle each piece. For example, if you wanted to practice the "Star-Spangled Banner," you might make the following list of things to practice first:

  - **Register transitions:** To help you manage the phrases that move between registers (see Chapter 11)

  - **Articulation of consonants and vowels:** To help you make sure the right shapes and sounds happen throughout the song (see Chapters 3 and 4)

  - **Range:** To help you develop the high notes in the song (see Part III)

  - **Breath coordination:** To help you handle the long phrases (see Chapter 2)

  - **Sustained tones and vibrato:** To help you manage the vibrato on the notes that sustain (see Chapter 12)

After you make a list of the skills that are important for the song you want to sing, you can make a list of exercises that address these skills so that you can gradually improve your technique and sing the song better by the time of the performance.

Cool Down after Practicing

After working out at the gym, many people take time to cool off before going back outside. You need to do the same thing after you sing, especially when your practice session was long and challenging. Use the exercise on Track 1 that helped you warm up to cool down, too (see Chapter 1 for this track). You want to go from making big noisy sounds to gradually winding down to making softer and lighter middle voice sounds to get your voice back to neutral.

Know When to Rest

You know you're vocally tired after a singing session if your muscles feel warm like they do when you work out. Muscles that are tired after a practice session recoup pretty fast; you can rest for a few hours and then practice again. But if your muscles are hurting or you feel strain after your session, you need to review your session to find out what went wrong:

- ✔ Double-check your breathing to make sure you were really consistent with keeping the breath flowing.

- ✔ Monitor how you were changing registers to make sure you weren't pushing the boundaries of a register too far and causing strain.

- ✔ Make sure the song you're singing isn't too taxing for you. If your song just exhausts your voice, consider taking it down to a lower key until you develop your technique enough to manage the higher key.

Being tired after practicing is different from the vocal fatigue you feel when you've been singing incorrectly.

At the first sign of sickness, your voice may feel different. Observe the sensations you feel in your throat, such as scratching, burning, or itching. Itching may just mean your allergies are acting up and you need to get out your Neti pot or your nasal saline solution to keep the pollens out of your nasal passages. A burning sensation may mean you're getting sick and your body is trying to fight off whatever is coming on. A scratchy throat can mean your vocal cords are slightly swollen and are having difficulty moving as easily as normal. If you feel an illness coming on, rest your voice for a few days.

If you've done something foolish like scream at a game or yell over the music at a club, rest your voice. Your voice may need several days to return to normal after screaming. Allow your voice to rest by keeping quiet — no talking, no whispering, no sound coming out of your mouth. Try not to scream too much on a regular basis. Those little muscles usually recover with rest, but they may not recover 100 percent every time if you continue to abuse your voice.

Get to Know Your Song and Your Story

Practicing your song involves working on the melody, rhythm, text, phrasing, and all kinds of other details. As you practice your song, focus on one element at a time:

1. **Memorize the text as a monologue.**

   Write out the text and study the punctuation and meaning of the words so you know exactly what the story is about. After you know the story of the text, memorize the text by memorizing one line at a time. Memorize the first line and say it aloud to make sure you know it. Then memorize the second line and say it aloud.

Say the first two lines aloud from memory. Continue to memorize one new line at a time and add it to the previous lines. When you have the whole song memorized, practice speaking the text aloud to make sure you don't stumble or forget any sections. Then speak through the words quickly without stopping to pause. Doing so forces you to think ahead and simulates what happens in a performance.

2. **Explore the rhythm.**

   Tap out the rhythm (without singing) so you know exactly how much time to give each note. (See Chapter 6 for more on rhythm.)

3. **Speak the text in the rhythm of the melody.**

   Don't sing the song yet; just focus on getting the timing of the words.

4. **Learn the melody without the words.**

   Take time to focus on the melody line and intervals so you can drill the musical precision without having to worry about anything else. Sing through the melody on a vowel to explore the phrasing and breath control you need to sing the song. (Turn to Chapter 5 for details on intervals and Chapter 2 for help with breath control.)

5. **Put everything together.**

   Now that you know the many parts of the song, you can put them all together and practice singing the song as a whole. If you try to put everything together before you know the individual parts, you'll need a lot more time to learn a new song.

After you have the song going, take some time to prepare the story behind the song. Use your acting skills to decide the full story you want to tell so you know the sounds you need to make as you sing. You could just vocalize and show off your beautiful voice, but your audience wants to experience the story you tell, not just hear your voice.

After you know the words of the song and the story behind them, you're ready to explore the song physically. Depending on the type of song you sing, your physical portrayal of the song may vary. Performing a rock song is much more laid back than performing a musical theater or classical song. Watch other performers to know what's customary for the style of music you're singing and then prepare what you plan to do as you sing. Here are some examples of what you may want to do:

- ✔ **Make hand and arm gestures.** When you gesture, make sure each gesture enhances the story. Random gestures may be fun to make, but they don't enhance the story, and they may make you look like you choreographed the song without a purpose.

- ✔ **Move around the stage.** Decide how much space you have in the performance to determine how much movement you can add to your song. Moving around is customary in a lot of styles of music, but you want the movement to enhance the story or you'll look like you're wandering aimlessly around the stage.

When you've finished all the physical preparation for the song — from the gestures to the technical skills — then you're ready to prepare the song for the performance.

Prepare for the Performance

Practicing for a performance gives you the opportunity not only to practice your technical skills but also to apply them in front of an audience. To prepare for a performance, you want to practice your song and then practice what you're going to experience at the performance.

The week prior to the event try to run through the song each day to simulate the performance. That means you have to memorize your song at least one week before the event. (Don't memorize the song the day before the event; you want the song to be in your long-term memory rather than just your short-term memory.)

Schedule several run-through simulations the week before the performance. If you can do the run-through in the room where you'll perform, go for it! If you can't get into the performance space, don't worry. You can simulate the room at home. Practice the entrance onto the stage or into the room and then sing your song and exit. As you practice your entrance, be sure to practice breathing while you're moving. You don't want to hold your breath as you enter because if you do, you have to start the song out of breath. Time the breath so you inhale with the first step, and continue to inhale and exhale as you enter. After singing through the song, practice your bow or your acknowledgment to the applause and then take a breath and make your exit.

Practice singing through your song when you're flustered rather than just when you're calm. Practicing your song when you're slightly out of breath is more similar to what you'll experience in the performance.

Find Help from a Voice Teacher

Finding a voice teacher may seem daunting, but it's really not. Just start by asking your friends and colleagues whether they have a singing teacher they like. If they're really nice, your friends or colleagues may even allow you to observe one of their lessons so you know what to expect going into your own first voice lesson. Or you can call the local music store, music college, or conservatory and ask for suggestions for voice teachers. After you find a possible teacher, make a list of what you want to find out about, including the following:

- ✔ Cost of lessons
- ✔ Length of each lesson
- ✔ Payment plan options (cash only, credit cards, checks, online payment options)
- ✔ Frequency of lessons
- ✔ Cancellation policy

After you know the logistics, ask what you need to bring to each lesson, such as sheet music or audio recordings of your songs, a recording device, and a notebook or practice journal. Expect to answer a few questions at the first lesson so that your teacher knows what your goals are and how to best structure your lessons. You may want to try a few lessons to decide whether the teacher is the right fit for you.

Chapter 16

Ten Questions Singers Ask Frequently

In This Chapter

▶ Blending your voice with other singers and instruments

▶ Preparing your mind and body before your performance

▶ Discovering what you can do to keep your voice healthy

This chapter offers answers to ten common questions that singers ask. Knowing the answers to these questions now can help you make good choices to keep your singing voice healthy for years to come. These choices range from how you develop and use your technique to how you prepare for your performance.

What Style of Music Is Right for My Voice?

The style of music you like to listen to may be different from the style you're able to sing. Listen to various styles of music to determine what you like. Pay attention to the sounds of the singers you hear. Listen for voices like yours, and then listen to the songs they sing. If you like the sounds of the style, record yourself singing along and play back your recording to see how you sound.

You can't change your voice type, but you can vary the sounds you make to match the style you're singing. Doing so can help you develop your technique, and the more developed your technique, the more confident you can be in determining which style of music best suits your skills.

Singing classical music calls for singing long phrases, big, bold sounds, and the exact words on the page, while singing rock music calls for a lot less precision. Know your voice and the sounds you do well and be aware of what sounds different music styles require. Being able to change your sound enough for a classical song and then a rock song takes practice. You have to practice making the right sounds in different songs, and you have to know what's right for different styles of music.

When Is a Song out of My Range?

When you hear a song on the radio that you absolutely love, you're probably tempted to order the sheet music right away so that you can learn the song, but not every song is in your singing range. Looking at a sheet of music to find out whether a song is within your range takes a little practice, but it's pretty easy after you get the hang of it. You can start by practicing the exercises in this book and noticing which high or low notes are comfortable for you to sing. Compare the high notes in your sheet music to the high notes in the exercises in this book to see if they're the same; if they are, you're probably good to go with the song you've picked. If the notes in the sheet music are way higher, you may need to pick a new song. Check out Chapter 5 for info on naming notes. You can also find out more about reading music in *Music Theory for Dummies* by Holly Day and Michael Pilhofer (Wiley).

At some point, you may find that you're comfortable singing a really high note in an exercise but not so comfortable singing the same note in a song. You can challenge yourself to develop the technical skills needed to sing the note in the song, but you need to be realistic and not choose a song with a high note that's well beyond your comfort zone. You need time and patience to develop your range, and you want to gradually extend your range instead of pushing your way up to the high notes too quickly. Trying to push your way up too quickly may cause your tone to be strained.

In addition to looking at the notes themselves in the sheet music, you need to recognize the rhythm of those notes. For example, singing a high note that's sustained or that requires difficult articulation for consonants is a very different experience than just quickly singing through the note. To decide whether you can sing the high note as it's written, try sustaining the note to see whether you feel confident and the note sounds comfortable. You may want to record yourself to hear just how comfortable the note sounds. Then sing the note by adding words from the song to see whether you can manage sustaining the note and articulating at the same time.

The same is true for low notes. You may be able to vocalize to a really low note on just the right vowel, but that same note may be difficult to reach in a song because of the vowel in the word. Notice which low notes you're comfortable singing in your vocal exercises; then test those notes out by singing different vowels or by adding different words to the exercise. Doing so can help you determine whether you can sing that particular note on any vowel.

Am I Tone Deaf or Just Singing Out of Tune?

If you're *tone deaf,* you haven't discovered how to hear whether your voice matches the pitches played on the accompanying piano or the pitches you hear in a song. If you sing *out of tune,* you can sing the right notes, but you don't sing them exactly in tune (you're slightly higher or lower than the actual pitch). Singers who are tone deaf may not notice that they aren't matching the pitches. Singers who sing out of tune, on the other hand, know they hit the right notes but just don't sing them exactly on pitch.

To practice matching your pitches to the pitches in the songs you sing, play a note on the piano and slide around on pitch until you hear how your voice vibrates the same as the pitch you play. When your voice matches that of the piano, the vibrations sound the same; when your pitches don't match, your voice clashes with the pitch the piano plays. You may not match the piano's pitch perfectly the first few times you try, but keep at it because with each attempt, you improve your sense of pitch.

If you have trouble singing in tune, you need to check your technique instead of trying to fix each note. Focus on your breath coordination as you sing to make sure you're moving breath consistently as you sing. Sing very specific vowels with very specific shapes. Monitor how your sound resonates. If the sound is too dark and the resonance is really far back in your mouth and throat, you may be singing flat. If you push too much, you may be singing sharp. Developing your sense of pitch takes time and patience, so don't give up if you have a hard time singing in tune at first. Focus on improving your overall technique to develop the physical coordination you need to be able to sing different pitches accurately.

How Do I Blend with Other Singers?

When you perform a solo, it's all about you, but when you're singing in a choir or other musical group, you must blend your voice with the group to create a cohesive sound. *Blending with other singers* means creating a tone that's similar to the other voices.

To blend with other singers, you want to

- **Match your volume to that of those around you.** Singing too loudly makes your voice stick out, which isn't good for group singing unless the choir director or group leader has specifically asked you to sing out to lead the others. (If that happens, the other singers need to blend with you.) On the other hand, singing too softly keeps you from being heard at all.

- **Blend your vibrato with the other singers.** Most choir directors ask the singers to blend their vibrato. For most singers, blending their vibrato means using less vibrato than they do when they sing solo. Matching the group's vibrato is especially important when you sing high notes. Listen to the other singers and allow your vibrato to match theirs, or use straight tone if that's what your director prefers. (*Straight tone* is when a singer chooses not to allow the vibrato to start. For more about straight tone and vibrato, flip to Chapter 12.)

- **Blend your articulation with the other singers.** Listen to the other singers in your group so that you can articulate the consonants — especially the ending consonants — at the same time.

How Do 1 Blend My Voice with Instruments?

If you want to blend your voice with an instrument, you have to listen to the sounds in the room rather than just the ones inside your head, and you have to focus on two main points:

- **Volume:** Some instruments make a lot of noise while others are softer. You have to vary your volume to blend with the volume of whatever instrument you're singing with, but your audience needs to hear your sound slightly louder than the instrument.

- **Tone:** Some instruments, like the flute, have a really high pitch (or frequency of sound); others, like the string bass, have a low pitch. Be sure to blend your resonance with that of the instrument accompanying you. To blend with a higher instrument such as the flute, allow the resonance to shift higher and lighter; to blend with the string bass, allow the resonance to shift lower.

The following instrumental accompaniments require a little extra work on your part:

- **Organ:** With some organs, particularly those in churches, the sounds they make come out of pipes that are far away from the console. If the organ pipes are at the other end of the place where you're singing, ask the organist for a rehearsal time when no one is around so you can calmly listen to and sing along with the sounds of the organ without worrying about making mistakes. It's perfectly normal to have trouble hearing the notes the first time you sing with an organ. Be patient; you'll gradually discover how to hear your notes and blend your voice with the organ.

- **Symphony or band:** If you're singing with a symphony or band, one of the instruments will play the note you need to hear to start singing. For symphonies, you can usually find your note written in the score, or you can ask the director to tell you which instrument plays your starting note. For bands, the music may not be written down, so you may just have to listen to hear the note or ask one of the musicians to play your starting note. Whether you're singing with a band or a symphony, you want to blend in musically, but you don't want to blend so well that the audience can't hear you over the instruments. Use your knowledge of resonance to be heard so you don't end up pushing out notes to be louder. For more on resonance, see Chapter 12.

What's the Best Way to Develop Vocal Endurance?

If you plan to sing in a show or performance at some point, you need to build up your vocal endurance well before the first rehearsal so that your voice can last for the entire show. After all, you don't want to get too tired before the end of the show. To build up your endurance, start with shorter practice sessions and gradually extend them to the length of your show. For example, start out with a 15- to 20-minute practice session and extend it to 30 minutes when you can easily sing for 20 minutes.

Feeling tired at the end of a practice session is perfectly normal when you're working on improving your endurance. You may need several weeks to build up your endurance to last the total length of your show, so give yourself plenty of time to practice in the weeks leading up to your show.

How Can 1 Maintain Proper Singing Posture While Playing an Instrument?

Instruments vary in shape and size, so the type of instrument you plan to play makes a difference in how you maintain your posture for singing. If you normally sit while you play your instrument, practice singing while standing to notice your posture. Notice how your body is aligned and your weight is balanced evenly throughout your body. Check out Chapter 1 for help with aligning your body. Then practice finding that same alignment when sitting in a chair without your instrument. The alignment in your torso should be the same while seated; the difference is that your legs are now bent and your feet are flat on the floor. Notice how you coordinate your breath (see Chapter 2) and align your body when you're sitting but not holding your instrument. Try to maintain this same breath coordination and body alignment when you hold your instrument.

Singing while playing the piano is slightly different than playing other instruments while sitting down. To help you develop the right posture for playing and singing, play the piano first without singing and really focus on your posture. Notice how you align your spine, how you extend your arms without any tension, and how you position your head. After you're familiar with your normal playing position, sing your song as you play to find out if you can maintain the same alignment. *Tip:* Pay special attention to how you hold your head as you sing if you're using a microphone at the piano. Angle your body so that you don't have to jut your head forward to face the audience because jutting your head forward can cause you to tighten your throat. Instead, angle your body or change the position of the microphone so you can maintain better alignment.

If you play an instrument while standing, you have to hold up both your body weight and the weight of the instrument. First, practice singing your song without your instrument. Then play your song on your instrument without singing. Pay attention to your posture as you hold your instrument. Make sure that you keep your muscles flexible and not locked. For example, check the muscles in your arms to make sure they're comfortable holding your instrument but not locked. Locking the muscles in your arms locks the muscles in your back, which affects your ability to breathe.

When (And What) Should I Eat before a Performance?

If you have a big performance coming up, you need to eat a good meal before it so that you have enough energy to carry you through the event. But you can't eat just anything anytime; you need to be smart about when and what you eat before you sing. If you try to sing a big concert right after you eat a huge meal, for example, you'll have a hard time moving the muscles in your torso. I recommend that you eat about two hours before a performance so that you have plenty of time to digest your food. (If you need some energy later on, you can always have a light snack at intermission.)

On the day of a big concert, always make sure you eat foods you've tried before. Save trying out new dishes for *after* your performance. Also, keep in mind that dairy foods may cause phlegm and spicy foods may cause bloating or indigestion, so avoid eating them on the day of a performance if they cause you problems. If you know your performance is going to be taxing with a lot of movement, you may want to eat a mix of protein for long-term energy and carbohydrates for short-term energy.

What you eat the night before may also help you on the day of the performance. If you get nervous before a performance and the butterflies in your stomach discourage you from eating much, make sure you plan the meals the day before the performance so you get some long-term energy to help carry you through the big day.

How Do I Get Over Stage Fright?

Stage fright is a big deal for a lot of singers. But you can conquer those butterflies in your stomach, your hot and sweaty palms, and even your racing heart by following these helpful tips:

- **Make sure you're really prepared for the performance.** Work on your technical skills so you can feel confident you're making all the right sounds. Then practice applying those technical skills to the song(s) you're going to sing at your performance.

- **Prepare for the inevitable adrenaline rush of a live performance by simulating the performance experience.** Invite some friends over and practice singing for them so you can get a boost of adrenaline before the performance. If you do this at least three times before the performance, you won't be as surprised when the adrenaline hits at the performance because you'll have experienced it when your friends came over to watch you perform the song. Adrenaline doesn't go away, so you might as well figure out how to use it instead of dreading it.

- **Pay attention to how you talk to yourself.** If you keep telling yourself that you're going to be terrified and sing poorly, your performance may not go nearly as well as you may have liked simply because you keep thinking negatively about it. Instead, talk positively to yourself in the weeks leading up to the performance; doing so really helps you retrain your brain to not attack you right before you go on stage. The more positively you talk about your practicing and performing, the more you train your brain to stop the negative talk.

Try writing down the negative things you say to yourself and then rephrasing them. For example, if you tend to say to yourself, "You are going to suck and everybody is going to laugh," change that negative thought to a more positive one: "I am prepared, and I can confidently apply my technique in front of an audience."

✔ **Choose the companionship you need before the performance.** Either keep to yourself before the performance or surround yourself with a friend or two who will encourage you. Ask your friends to help you stay positive.

Be prepared for people to ask you if you're nervous before a performance; it's a very common question backstage. And if you *are* nervous, that question can just make you feel worse! The good news is that you don't have to answer yes or no. Instead, you can answer with a different kind of statement like, "I'm really excited." Remember that being nervous at a performance or audition is perfectly normal, so don't panic if you are nervous. Just try not to dwell on your nerves; instead, think positive (see the preceding bullet).

Singers often ask whether they can have a drink to calm their nerves before a performance. Because alcohol dehydrates you and your vocal cords need moisture in the tissue to vibrate properly, alcohol isn't the best drink of choice right before you sing. Although using alcohol to calm your nerves may help your anxiety, doing so creates an entirely different problem that you'll have to deal with after you take the stage.

What Do I Have to Do to Keep My Voice Healthy?

Keeping your singing voice healthy starts with how you treat your speaking voice. For example, if you scream at a sporting event, you may be hoarse the next day (and that's not going to help you in the healthy voice department). One way to keep your speaking voice healthy is to use the same habits for speaking that you use for singing. For example, use your breath to speak, speak on a pitch that isn't too low or too high for you, and don't growl or make scratchy sounds when you speak. Create a clear tone just like the one you use when singing.

Medications that you take can greatly affect the singing voice. The side effect of most medications is that they dry out your throat. Check with your doctor and do a little research if you suspect that your medication may be drying out your throat. You know your throat is dry when your voice feels sluggish and starting the tone is difficult and sounds scratchy.

Here are some other tips that can help you keep your voice healthy:

✔ **Get plenty of sleep.** Many singers need at least eight hours of sleep each night. After you've been singing for a little while, you'll have a pretty good idea of just how much sleep you need to sing at your best. Experiment with your sleep pattern to figure out if sleeping six hours makes your voice feel fantastic or if you need at least eight hours. After you know how many hours you really need, you can make sure you get that amount of sleep as often as possible but especially when you're preparing for a performance.

✔ **Keep your body healthy.** Your physical workout sessions (like running, biking, and so on) help keep your cardiovascular system strong. Singing is similar to other sports in that you need a strong body to make your best sounds.

✔ **Don't smoke.** Smoking isn't a good habit for singers. When you inhale, the smoke passes over the vocal cords. If you're serious about taking the best care of your voice, avoid smoking anything and stay away from secondhand smoke as much as possible.

Appendix

About the CD

In This Appendix
▶ Identifying the tracks on the CD
▶ Troubleshooting the CD

The CD that accompanies this book is a normal audio CD that you can play in any CD player, including your computer.

Note: If you're using a digital or enhanced digital version of this book, this appendix does not apply. Please go to `http://booksupport.wiley.com` for access to the additional content.

Listening to the CD

In addition to the printed music, every exercise in this book features a black box that lets you know on which CD track you can find the accompanying music. Most of the tracks have a singer demonstrating the sounds for you and a piano playing the figure. However, a few tracks have just the piano playing the track for you. The description of the track in the chapter tells you which figures have only the piano.

The following table tells you the location of the exercises so you can easily find the exercise on a particular topic. The practice pieces are also included on the CD and are marked *Practice Piece* in the table.

Track	Chapter	Section Where You Find the Exercise
1	1	Putting It All Together with a Vocal Warm-Up
2	2	Practicing short phrases
3	2	Practicing longer phrases
4	2	Testing your breath control
5	3	Shifting the arch around for *ooh* and *ah*
5	3	Altering your lip shape for *oh* and *ah*
5	3	Tackling the tricky vowels *aw* and *OOh*
6	3	Singing through the five back vowels
7	3	Dropping the arch between *ee* and *ih*
7	3	Moving between *ee* and *ay*
7	3	Distinguishing between *ee* and *eh*
7	3	Comparing *eh* and *a*
8	3	Singing through the five front vowels

(continued)

Track	Chapter	Section Where You Find the Exercise
9	3	Alternating between Front and Back Vowels
10	3	Presenting the Middle Vowel, *Uh*
11	3	Singing Combination Vowels
12	4	Exploring the voiced consonants *L, N,* and *D*
12	4	Distinguishing between voiced *D* and unvoiced *T*
12	4	Sounding out the voiced *R*
12	4	Singing unvoiced *S* and voiced *Z*
12	4	Moving the tip of the tongue to the teeth for *TH*
13	4	Singing through the consonants *L, N, D, T, S, Z,* and *TH*
14	4	Practicing voiced *G,* unvoiced *K,* and voiced *NG*
15	4	Singing through the consonants *K, G,* and *NG*
16	4	Practicing voiced consonants *W* and *M*
16	4	Alternating between voiced *B* and unvoiced *P*
16	4	Moving only the bottom lip for *F* and *V*
17	4	Singing through *W, M, P, B, F,* and *V*
16	4	Puckering for voiced *J* and unvoiced *CH*
16	4	Moving air through *SH* and *ZH*
18	4	Singing through the consonants *J, CH, SH,* and *ZH*
19	5	Seconds and thirds in action
20	5	Singing perfect intervals
21	5	Singing sixths and sevenths
22	5	Building scales with triads
23	5	Singing major scales
24	5	Singing minor scales
25	5	Practice Piece: "Singing All the Intervals"
26	6	Practice piece: "The Rhythm Song"
27	6	Practice piece: "Checking Out Rhythm"
28	7	Making a smooth crescendo
29	7	Gradually singing softer with a decrescendo
30	7	Mastering dynamic contrast
31	7	Practice Piece: "I Sing Out!"
32	8	Exploring the sounds of chest voice
33	8	Varying the heaviness in your chest voice
34	8	Strengthening your chest voice
35	8	Modifying vowels in chest voice
36	8	Practice Piece: "Finding My Chest Voice"
37	9	Working out your falsetto
38	9	Taking falsetto down
39	9	Exploring various vowels in falsetto

Track	Chapter	Section Where You Find the Exercise
40	9	Getting a feel for head voice
41	9	Exploring high resonance in head voice
42	9	Singing through consonants in head voice
43	9	Monitoring your larynx while singing
44	9	Managing many high phrases
45	9	Creating spinning tone
46	9	Sustaining notes in your head voice
47	9	Practice Piece: "A Bejeweled Love Song"
48	10	Getting to know your middle voice
49	10	Strengthening your middle voice
50	10	Finding clear vowels in middle voice
51	10	Rolling into a mix
52	10	Changing around the mix
53	10	Practice Piece: For the guys: "Don't Let It Go"
54	10	Practice Piece: For the guys: "I'm Dyin'"
55	10	Practice Piece: For the gals: "How Will I Know"
56	10	Practice Piece: For the gals: "My Baby"
57	11	Dropping into chest voice
58	11	Changing back and forth from chest voice to middle voice
59	11	Climbing from middle voice to head voice
60	11	Singing from falsetto into chest voice
61	11	Changing from chest voice to falsetto
62	11	Rolling back and forth from chest voice to falsetto
63	11	Shifting from middle voice to chest voice
64	11	Shifting from middle voice to head voice
65	11	Practice Piece: "Marching Forth"
66	12	Practicing the onset of tone
67	12	Finding your resonance
68	12	Using vowels to explore resonance
69	12	Varying where tone resonates in your body
70	12	Changing between vibrato and straight tone
71	12	Practice Piece: "Changing Tone"
72	13	Taking a quick breath
73	13	Giving up control to get a feeling for agility
74	13	Stepping up the pace
75	13	Turning around on the tonic
76	13	Running to the top of the scale
77	13	Singing every other step of the scale
78	13	Gaining momentum

(continued)

Track	Chapter	Section Where You Find the Exercise
79	13	Starting on the top
80	13	Jumping up (or down) an octave
81	13	Practice Piece: "A Joyful Noise"
82	14	Speaking chatty sounds on specific pitches
83	14	Working on your speaking range
84	14	Using different phrases to expand your speaking range
85	14	Changing from mix to belt on one note
86	14	Applying your belt sounds to a tune
87	14	Increasing your belt range
88	14	Developing vocal stamina
89	14	Practice Piece: "Don't You Tell Me No Lie"
90	14	Practice Piece: "It's Time"

Customer Care

If you have trouble with the CD, please call Wiley Product Technical Support at 877-762-2974. Outside the United States, call 317-572-3993. You can also contact Wiley Product Technical Support at `http://support.wiley.com`. Wiley will provide technical support only for installation and other general quality control items.

To place additional orders or to request information about other Wiley products, please call 877-762-2974.

John Wiley & Sons, Inc.
End-User License Agreement